Magento 2 Development Cookbook

Over 60 recipes that will tailor and customize
your experience with Magento 2

Bart Delvaux

BIRMINGHAM - MUMBAI

Magento 2 Development Cookbook

First published: December 2015

Production reference: 1171215

Published by Packt Publishing Ltd.
Livery Place
35 Livery Street
Birmingham B3 2PB, UK.

ISBN 978-1-78588-219-7

www.packtpub.com

Credits

Authors

Bart Delvaux

Reviewers

Karen Kilroy

Pankaj Pareek

David Parloir

Marius Strajeru

Commissioning Editor

Veena Pagare

Acquisition Editor

Prachi Bisht

Content Development Editor

Aparna Mitra

Technical Editor

Abhishek R. Kotian

Copy Editor

Pranjali Chury

Project Coordinator

Izzat Contractor

Proofreader

Safis Editing

Indexer

Mariammal Chettiyar

Graphics

Disha Haria

Production Coordinator

Conidon Miranda

Cover Work

Conidon Miranda

About the Author

Bart Delvaux is an experienced web developer with several years of experience in the PHP world. He has worked with the most important frameworks in PHP, such as Drupal and Zend Framework, but Magento is his specialization.

Bart has obtained all the Magento developer certifications: Front End Developer, Developer, as well as Developer Plus. He currently works for ISAAC Software Solutions, a company that specializes in software solutions such as web shops, apps, system integrations, and more.

Bart finished a large variety of Magento projects in his Magento career that started in 2010 with the principle "quality above quantity". Having gone from handling a basic shop to shipping modules and large, complex Magento stores, Magento holds no secrets from him.

Bart has also worked on *Magento 1.8 Development Cookbook, Packt Publishing*. Now that Magento 2 is out, it is time for the next one!

I want to thank everyone who made it possible for me to complete this book. I would like to extend thanks to the people at Packt Publishing for the support and to my colleagues for their vision and support.

Lastly, I want to thank the people who contributed to Magento 2. They did a good job creating a new version of the popular Magento system, which is future-proof!

About the Reviewers

Karen Kilroy is a highly experienced developer, administrator, and instructor. She is a Magento-certified Front End Developer. As a hands-on developer and systems administrator with more than 25 years of experience in IT, which includes 20 years in web development, Karen has focused primarily on Magento for the past 7 years. Currently, she is employed at Amplifi as a Magento technical lead and works on several well-known commerce sites.

Karen got her start in Magento at a direct marketing company selling EdenPURE Heaters (`edenpure.com`), a site that generates millions of dollars in sales. Additionally, she was a courseware author and instructor for Magento's official training arm, Magento U, between 2010 and 2014. Karen is also a reviewer of *Mastering Magento, 2nd Edition, Packt Publishing*.

Prior to becoming involved with Magento, she customized LAMP content management systems, such as Joomla, Drupal, and WordPress. In the early days of web development, Karen led her own company, where she employed 20 developers doing Java and Lotus Notes/Domino work for large clients.

In her spare time, she is also a professional dragon boat coach and steersperson.

Pankaj Pareek is a certified software professional who has expertise in Magento, PHP, and other frameworks. He has provided his professional services in this field for more than 7 years.

A true professional, Pankaj works with the motto that knowledge increases when you share it with others. He is a person who has explored different aspects of the software field suo moto. Pankaj is a quick, curious learner who received various recognized certifications in the IT field in a very short span of time, namely Magento Developer (2013), Magento Solution Specialist (2015), and Zend Certified Engineer (2014).

> I would like to express my gratitude toward my loving grandmother, family, colleagues, and the almighty god.

David Parloir has been a freelance Magento developer since the first version was released in 2008, and through this, he has also been the lead developer for several large global projects. Prior to this, David worked for several companies that focused on the development of e-commerce websites and even worked as a teacher of Magento for a short period. He is a self-taught developer who sees web development as more than a job—he sees it as a passion. David considers himself a craftsman, keeping up to date with the latest trends in this area while balancing the new skills he develops, with a desire for his code to be efficient, simple, and elegant.

Marius Strajeru is 32 years old and finished as a faculty of computer science in Iasi, Romania, in 2006. Since then, he has worked as a PHP developer for various software companies.

Marius' area of expertise is Magento; he has been working with Magento since version 1.0 came out in 2008. He started looking at Magento 2 as soon as he heard that the source code is available in a dev version.

www.PacktPub.com

Support files, eBooks, discount offers, and more

For support files and downloads related to your book, please visit www.PacktPub.com.

Did you know that Packt offers eBook versions of every book published, with PDF and ePub files available? You can upgrade to the eBook version at www.PacktPub.com and as a print book customer, you are entitled to a discount on the eBook copy. Get in touch with us at service@packtpub.com for more details.

At www.PacktPub.com, you can also read a collection of free technical articles, sign up for a range of free newsletters and receive exclusive discounts and offers on Packt books and eBooks.

https://www2.packtpub.com/books/subscription/packtlib

Do you need instant solutions to your IT questions? PacktLib is Packt's online digital book library. Here, you can search, access, and read Packt's entire library of books.

Why subscribe?

- ▸ Fully searchable across every book published by Packt
- ▸ Copy and paste, print, and bookmark content
- ▸ On demand and accessible via a web browser

Free access for Packt account holders

If you have an account with Packt at www.PacktPub.com, you can use this to access PacktLib today and view 9 entirely free books. Simply use your login credentials for immediate access.

Table of Contents

Preface

Magento is one of the most popular e-commerce platforms on the market. It contains a lot of e-commerce functionality, it is stable, and it is free. This means that a lot of people choose Magento for their online business.

The first stable version of Magento was released in 2008. The later releases were based on the first version of Magento. Technology changes quickly and Magento needed a big update—a big release Magento 2 is now ready.

Developing in Magento is not as easy as you would expect. Even if you have knowledge of Magento 1, a good guide with practical examples that shows you the best practice is a must have, and this is exactly what this book will do.

With Magento 2 Development Cookbook, we will cover the most important topics that will help you become a good Magento 2 developer. We will start with the basics and we will end with the more advanced topics.

This book is divided into several recipes, which show you which steps to take to complete a specific action. In each recipe, we have a section that explains how everything works.

We will start this book with the creation of a good development environment. For a good development environment, we need the right tools. We will install Magento and we will discuss how we can migrate data from a Magento 1 to a Magento 2 shop. Next, we will see some functional stuff. You will learn how the catalog system works, which product types are available, and a lot more.

After this, you will learn how we can create a Magento theme to change the look and feel of the Magento shop. But the main focus of this book will be the development part. We will create a custom module that we will extend with a lot of common features that are used in Magento projects, such as extra controller pages, database integrations, custom shipping methods, and extra backend interfaces.

At the end of this book, we will see how we can improve the performance of a Magento shop. Finally, we will see some debugging techniques, such as Xdebug and creating unit tests using the Magento test framework.

What this book covers

Chapter 1, Upgrading from Magento 1, provides an introduction to how you can install and migrate the data from a Magento 1 to a Magento 2 shop. We will also prepare our development environment in this chapter.

Chapter 2, Working with Products, gives you a more functional information about the possibilities of displaying products in your Magento shop.

Chapter 3, Theming, explains how you can customize the look and feel of your webshop using a custom Magento theme.

Chapter 4, Creating a Module, describes how to create a basic Magento module; how to extend that module with custom configurations, such as a custom page, translations, and blocks; and how to change behavior of standard Magento classes.

Chapter 5, Databases and Modules, demonstrates how you can extend a Magento module with database interactions, such as install and upgrade scripts, a custom entity that represents a database table.

Chapter 6, Magento Backend, shows you how to integrate a Magento module with the backend, such as adding configuration pages, creating overview pages, and extending the admin menu.

Chapter 7, Event Handlers and Cronjobs, describes how the event-driven architecture is implemented in Magento and how to integrate this in your module. Later in this chapter, you will learn how to create cronjobs and how to test them.

Chapter 8, Creating a Shipping Module, shows you how to create a module with the configurations that are required for a new shipping method.

Chapter 9, Creating a Product Slider Widget, will cover how to create a module with a custom widget, how to build the backend interface, and how to provide a good UI in the frontend of that widget.

Chapter 10, Performance Optimization, describes how to benchmark a site to explore the limits and how to improve the performance using different techniques such as Redis and Memcached.

Chapter 11, Debugging and Unit Testing, shows you how to use the PHP debugger Xdebug and how we can create automated tests using the Magento 2 testing framework.

What you need for this book

- ▸ Magento 2 source code
- ▸ A virtual Linux server (Ubuntu 15.10 or higher)
- ▸ On that virtual server, you need the following:
    - ◦ Apache 2.4
    - ◦ PHP 5.5 or higher
    - ◦ MySQL Server 5.6 or higher
    - ◦ SSH access
- ▸ NetBeans IDE (or any other good PHP editor like PhpStorm)
- ▸ A database client (such a phpMyAdmin)
- ▸ A standard web browser
- ▸ Xdebug
- ▸ Git SCM

Who this book is for

This book is for web programmers who are familiar with PHP and want to start with Magento 2. This book is also for Magento 1 developers who want to know how everything works in Magento 2.

This book will start with the basics of Magento 2 development and will end with the more advanced topics. Even if you knowledge about Magento development, this book is a good reference if you want to more about a particular topic in Magento.

Sections

In this book, you will find several headings that appear frequently (Getting ready, How to do it, How it works, There's more, and See also).

To give clear instructions on how to complete a recipe, we use these sections as follows:

Getting ready

This section tells you what to expect in the recipe, and describes how to set up any software or any preliminary settings required for the recipe.

How to do it...

This section contains the steps required to follow the recipe.

How it works...

This section usually consists of a detailed explanation of what happened in the previous section.

There's more...

This section consists of additional information about the recipe in order to make the reader more knowledgeable about the recipe.

See also

This section provides helpful links to other useful information for the recipe.

Conventions

In this book, you will find a number of text styles that distinguish between different kinds of information. Here are some examples of these styles and an explanation of their meaning.

Code words in text, database table names, folder names, filenames, file extensions, pathnames, dummy URLs, user input, and Twitter handles are shown as follows: "The `widget.xml` file is used to define widgets in the Magento installation."

A block of code is set as follows:

```xml
<?xml version="1.0"?>
<config xmlns:xsi="http://www.w3.org/2001/XMLSchema-
instance" xsi:noNamespaceSchemaLocation=
"urn:magento:framework:App/etc/routes.xsd">
    <router id="standard">
        <route id="helloworld" frontName="helloworld">
            <module name="Packt_HelloWorld" />
        </route>
    </router>
</config>
```

New terms and **important words** are shown in bold. Words that you see on the screen, for example, in menus or dialog boxes, appear in the text like this: "Clicking the **Next** button moves you to the next screen."

> Warnings or important notes appear in a box like this.

> Tips and tricks appear like this.

Reader feedback

Feedback from our readers is always welcome. Let us know what you think about this book—what you liked or disliked. Reader feedback is important for us as it helps us develop titles that you will really get the most out of.

To send us general feedback, simply e-mail `feedback@packtpub.com`, and mention the book's title in the subject of your message.

If there is a topic that you have expertise in and you are interested in either writing or contributing to a book, see our author guide at `www.packtpub.com/authors`.

Customer support

Now that you are the proud owner of a Packt book, we have a number of things to help you to get the most from your purchase.

Downloading the example code

You can download the example code files from your account at `http://www.packtpub.com` for all the Packt Publishing books you have purchased. If you purchased this book elsewhere, you can visit `http://www.packtpub.com/support` and register to have the files e-mailed directly to you.

Downloading the color images of this book

We also provide you with a PDF file that has color images of the screenshots/diagrams used in this book. The color images will help you better understand the changes in the output. You can download this file from `http://www.packtpub.com/sites/default/files/downloads/1234OT_ColorImages.pdf`.

Errata

Although we have taken every care to ensure the accuracy of our content, mistakes do happen. If you find a mistake in one of our books—maybe a mistake in the text or the code—we would be grateful if you could report this to us. By doing so, you can save other readers from frustration and help us improve subsequent versions of this book. If you find any errata, please report them by visiting http://www.packtpub.com/submit-errata, selecting your book, clicking on the **Errata Submission Form** link, and entering the details of your errata. Once your errata are verified, your submission will be accepted and the errata will be uploaded to our website or added to any list of existing errata under the Errata section of that title.

To view the previously submitted errata, go to https://www.packtpub.com/books/content/support and enter the name of the book in the search field. The required information will appear under the **Errata** section.

Piracy

Piracy of copyrighted material on the Internet is an ongoing problem across all media. At Packt, we take the protection of our copyright and licenses very seriously. If you come across any illegal copies of our works in any form on the Internet, please provide us with the location address or website name immediately so that we can pursue a remedy.

Please contact us at copyright@packtpub.com with a link to the suspected pirated material.

We appreciate your help in protecting our authors and our ability to bring you valuable content.

Questions

If you have a problem with any aspect of this book, you can contact us at questions@packtpub.com, and we will do our best to address the problem.

1
Upgrading from Magento 1

In this chapter, we will cover:

- Creating a Magento 1 website with sample data
- Creating a Magento 2 website
- Preparing an upgrade from Magento 1
- Upgrading the database
- Using an IDE
- Writing clean code with PHP MD and PHP CS

Introduction

Magento is one of the most complete e-commerce platforms on the open source market. With a default Magento installation, all the common e-commerce features, such as catalog navigation, promotion rules, tax settings, online payments, and so on are available.

The first version of Magento was released in 2008 after one year of development. Magento was initially designed as an e-commerce system that could be used for a wide range of uses. In later years, Magento became very popular as an out-of-the-box e-commerce system and a lot of minor versions of the 1.x series have been released in the last few years.

To be future proof, Magento started the development of a major upgrade of the system, also known as Magento 2. Magento 2 is a big improvement on every part of Magento. Every aspect is analyzed and rewritten with up-to-date technologies to be ready for the future. Everything, including the developer experience, maintainability, performance, and technologies will be improved.

In this chapter, we will upgrade the data of a Magento 1 installation to a Magento 2 installation. We will also prepare some tools that we can use in the following chapters of this book.

Creating a Magento 1 website with sample data

To start a Magento 2 upgrade, we need a Magento 1 webshop with some data. In this recipe, we will install the latest Magento version, 1.9, with the sample data for the new responsive theme.

Getting ready

To install a Magento 1 website, we need the following stuff:

- A web server (Linux, Apache2, PHP, or MySQL)
- The Magento 1.9 codebase
- The Magento 1.9 sample data

> The Magento 1.9 codebase and sample data can be downloaded from the Magento site at http://www.magentocommerce.com/download.

The following stuff is recommended for the installation:

- Command-line access
- A virtual host (domain name) that is going to be your web root

> We recommend that you use a test server that is on your development machine. If you use a Linux or a Mac operating system, you can install the webserver on your local machine. If you have a Windows machine, you can use a virtual Linux server for your development.

How to do it...

1. Extract the Magento code archive in your webroot (the directory of the virtualhost). An `ls -la` command should give you the following output:

```
api.php

app

cron.php

cron.sh

downloader

errors

favicon.ico

get.php

includes

index.php

index.php.sample

install.php

js

lib

LICENSE_AFL.txt

LICENSE.html

LICENSE.txt

mage

media

php.ini.sample

pkginfo

RELEASE_NOTES.txt

shell

skin

var
```

2. Extract the sample data archive to a different folder from the webroot. Copy the contents of the `media` and `skin` folders to the `media` and `skin` folders in your webroot. We can do this by using the following `cp` command:

```
cp -R <path_to_sampledata_folder>/media/*
<path_to_magento_folder>/media/

cp -R <path_to_sampledata_folder/skin/*
<path_to_magento_folder>/skin/
```

3. Create a database for the Magento 1 installation and name it `magento1`. We can do this by running the following commands:

```
mysql -u <username> -p

create database magento1;

exit;
```

4. Import the `sql` file that is in the sample data directory. This file contains a database that we will import into the `magento1` database. We can do this by running the following command:

```
mysql -u <username> -p magento1< "path_to_sample_data.sql"
```

To avoid permission problems, ensure that all files and folders have the right permissions. For security reasons, it is recommended that all files have just enough permissions so that only the right users can access the right files. When you give all the rights (777), you don't have permission problems because each user can read, write and, execute each file of your application. More information about file permissions can be found at `http://devdocs.magento.com/guides/m1x/install/installer-privileges_after.html`.

5. When the files are in the right place and the database is imported, we can run the Magento installer. Open your browser and go to the domain that is configured for your website. You should see the installer as in the following screenshot:

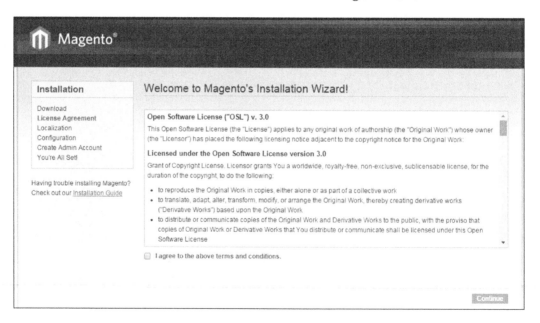

6. Continue with the installation process by accepting the terms and conditions.

7. On the next screen, choose the correct language, locale, and currency for your store.

8. On the configuration page, fill in the form with the right data:

   ❑ **Database Type**: MySQL.

   ❑ **Host**: Enter the hostname or IP address of your database server (localhost if it is on the same machine).

   ❑ **Database name**: Enter magento1 in this field (or another name if you have a different name for your database).

   ❑ **User name**: Enter your database username.

   ❑ **User password**: Enter your database password.

   ❑ **Tables prefix**: Leave this field empty (the string in this field will be used to prefix all tables of your database).

   ❑ **Base URL**: Enter the URL of your website in this field.

   ❑ **Admin path**: Enter admin in this field. This will be the path of the backend.

   ❑ **Enable charts**: For development, it is recommended that this be unchecked.

   ❑ **Skip Base URL Validation Before the Next Step**: When checked, the wizard will check for a valid URL when processing this form.

   ❑ **Use Web Server (Apache) rewrites**: Check this when the apache module mod_rewrite is enabled.

   ❑ **Use Secure URL's (SSL)**: This checkbox must be unchecked if you don't use HTTPS.

9. Submit this form and we will be forwarded to the next step. In this step, you can configure the administrator account. Fill in the right data and remember the username and password because this is required to manage the store. Leave the **encryption key** field empty.

10. After submitting this form, the installation is complete. Optionally, you can submit the Magento survey. At the bottom of the page, there are buttons to navigate to the frontend and backend. When going to the frontend, you can see a demo shop with sample data as in the following screenshot:

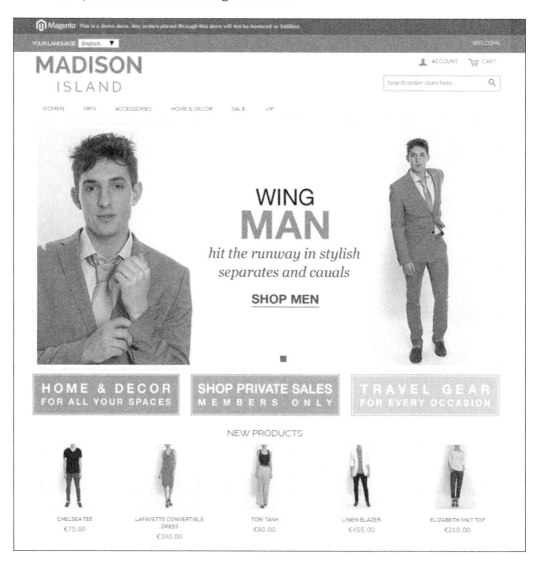

11. The layout is responsive. When scaling your browser to a smaller width, the website will switch to the mobile layout like in the following screenshot:

How it works...

We have just created a fully functional Magento 1 store. The webshop is fully configured and filled with data about products, customers, and orders, just the data we need to migrate to Magento 2 (in the upcoming recipes).

When installing a new shop, you have to follow the installer. This interface creates a configuration file `app/etc/local.xml`. If the file doesn't exist, Magento will launch the installer wizard. If the file is there, Magento will run the shop.

With a valid `local.xml` file, it is technically possible to install a new Magento shop, but this is not recommended because some settings such as a backend user, time zone, and currency are not set. These are actions that you have to do manually when choosing for this method.

Creating a Magento 2 website

In the previous recipe, we created a Magento 1 website with sample data that we will use for an upgrade. In this recipe, we will do the same, but we will create a Magento 2 website with the sample data for Magento 2.

Getting ready

To install Magento 2, we need the newest tools to run that application. Make sure your webserver has the following stuff installed:

- **PHP 5.5** or higher
- **MySQL 5.6** or higher
- **Apache 2.2** or higher
- Command line access
- Composer

We can install Magento 2 in different ways. In this recipe, we will install Magento 2 using Composer. The advantage of this is that we can use GIT to add version control to our custom development.

How to do it...

1. We will install Magento 2 with Composer. For this, we need authentication keys. With an account on the `magento.com` site, go to **Developers | Secure keys** in the **My Account** section. On this page, you can generate public and private keys that will be your username and password in the next step.

2. To install Magento 2 with composer, we have to run the following command:

   ```
   composer create-project --repository-url=
   https://repo.magento.com magento/project-community-edition
   <installation_dir>
   ```

3. You will be prompted for a username and password. The username is the public key and the password is the private key that we generated in the previous step. When the command has run, the installation directory will have the following structure:

```
app
bin
CHANGELOG.md
composer.json
composer.lock
CONTRIBUTING.md
CONTRIBUTOR_LICENSE_AGREEMENT.html
COPYING.txt
dev
.gitignore
Gruntfile.js
.htaccess
.htaccess.sample
index.php
lib
LICENSE_AFL.txt
LICENSE.txt
nginx.conf.sample
package.json
.php_cs
php.ini.sample
pub
README.md
setup
.travis.yml
update
var
vendor
```

 Check that the user and group of these files are the same as your Apache user. One recommendation is to execute all the commands as your apache user.

4. We have installed the codebase with composer. Now we can run the installation wizard. Open your browser and enter the URL of your site. You should see the following welcome screen:

Version 2.0.0

Welcome to Magento Admin, your online store headquarters. Click 'Agree and Set Up Magento' or read Getting Started to learn more.

Terms & Agreement

Agree and Setup Magento

5. Hit the **Agree and Setup Magento** button and start the environment check.

6. Click on **Next** and enter your database information as follows:

    ❑   **Database Server Host**: The hostname or IP address of the database server

    ❑   **Database Server Username**: The username of the database account

    ❑   **Database Server Password**: The password for the account

    ❑   **Database Name**: The name of the database

    ❑   **Table Prefix**: Optionally, you can give a prefix for each table

7. Go to the next step and check if the right information is filled for the URL part. In the advanced section, you can optionally configure HTTPS, apache rewrites, and your encryption key. For our test environment, we can leave these settings as they are configured.

Make sure that the `mod_rewrite` option is enabled for the apache server. When not enabled, the URL rewrites will not work correctly.

8. In the next step, you can configure your time zone, currency, and default language.

9. In the last step, you can configure your administration account. After clicking on the **Next** button, you are ready to install. Click on the **Install Now** button and the installer will start. This will take some time because the installer will add the sample data during the installation. You can open the Console Log to see what is currently happening.

10. When the installer is ready, you will see the following success message:

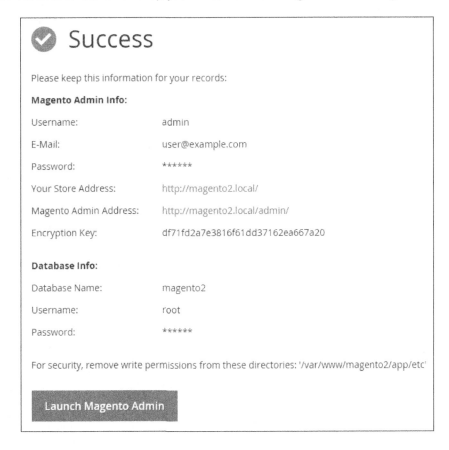

11. Run the following commands in your Magento installation directory to configure the sample data:

```
php bin/magento sampledata:deploy
composer update
php bin/magento setup:upgrade
```

12. The preceding commands will download and install the sample data packages. Because they contain a lot of images, this could take some time. The `setup:upgrade` command will install the sample data, and this also takes some time.

13. The installation of the webshop is now complete. You now have an up-and-running Magento 2 webshop. When you navigate to the category **Gear | Bags**, you should see something like in the following screenshot:

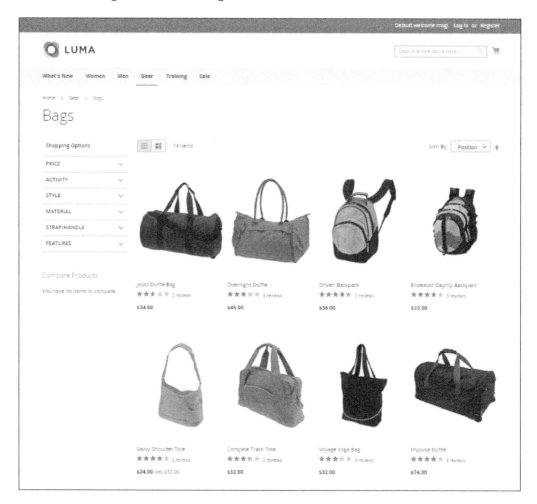

How it works...

We have now installed a Magento 2 website. Like we did in the previous recipe for Magento 1.9, we downloaded the codebase (using composer), created a database, and installed Magento.

For Magento 2, we used composer to download the codebase. Composer is a PHP dependency manager. All the dependencies are set in the `composer.json` file. For this recipe, there are the `Magento` and the `magento-sample-data` dependencies in the `composer.json` file. There is also a `composer.lock` file generated. In that file, the versions of the installed dependencies are stored.

 When working with GIT, we only have to commit the `composer.json`, `composer.lock`, and `.gitignore` files for a working Magento 2 project. When another person does a Git clone of the repository and runs the composer's `install` command, Magento 2 will be installed with the version that is in the `composer.lock` file.

The sample data for Magento 2 is now a script that will be executed after the installation of Magento. That script will add products, customers, orders, CMS data, and more configurations to populate the shop.

The shop is installed and the configuration settings (database, encryption key, and so on) are now stored in `app/etc/env.php` instead of in the `app/etc/local.xml` file in Magento 1.

There's more...

When installing Magento 2, here are some common issues that can occur and their fixes:

- When you don't see CSS in your browser, you have to check the following things:
    - Make sure the `pub/` folder is writable
    - Run the command `php bin/magento setup:static-content:deploy` to generate the static content

- You forget to install the sample data:
    - You can install the sample data after the installation of Magento with the command `php bin/magento sampledata:deploy`

- The installation is not responding anymore:
    - This could be caused by an Apache timeout. If this occurs, you can maybe try the command-line installation. This works as follows:

To run the Magento installer from the command line, we can use the command `php bin/magento setup:install`. We have to add the following required parameters to the command to configure the installation:

- `base-url`: The base URL, for example `http://magento2.local/`
- `db-host`: The database host or IP address

- ▸ `db-user`: The database username

- ▸ `db-name`: The database name

- ▸ `db-password`: The database password

- ▸ `admin-firstname`: The first name of the administrator user

- ▸ `admin-lastname`: The last name of the admin user

- ▸ `admin-email`: The e-mail address of the admin user

- ▸ `admin-user`: The username (login name) of the admin user

- ▸ `admin-password`: The password for the admin user

- ▸ `language`: The language of the shop

- ▸ `currency`: The currency code of the shop

- ▸ `timezone`: The time zone of the shop

- ▸ `use-rewrites`: Whether to use the apache rewrites or not

- ▸ `use-sample-data`: Install the sample data (optional)

Look at the following code for a working example of the install command:

```
php bin/magento setup:install --base-url=http://magento2.local/ --db-
host=localhost --db-user=magento2 --db-name=magento2 --db-
password=yourpassword --admin-firstname=John --admin-lastname=Doe --
admin-email=john.doe@example.com --admin-user=admin --language=en_US
--currency=USD --timezone=UTC --use-rewrites=1
```

Preparing an upgrade from Magento 1

The differences between Magento 1 and Magento 2 are huge. The code has a whole new structure with a lot of improvements but there is one big disadvantage. What do I do if I want to upgrade my Magento 1 shop to a Magento 2 shop?

Magento created an upgrade tool that migrates the data from a Magento 1 database to the right structure for a Magento 2 database.

The custom modules in your Magento 1 shop will not work in Magento 2. It is possible that some of your modules will have a Magento 2 version, and depending on the module, the module author will have a migration tool to migrate the data that is in the module.

Getting ready

Before we get started, make sure you have an empty (without sample data) Magento 2 installation with the same version as the Migration tool that is available at:

`https://github.com/magento/data-migration-tool-ce.`

How to do it...

1. In your Magento 2 version (with the same version as the migration tool), run the following commands:

```
composer config repositories.data-migration-tool git
https://github.com/magento/data-migration-tool-ce

composer require magento/data-migration-tool:2.0.0
```

2. Install Magento 2 with an empty database by running the installer. Make sure you configure it with the right time zone and currencies.

3. When these steps are done, you can test the tool by running the following command:

```
php bin/magento migrate:data --help
```

4. The next thing is creating the configuration files. Examples of the configuration files are in vendor/magento/data-migration-tool/etc/<version>. We can create a copy of this folder where we can set our custom configuration values. For a Magento 1.9 installation, we have to run the following cp command:

```
cp -R vendor/magento/data-migration-tool/etc/
ce-to-ce/1.9.1.0/ vendor/magento/data-migration-tool/
etc/ce-to-ce/packt-migration
```

5. Open the vendor/magento/data-migration-tool/etc/ce-to-ce/packt-migration/config.xml.dist file and search for the source/database and destination/database tags. Change the values of these database settings to your database settings like in the following code:

```
<source>
  <database host="localhost" name="magento1" user="root"/>
</source>
<destination>
  <database host="localhost" name="magento2_migration"
  user="root"/>
</destination>
```

6. Rename that file to config.xml with the following command:

```
mv vendor/magento/data-migration-tool/etc/ce-to-ce/
packt-migration/config.xml.dist vendor/magento/
data-migration-tool/etc/ce-to-ce/packt-migration/config.xml
```

How it works...

By adding a composer dependency, we installed the data migration tool for Magento 2 in the codebase. This migration tool is a Magento console command that will handle the migration steps from a Magento 1 shop.

In the `etc` folder of the migration module, there is a sample configuration of an empty Magento 1.9 shop.

If you want to migrate an existing Magento 1 shop, you have to customize these configuration files so it matches your preferred state.

In the next recipe, we will learn how we can use the script to start the migration.

Upgrading the database

In the previous recipe, we configured the database migration tool. In this recipe, we will run the migration tool so that we can migrate parts from a Magento 1 shop to a Magento 2 shop.

Getting ready

You need a Magento 1 website and a Magento 2 website. The Magento 2 website needs to have the database migration tool installed and configured as described in the previous recipe.

In this recipe, we will do a migration from a clean Magento 1 site, to a Magento 2 site without sample data.

We did a migration from a clean Magento 1 database with some test products. Make sure you have a cleanly installed Magento 1 shop with some test data (products, orders, and so on) in it.

How to do it...

1. First we need to make sure that the database settings are correct in the `vendor/magento/data-migration-tool/etc/ce-to-ce/packt-migration/config.xml` file. Open that file and check that the database credentials are correct. We created this file in the previous recipe:

   ```
   <source version="1.9.1">
   <database host="localhost" name="magento1_migration"
   user="root"/>
   </source>
   ```

```
<destination version="2.0.0.0">
<database host="localhost" name="magento2_migration"
user="root"/>
</destination>
```

 If you have a database prefix in your source or destination database, you can optionally configure source_prefix and dest_prefix in the <options> section of the same configuration file.

 Test the migration first with a clean Magento 1.9 database. The mapping that we will use in this recipe is for a clean Magento 1.9 installation. With an existing shop, you will have custom attributes and entities that need more configuration to make the migration work.

2. If these settings are correct, we can run the upgrade tool. Run the following command:

   php bin/magento migrate:data --help

3. This gives us the following output:

```
www-data@ubuntu1:~/magento2$ php bin/magento migrate:data --help
Usage:
 migrate:data [-r|--reset] config

Arguments:
 config                 Path to main configuration file, i.e.: etc/m1_version/config.xml

Options:
 --reset (-r)           Reset the current position of migration to start from the beginning
 --help (-h)            Display this help message
 --quiet (-q)           Do not output any message
 --verbose (-v|vv|vvv)  Increase the verbosity of messages: 1 for normal output, 2 for more
verbose output and 3 for debug
 --version (-V)         Display this application version
 --ansi                 Force ANSI output
 --no-ansi              Disable ANSI output
 --no-interaction (-n)  Do not ask any interactive question

www-data@ubuntu1:~/magento2$
```

4. To start or test a migration, we have to run the following command:

   php bin/magento migrate:data vendor/magento/data-migration-tool/etc/ce-to-ce/packt-migration/config.xml

5. The migration will start and will give the following output:

```
[2015-10-25 13:51:40][INFO][mode: data][stage: integrity check][step: EAV Step]: started
[2015-10-25 13:51:40][INFO][mode: data][stage: integrity check][step: Customer Attributes Step]: started
[2015-10-25 13:51:40][INFO][mode: data][stage: integrity check][step: Map Step]: started
[2015-10-25 13:51:40][INFO][mode: data][stage: integrity check][step: Url Rewrite Step]: started
[2015-10-25 13:51:40][INFO][mode: data][stage: integrity check][step: Log Step]: started
[2015-10-25 13:51:40][INFO][mode: data][stage: integrity check][step: Ratings Step]: started
[2015-10-25 13:51:40][INFO][mode: data][stage: integrity check][step: ConfigurablePrices step]: started
[2015-10-25 13:51:40][INFO][mode: data][stage: integrity check][step: OrderGrids Step]: started
[2015-10-25 13:51:40][INFO][mode: data][stage: setup triggers][step: Stage]: started
[2015-10-25 13:51:40][INFO][mode: data][stage: data migration][step: EAV Step]: started
100% [============================] Remaining Time: 1 sec
[2015-10-25 13:51:41][INFO][mode: data][stage: volume check][step: EAV Step]: started
100% [============================] Remaining Time: 1 sec
[2015-10-25 13:51:41][INFO][mode: data][stage: data migration][step: Customer Attributes Step]: started
100% [============================] Remaining Time: 1 sec
[2015-10-25 13:51:42][INFO][mode: data][stage: volume check][step: Customer Attributes Step]: started
100% [============================] Remaining Time: 1 sec
[2015-10-25 13:51:42][INFO][mode: data][stage: data migration][step: Map Step]: started
100% [============================] Remaining Time: 1 sec
[2015-10-25 13:51:53][INFO][mode: data][stage: volume check][step: Map Step]: started
100% [============================] Remaining Time: 1 sec
[2015-10-25 13:51:54][INFO][mode: data][stage: data migration][step: Url Rewrite Step]: started
100% [============================] Remaining Time: 1 sec
[2015-10-25 13:51:54][INFO][mode: data][stage: volume check][step: Url Rewrite Step]: started
100% [============================] Remaining Time: 1 sec
[2015-10-25 13:51:54][INFO][mode: data][stage: data migration][step: Log Step]: started
100% [============================] Remaining Time: 1 sec
[2015-10-25 13:51:54][INFO][mode: data][stage: volume check][step: Log Step]: started
100% [============================] Remaining Time: 1 sec
[2015-10-25 13:51:54][INFO][mode: data][stage: data migration][step: Ratings Step]: started
100% [============================] Remaining Time: 1 sec
[2015-10-25 13:51:54][INFO][mode: data][stage: volume check][step: Ratings Step]: started
100% [============================] Remaining Time: 1 sec
[2015-10-25 13:51:54][INFO][mode: data][stage: data migration][step: ConfigurablePrices step]: started
100% [============================] Remaining Time: 1 sec
[2015-10-25 13:51:54][INFO][mode: data][stage: volume check][step: ConfigurablePrices step]: started
100% [============================] Remaining Time: 1 sec
[2015-10-25 13:51:54][INFO][mode: data][stage: data migration][step: OrderGrids Step]: started
100% [============================] Remaining Time: 1 sec
[2015-10-25 13:51:54][INFO][mode: data][stage: volume check][step: OrderGrids Step]: started
100% [============================] Remaining Time: 1 sec
[2015-10-25 13:51:54][INFO][mode: data][stage: volume check][step: OrderGrids Step]: Migration completed
/magento2-migration/vendor/magento/data-migration-tool$
www-data@ubuntu1:~/magento2-migration/vendor/magento/data-migration-tool$
```

6. The migration is now complete. If you check your database for the Magento 2 website, you will see that the data (products, categories, and so on) is migrated from Magento 1.

 If you want to rerun the migration tool, you have to remove the `var/migration-tool-progress.lock` file.

7. We can also migrate the settings from the Magento 1 website. To do this, you have to replace the `data` parameter in the command using `settings`.

8. To check if the upgrade works, you have to look at the data of the Magento 2 installation. We can check the following things in the backend:

   ❏ The orders (**Sales | Orders**)

   ❏ The products (**Products | Catalog**)

   ❏ The customers (**Customers | All Customers**)

9. You can also check in the database if you look at the following tables:

   ❏ `sales_order`

   ❏ `customer_entity`

   ❏ `catalog_product_entity`

   ❏ `url_rewrite`

How it works...

When the migration tool starts, it starts checking all the configurations that are in the configuration files of the migration tool. If there are more things available in the Magento 1 database than the things that are configured, the migration tool will give a notification and stop the migration.

It's likely that every existing Magento 1 shop works with custom attributes, custom entities, and so on. Each entity, attribute, and so on needs to be declared in the configuration files.

The most time-consuming part of a migration is to create a good configuration file so that the migration tool won't fail on missing stuff. It is on you to decide what to ignore and what to migrate. If the configuration files are valid, the migration will start and the data will come into the Magento 2 database. The same principle applies when migrating the settings, but you have to think about whether you want it.

 With the migration tool, it is only possible to migrate data and settings. The code of Magento 1 modules will not work in Magento 2. So for your modules, you need to see if there is a Magento 2 version/alternative available.

There's more...

In this recipe, we did a migration of a clean Magento 1 installation to a clean Magento 2 installation. However almost every running Magento 1 shop is not clean. It contains custom attributes, custom modules, and a custom configuration.

When migrating such a shop to a new shop, the migration is a bit more complex. The first question is: *What needs to be migrated?* With the tool, you can migrate every entity, from products, customers, and orders to reviews, settings, and more.

If you want to skip data that must be migrated, you can use the `map.xml` file. If you open the file `vendor/magento/data-migration-tool/etc/ce-to-ce/packt-migration/map.xml`, you see that a lot of entities are ignored in the `map/source/document_rules` tag.

 If you want to change something in the `map.xml` file, you have to make sure that the right `map.xml` file is loaded. This file is configured in the `config.xml` file (where you did your database configuration). In that file, you have to look for the XML tag `config/options/map_file`.

If you have an error such as **Source documents not mapped**, you have to add the configuration for these entities in the `map/source/document_rules` tag of the `map.xml` file. If the error is something like **Destination documents not mapped**, you have to add configuration in the `map/destination/document` tag of the `map.xml` file.

To solve errors such as **Source fields not mapped** you have to add configuration in the `map-eav.xml` file.

See also

Migrating configuration files is the most time consuming part of a data migration. If you want more information on the migration tool, you can have a look at the Magento Migration Whitepaper, available at

`http://magento.com/resources/magento-2-migration-whitepaper.`

Using an IDE

Writing good code starts with a good development environment. An **Integrated Development Environment** (**IDE**) is the main part of a good development environment. **NetBeans** is a free and open source PHP editor that can be used for Magento development. In this recipe, we will set up a Magento 2 project in NetBeans.

Getting ready

Install the latest version of NetBeans IDE on your computer. You can download it from the following URL:

`https://netbeans.org/downloads/`

For PHP development, you need to download the `HTML5 & PHP` bundle.

How to do it...

1. To create a new project, open NetBeans and navigate to **File | New Project**.

2. A window like the one in the following screenshot will appear on your screen. Click on **PHP** and **PHP Application with Existing Sources**.

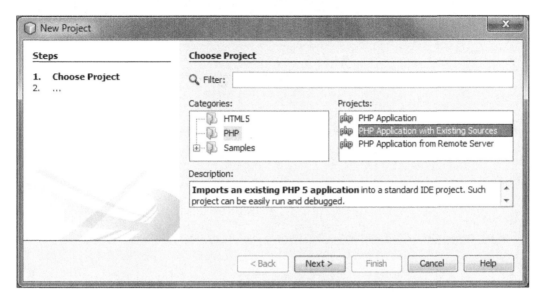

3. Click on **Next** and configure the following settings:

   ❑ **Source Folder**: This field is set to the location of your Magento code (like /var/www/html/magento2/)

   ❑ **Project Name**: The NetBeans project name is entered in this field

   ❑ **PHP Version**: This field is set to **PHP 5.5**

   ❑ **Default Encoding**: This field is set to **UTF-8**

4. In the next screenshot, you can see how everything is configured:

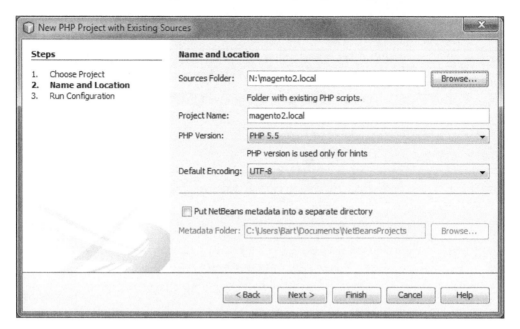

When you are working with a version control system like GIT, it is recommended that you check the checkbox. Put NetBeans metadata into a separate directory. If not checked, a `.nbproject` folder is created in your Magento root, and you don't want to have that folder in your version control system. Another possibility is to add the `.nbproject` folder in the `.gitignore` file.

5. Click on **Next** and configure the final settings:

- ❑ **Run as**: If you are developing on a local PC, choose **Local Web Server**
- ❑ **Project URL**: The URL of your website
- ❑ **Index file**: Set this to `index.php`

The settings are shown in the following screenshot:

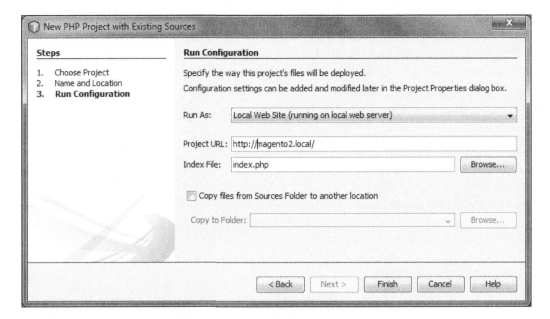

6. Click on the **Finish** button and your NetBeans project is ready. You can now start developing.

There's more...

In this recipe, we used the free code editor NetBeans, but there are also some other good alternatives on the market, such as:

- PHPStorm
- Eclipse with PDT (PHP Development Tools)
- Zend Studio

Writing clean code with PHP MD and PHP CS

Maintaining clean code is much more efficient than maintaining spaghetti code, but writing clean code is not as easy as it sounds. These days there are some tools that help you with writing clean code, such as **PHPMD** and **PHP_CodeSniffer**.

PHPMD stands for PHP Mess Detector; this tool will check your code on complexity and how variables are used and will detect some possible bugs. It goes a bit further than the syntax check in your IDE.

PHP_CodeSniffer or PHPCS checks your code on coding standards such as PSR-1 and PSR-2.

Getting ready

We will install PHPMD and PHP_CodeSniffer in our development environment. Make sure you have command-line access to your development environment.

How to do it...

1. Before installing PHPMD and PHP_CodeSniffer, we have to make sure that PHP is installed on our development machine. Especially if you are developing on a remote server, it could be that PHP is not installed.

2. Download and install PHPMD. Depending on your OS, the protocol could be different. You can find instructions at:

    ```
    http://phpmd.org/download/index.html
    ```

3. Download and install PHP_CodeSniffer. You can find the installation instructions at:

    ```
    https://github.com/squizlabs/PHP_CodeSniffer
    ```

4. Everything is installed, so we can run a test for PHPMD. For the PHPMD command, these are the required options:

    - Filename or directory
    - The format of the report
    - The ruleset

5. Let's run the following command to check the file on clean code and output text:

    ```
    phpmd app/code/Magento/Cms/Model/Observer.php text
    cleancode
    ```

6. It gives us the following output:

```
/var/www/magento2/app/code/Magento/Cms/Model/Observer.php:7
0    Avoid using static access to class
'\Magento\Cms\Helper\Page' in method 'noCookies'

/var/www/magento2/app/code/Magento/Cms/Model/Observer.php:7
1    Avoid using static access to class
'\Magento\Store\Model\ScopeInterface' in method
'noCookies'.

/var/www/magento2/app/code/Magento/Cms/Model/Observer.php:7
7    The method noCookies uses an else expression. Else is
never necessary and you can simplify the code to work
without else.
```

7. There are a lot of errors, but Magento 2 defines its own rules for PHPMD. To run a test with these rules, we can run the following command:

```
phpmd app/code/Magento/Cms/Model/Observer.php text
dev/tests/static/testsuite/Magento/Test/Php/_files/phpmd/
ruleset.xml
```

8. This command gives empty output, which means that this file is valid.

9. We will now run a test on the same file with PHP_CodeSniffer. With the next command, we will run a test on the same file we used for PHPMD.

```
phpcs app/code/Magento/Cms/Model/Observer.php
```

10. This test gives us the following output:

```
FILE: /var/www/magento2/app/code/Magento/Cms/Model/Observer.php
--------------------------------------------------------------------
----
FOUND 22 ERRORS AND 2 WARNINGS AFFECTING 12 LINES
--------------------------------------------------------------------
----
     5 | WARNING | [ ] PHP version not specified
     5 | ERROR   | [ ] Missing @category tag in file comment
     5 | ERROR   | [ ] Missing @package tag in file comment
     5 | ERROR   | [ ] Missing @author tag in file comment
     5 | ERROR   | [ ] Missing @license tag in file comment
     5 | ERROR   | [ ] Missing @link tag in file comment
    10 | ERROR   | [ ] Missing @category tag in class comment
    10 | ERROR   | [ ] Missing @package tag in class comment
    10 | ERROR   | [ ] Missing @author tag in class comment
```

```
 10 | ERROR   | [ ] Missing @license tag in class comment
 10 | ERROR   | [ ] Missing @link tag in class comment
 18 | ERROR   | [ ] Protected member variable "_cmsPage" must not
be
    |         |     prefixed with an underscore
 25 | ERROR   | [ ] Protected member variable "_scopeConfig" must
not
    |         |     be prefixed with an underscore
 27 | ERROR   | [ ] Missing short description in doc comment
 28 | ERROR   | [ ] Missing parameter comment
 28 | ERROR   | [x] Expected 27 spaces after parameter type; 1
found
 29 | ERROR   | [ ] Missing parameter comment
 42 | ERROR   | [ ] Missing parameter comment
 42 | ERROR   | [x] Tag value indented incorrectly; expected 2
spaces
    |         |     but found 1
 43 | ERROR   | [ ] Tag cannot be grouped with parameter tags in a
    |         |     doc comment
 62 | ERROR   | [ ] Missing parameter comment
 62 | ERROR   | [x] Tag value indented incorrectly; expected 2
spaces
    |         |     but found 1
 63 | ERROR   | [ ] Tag cannot be grouped with parameter tags in a
    |         |     doc comment
 78 | WARNING | [ ] Line exceeds 85 characters; contains 94
    |         |     characters
--------------------------------------------------------------------
----

PHPCBF CAN FIX THE 3 MARKED SNIFF VIOLATIONS AUTOMATICALLY
--------------------------------------------------------------------
----


Time: 28ms; Memory: 3.75Mb
```

 If the `phpmd` command is not working, you have to find the path to the `phpmd` executable and run it from there.

11. When we specify the ruleset of Magento 2, we have the following command:

```
phpcs app/code/Magento/Cms/Model/Observer.php --standard=
dev/tests/static/testsuite/Magento/Test/Php/_files/phpcs/
ruleset.xml
```

12. This command gives us the following output:

```
FILE: /var/www/magento2/app/code/Magento/Cms/Model/Observer.php
------------------------------------------------------------------
----
FOUND 5 ERRORS AFFECTING 5 LINES
------------------------------------------------------------------
----
 18 | ERROR | Missing variable doc comment
 25 | ERROR | Missing variable doc comment
 31 | ERROR | Missing function doc comment
 45 | ERROR | Missing function doc comment
 65 | ERROR | Missing function doc comment
------------------------------------------------------------------
----


Time: 35ms; Memory: 3.75Mb
```

How it works...

PHPMD and PHP_CodeSniffer are tools that checks PHP files on code style. These tools have defined their default rulesets for common usage.

Magento has created its own rulesets; they can be found in the directory `dev/tests/static/testsuite/Magento/Test/Php/_files/phpcs/ruleset.xml`.

When developing custom code in Magento 2, it is recommended that you configure these rulesets when working with PHPMD and PHP_CodeSniffer.

There's more...

Some IDE's have built-in support for PHPMD and PHP_CodeSniffer. These plugins will run a test when saving a file.

In NetBeans, you have the **phpcsmd** plugin that allows you to integrate these tools in your IDE. For more details visit the following URL:

`http://plugins.netbeans.org/plugin/40282/phpmd-php-codesniffer-plugin`

In **PHPStorm**, there is built-in support for PHPMD and PHP_CodeSniffer. If it is configured, there is a color indicator that says how clean your code is. More information can be found at `https://www.jetbrains.com/phpstorm/help/using-php-mess-detector.html`.

When configuring PHPMD and PHP_CodeSniffer in an IDE, these tools and PHP need to be installed on the machine on which the IDE is running.

Working with Products

2

In this chapter, we will cover the following recipes:

- ▸ Configuring the catalog defaults
- ▸ Working with attribute sets
- ▸ Working with product types
- ▸ Adding social media buttons
- ▸ Embedding an HTML object
- ▸ Changing the URL of a product page

Introduction

How products are displayed in the frontend is very important for making a web shop with good usability. Convincing the visitors to buy something from the shop is the main target of every shop owner.

Products need to be set in such a way that a visitor can quickly find what he is looking for. With good product content, a shop looks reliable, due to which a visitor is more likely to buy something.

In this chapter, we will explain what you can do to display products in your shop, and we will see some extra things, such as a video and add to cart links, to raise conversion from a prospective buyer to an actual buyer.

The goal of this chapter is to make your shop more user-friendly with just a little development.

Configuring the catalog defaults

One of the first things is to configure some default catalog settings to the preferred values. We will cover all the configuration values that are possible in a Magento 2 installation.

We will go through the available configurations and change some values to the recommended settings.

Getting ready

Open your frontend and log into the backend in a separate browser tab. We will modify some configuration values to the recommended settings. When changing a configuration value, we can check what happens in the frontend.

How to do it

In the next steps, we will take a look at the catalog settings:

1. In the backend, navigate to **Stores | Settings | Configuration**. Open the **Catalog** menu, as we can see in the following screenshot:

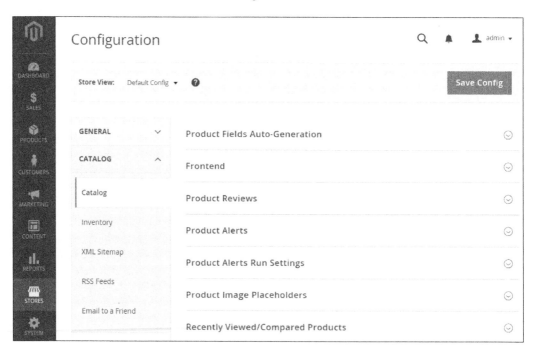

2. Open the **Product Fields Auto-Generation** section. In this section, we can configure the behavior of the generation of SKU and metadata. When we add the following values for **the Mask for Meta Keywords**, the SKU, name, and the string "Magento" will be generated when saving a product:

   ❑ **{{sku}}, {{name}}, Magento**

3. Open the **Storefront** section and set the following values:

   ❑ **List mode**: `grid` (by default, this shows the products in a grid or list)

   ❑ **Products per page on Grid allowed values**: `12, 24, 36`

   ❑ **Products per page on Grid default value**: `24`

> When changing the allowed and default value for a grid page, ensure that you can divide the numbers by the number of products that fit in a row in your theme. Otherwise, the last row of products will not be complete.

   ❑ **Products per page on List allowed values**: `10, 20, 30, 40`

   ❑ **Products per page on List default value**: `10`

   ❑ **Allow all products per page**: `No`

> When you have a large number of products, it is not recommended to set the **Allow all products per page option** to `Yes`. When you have 2000 products and you want to show all the products on a single page, you will generate an enormous HTML output that can cause memory issues.

   ❑ **Product listing Sort by**: `price`

   ❑ **Use Flat Catalog Category**: `No`

   ❑ **Use Flat Catalog Product**: `No`

   ❑ **Allow Dynamic Media URL's in Products and Categories**: `Yes`

4. Enable the product reviews for guests. This allows everyone to write a review about a product. When this is enabled, a review form will appear on the product review page.

5. Open the **Product Alerts** section to configure product alert e-mails that will be sent when the price or stock changes.

6. We will configure a stock alert with the following settings:

   ❑ **Allow alert when product price changes**: `No`

   ❑ **Allow alert when product comes back in stock**: `Yes`

The previous configurations will send stock alert e-mails (a stock alert is triggered when a product becomes available in stock) to the subscribed e-mail addresses.

7. We can set the values for **Product Alerts Run settings** in the next section. We will configure a daily task at 04:00 hours to send the alert e-mails:

   ❑ **Frequency**: Daily

   ❑ **Start time**: 04:00:00

8. Leave the **Product Image Placeholders** options as they are. If we want, we can set a default image that will be shown when a product has no image or the image is not found. The best way is to set the placeholder images in the theme.

9. In the **Recently Viewed/Compared Products** tab, set the following values:

   ❑ **Show for current**: Website

 This will show the recent products you viewed over all stores and store views in the website.

   ❑ **Default recently viewed count**: 5

   ❑ **Default recently compared count**: 5

10. In the **Price** tab, set the **Catalog Price Scope** option as Global. For this tutorial, we don't need different prices for each store view. When **Price Scope** is set to Global, we can only configure one global price for a product, which will be the same in all store views.

11. In the **Layered Navigation** section, we will modify some settings to customize the left navigation for the category pages:

    ❑ **Display product count**: Yes

    ❑ **Price navigation step calculation**: Automatic (this will equalize price ranges)

12. By making these settings, the price steps will always have the same increment.

13. Open the **Category Top Navigation** section, and set **Maximal Depth** to 3. This means that the navigation will be shown with a maximum of three levels.

14. In the *Changing the URL of a product page* recipe, we will look at the **Search Enginge Optimization** step.

15. Configure the **Catalog Search** section as follows:

   ❑ **Minimal Query Length**: 3

   ❑ **Maximum Query Length**: 128

   ❑ **Search Engine**: MySQL

   ❑ **Apply Layered Navigation if Search Results are Less Than**: 0

 If a search result shows a lot of products, the generation of the layered navigation slows down the pageload. With this setting, you can disable the layered navigation if the results count is higher than the configured value.

16. Don't forget to save the configuration by clicking on the **Save Config** button.

How it works

All these settings are saved in the configuration table of Magento. The frontend files for the catalog pages will pick up these settings and render the output based on these settings.

When you add extra functionality to the category page, you can easily extend the configuration with extra parameters. More information about extending the configurations is given in the *Extending the system configuration* recipe of *Chapter 6, Magento Backend*.

Working with attribute sets

Magento has a flexible system to work with products. When you sell, for example, a board game or a computer, the specifications of each product are different. For a board game, information such as age and duration is relevant. For a computer, a lot of technical specifications are relevant, such as the CPU power, disc size, and so on.

To cover this, Magento 2 comes with a system called **product templates**, which can be compared with **attribute sets** in Magento 1.

A product template is a specification of product attributes that you can assign to products.

Getting ready

In the backend, we will use the pages **Stores | Attributes | Product** and **Stores | Attributes | Attribute Set**.

We will create a newproduct attribute and a new product template (such as an attribute set) that we can use in new products.

How to do it

In the following steps, we will create an extra product attribute that we can use in a product template:

1. Navigate to **Stores | Attributes | Product** in the backend, and click on the **Add New Attribute** button.

2. Populate the form with the following instructions:

   ❑ **Default label**: `Available from` (This label will be used to identify the attribute)

   ❑ **Catalog Input Type for Store Owner**: `Date` (this is the type of the attribute)

3. Click on **Save and Continue Edit** and the attribute will be saved. You will see that the **Attribute Code** field is prepopulated with a code that is generated from the label.

4. Additionally, we can set the following values:

   ❑ **Values required**: `No`

   ❑ **Scope**: `Store View` (with this setting, we create the possibility to specify separate values for each store view)

   ❑ **Default value**: Leave this field empty

   ❑ **Unique value**: `No`

5. In the **Manage Labels** tab, we can set the label that will be displayed on the product detail page. If left empty, the attribute label will be used.

6. In the **Storefront Properties** tab, we can set the following properties:

   ❑ **Use in search**: `No`

   ❑ **Comparable on Storefront**: `No`

   ❑ **Use for Promo Rule Conditions**: `No`

   ❑ **Allow HTML Tags on frontend**: `No`

   ❑ **Visible on Catalog Pages on Storefront**: `No`

   ❑ **Used in Product Listing**: `No`

   ❑ **Used for Sorting in Product Listing**: `No`

7. Click on **Save Attribute**; this will save the attribute.

8. The next step is to create an **Attribute Set** to which will assign a product to. In the backend, navigate to **Stores | Attributes | Attribute Set**.

9. Click on the **Add Attribute Set** button and fill in the form, as follows:

10. Clicking on **Save** will open the overview page.
11. Create a group named **Game specific data** and drag the **available_from** and **manufacturer** attributes to it. The overview will look as follows:

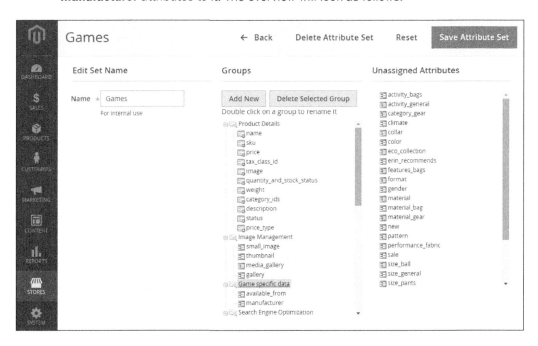

12. Save the Attribute Set.

13. Navigate to **Product | Catalog** and create a new product by clicking on the **New Product** button.

14. Select the right Attribute Set in the form, as shown in the following screenshot:

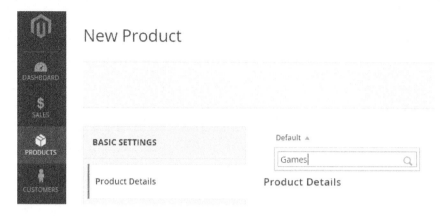

15. When selecting the **product template**, you will see that the **Game specific data** tab appears in the product tab, as shown in the following screenshot:

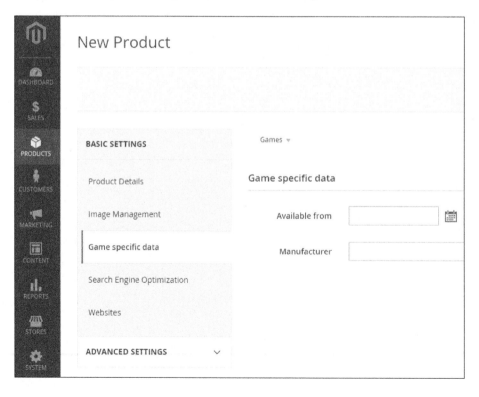

How it works

Product attributes and **Attribute Sets** are used when you work with multiple families of products. In the sample data of our shop, there are more attribute sets available for bags, clothing, and more.

With Attribute Sets, you can make groups of attributes for every product family. When creating a product attribute, you have to choose the type of the attribute, which can be one of the following:

- Text field
- Text area
- Date
- Yes/No
- Multiple select
- Dropdown
- Price
- Media image
- Fixed Product Tax

 When you want to use an attribute as a filter in the left navigation on the category pages, this attribute must have the type Dropdown, Multiple Select or Price.

Working with product types

In Magento 2, it is still possible to work with different types of products. The standard product is a simple product, which is used to sell basic products, but there are more types available, such as products, where you can choose a size and other options, or download products, virtual products (such as a license), and product combinations.

Getting ready

In this recipe, we will create a configurable product, for example, you want to buy a pair of shoes where you can choose their size and color. Open the Magento backend and navigate to **Products | Catalog**.

How to do it

In the following steps, we will create a product where we can specify a size on the product detail page:

1. Navigate to **Products | Catalog**, click on the arrow near the **Add Product** button, and choose **Configurable Product** as shown in the following screenshot:

2. Choose a name, SKU, and price for the product.

3. The next step is to decide the attribute on which we want to configure our product. Scroll down through the **New Products** page, and click on the **Create Configurations** button. In the grid, select the **Size** attribute and click on **Next**.

4. Select the sizes for your products and click on **Next**.

5. On the next screen, you can add images, prices, and quantities for the products, or you can do this later.

6. When you click on **Next**, you will get an overview. When you click on **Generate Products**, the products will be displayed as shown in the following screenshot:

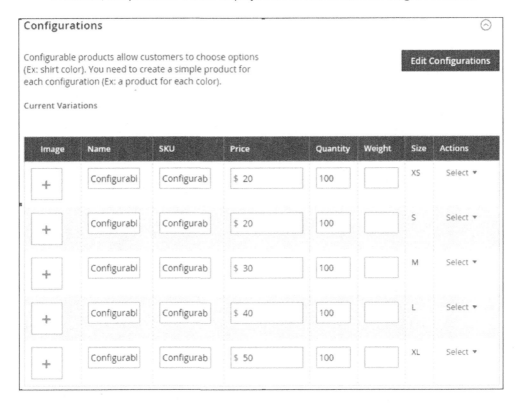

7. Click on the **Save** button and a popup will show up to create a specific attribute set for this configuration. Select the **Add configurable attributes to the new set based on current** option and select a Size for the name.

8. Click on **Confirm** to save the products in the database.

9. On the **Product Edit** page, select the category where you want to add the product, click on **Save**, and search for the product in the right category in the frontend. The product detail page will look as follows:

How it works...

A configurable product is a product where you can select one or more options on the product detail page. Each combination of selections leads to a simple product in the database. The customer chooses the options, and when adding the configurable product to the cart, a simple product is also added in the background.

This is the reason why we have generated simple products to be shown as options in our configurable product. The configurable product is a parent wrapper that is used to display in the frontend. The simple products are hidden in the frontend by the Visibility attribute.

When a product is sold, the SKU of the selected child product will be used to process the order. That's the reason why we have to configure a stock on the child products.

There's more...

In Magento, we can create six types of product. The following overview gives a short description of what is possible with the different product types.

A simple product

A simple product is just a product that you can sell in your web shop. Every product in Magento has a unique ID (**SKU**) that mostly has the same value as the article code of the suppliers.

A configurable product

In this recipe, we created a configurable product. This product has child products that you can configure on the product page (for example, to configure the size). The child products are simple products.

A bundle product

A bundled product is like a configurable product, but with this one, you can (optionally) specify more options.

In the sample data, you can find a good example by navigating to **Gear | Fitness Equipment | Sprite Yoga Companion Kit**.

 Every option of a bundle represents another product in the shop. When you add a bundle product to the cart, the products of the chosen configuration will also be added to the cart in the background.

A grouped product

A grouped product is a product that represents a set in which you can specify the number of child products. A good example of this can be found by navigating to **Gear | Fitness Equipment | Set of Sprite Yoga Straps**.

In a grouped product, you assign simple products. When adding a grouped product to the cart, the child products will be added as separate products with the configured quantity.

A virtual product

A virtual product is like a simple product but it is not physical. It has no inventory and can't be shipped. A good example of a virtual product is a software license.

A downloadable product

A downloadable product is a product that is not physical. When a customer buys a downloadable product, a download link will be sent to the customer so that they can download their product, which is in the form of a PDF, MP3, ZIP file, or any other type of file.

Adding social media buttons

These days, an increasing number of people are sharing their minds through different social media, such as Facebook, Twitter, and many more.

Every social media platform has the option to share pages on their platform. The most famous examples of this are the share buttons, such as the **Like** button of Facebook, the **Tweet** button, the **Google Plus** button, and many more.

Getting ready

In this recipe, we will add share buttons for the following platforms. You can take a look at the developer documentation of each platform as a preparatory step:

- Facebook (`https://developers.facebook.com/docs/plugins/like-button`)
- Twitter (`https://about.twitter.com/resources/buttons`)
- Google Plus (`https://developers.google.com/+/web/+1button/`)

To show a button on every product page, we have to do some code changes. Ensure that you have access to the code with your IDE.

How to do it

The following steps show you how to add social media buttons to the description of your product:

1. Open the page of the product where you want to add the social media buttons.
2. We will start with the **Like** button of Facebook. Visit `https://developers.facebook.com/docs/plugins/like-button` and configure the following form with your data:

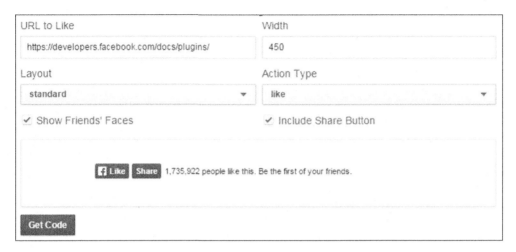

3. When clicking the **Get Code** button, you will see the code of the button. Place this code in the product description field.

4. Save the product and open the **Product Detail** page of that product in the frontend. You will see a **Like** button in the description field of the product.

5. We can also add buttons for sharing on other social media using the same principle. For Twitter, we can get the code of a button at `https://about.twitter.com/resources/buttons`. From here, copy the code and paste it after the code of the Facebook Like button.

6. Similarly, for Google Plus, we can get a button at `https://developers.google.com/+/web/+1button/` from where we can copy the code and paste it in the description field of the product.

7. When reloading the frontend, we can see the buttons on the detail page of that product. If we want to show it on every page, we will have to make a change in the code of the product detail template.

8. If you have a custom theme, copy and paste the `app/code/Magento/Catalog/view/frontend/templates/product/view/description.phtml` file to the configured `app/design/frontend/<package>/<theme>/Magento_Catalog/templates/product/view/description.phtml` theme.

 If you have no custom theme installed, take a look at the *Creating a Magento 2 theme* recipe of *Chapter 3, Theming*. In that recipe, all the steps are explained on how to do this.

9. Add the code of the social media buttons at the end of the file. You generate the product URL with the following code: `$block->getProduct()->getProductUrl()`. Use this code to generate the URL for the button. The code for the Facebook **Like** button code will look as follows:

```
<div class="fb-like"
    data-href="<?php echo $block->getProduct()->getProductUrl()
?>"
    data-width="450"
    data-layout="standard"
    data-action="like"
    data-show-faces="true"
    data-share="true">
</div>
```

10. Save the file, clean the cache, and you will see the **Like** button on every page.

How it works

A social media button is mostly a piece of external HTML that will render in your website. With this button, a page can be shared.

To render these buttons, external static resources from the social media website will be loaded. When you read the code of the buttons, you can see that additional JavaScript libraries are included in the code.

When sharing a page, the social media crawls the page to look for a title, image, and description for the post. In the first case, the crawler will search for the **Open Graph** meta tags.

These tags are generated by Magento on a product detail page, so a good title, image, and description will be displayed for the post.

Embedding an HTML object

In a product description, we can add HTML tags so that we can use the `<object>` tag. With an `<object>` tag, we can embed widgets, such as a YouTube video, social widgets, and more.

In this recipe, we will focus on how to add a YouTube video in a product description.

Getting ready

Go to `http://www.youtube.com`, and choose a video that you want to show on the product detail page.

How to do it

The next steps shows you how to embed a YouTube video on a product detail page.

1. On the YouTube video page, click on the **Embed** button. When you click this button, the following screen shows up:

2. Copy the HTML code and paste it in the description of the product.

3. Save the product.

4. Go to the product in the frontend. You will see the video on the **Product** page.

How it works

The ability to use HTML tags in product descriptions gives a lot of flexibility for this field. It is possible to use a WYSIWYG editor for the content because this allows us to use widgets, such as a YouTube video or other third-party widgets.

On a YouTube video page, we opened the embed options where we can configure the code that we will include in our site. We can specify options such as width, height, color and more.

When everything is configured, we can paste the Embed code in the HTML of the product description, and the video will be visible in the description of the product.

Changing the URL of a product page

When you are on a product page, the URL of every product always looks clean. The name in the URL makes it very **SEO** friendly.

In this recipe, we will explore the possibilities of URL rewrites in Magento.

Getting ready

In the backend, navigate to **Products | Inventory | Catalog** and look for a simple product with visibility **Catalog, Search**. This recipe is based on the **Endeavor Daytrip Backpack** product from the sample data.

How to do it

In the following steps, we will see the procedure for changing a URL of a product detail page.

1. Find the appropriate product in the frontend. You can find by navigating to **Gear | Bags**. If you open the product detail page, you will see the URL `/endeavor-daytrip-backpack.html`.

2. In the backend, change the URL key attribute to `buy-now-endeavor-daytrip-backpack`.

3. Reload the product in the frontend. The URL will change to the one we have just entered in the backend.

When you select the **Create Permanent Redirect** option for an old URL checkbox, Magento will create a permanent 301 redirect response for the old URL of the product. The checkbox is located in the product edit page in the backend under the URL Key attribute.

4. Empty the URL key attribute at the backend and save the product again. You will see that Magento autogenerates the URL key attribute based on the name of the product.

5. At the backend, navigate to **Stores | Configuration | Catalog | Search Engine Optimizations**. Clear the product **URL Suffix** field and save the configuration.

6. Clear the cache by navigating to **System | Cache Management**.

7. Reload the product in the frontend, and you will see that the `.html` suffix is gone.

> In Magento 1, there was a URL rewrite index, in Magento 2, this index is replaced by a new system to generate the URLs.

How it works

In Magento, there is a URL rewrite system that maps an SEO-friendly URL to the system's URL. In technical terms, this is also called **routing**. In the backend, you can see all the URL rewrites that are available in the installation.

You can see this by navigating to **Marketing | SEO & Search | URL Rewrites** in the backend. On this page, you can see the complete list of the URLs that are available in the web shop. If we search for `endeavor-daytrip-backpack`, we will see a list of all the URLs, which looks like this.

What we see is the following:

- ▸ Permanent 301 redirect responses (rows where the Redirect Type column is Permanent (301))
- ▸ The Product URL
- ▸ The URL of a product in every category

All the URLs are generated separately for each store views. When a product is enabled in multiple stores, it is normal that a product has more than one URL.

There's more

On the URL rewrite page, it is also possible to add custom URL rewrites. For example, a URL rewrite for the contact page.

When adding the **Add new URL Rewrite** button, a form shows up. The following screenshot shows us how we can create an alias from the `contact-us.html` URL to the `/contact` page:

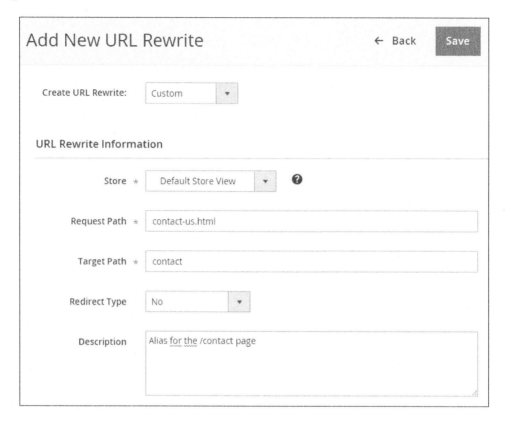

In the **Store** option, you can configure the store for the URL rewrite.

The value in the **Request Path** field is the path that you want to rewrite; in this case, we want to rewrite something on the `/contact-us.html` path.

The value in the **Target Path** field is the path where the request will end; in this case, it is the `/contact` page.

If the value in **Redirect Type** is set to `No`, the target path will be rendered on the request path (so, the URL doesn't change). You also have the choice to redirect the page with a permanent (301) or temporary (302) redirect.

3
Theming

In this chapter, we will cover:

- ▶ Exploring the default Magento 2 themes
- ▶ Creating a Magento 2 theme
- ▶ Customizing the HTML output
- ▶ Adding extra files to the theme
- ▶ Working with LESS
- ▶ Changing a page title
- ▶ Working with translations
- ▶ Adding widgets to the layout
- ▶ Customizing email templates

Introduction

The most common customization on a Magento shop is the theming. Making a good first impression to your customers is an important point to raise the conversion. Almost every store owner wants a look and feel of their company in their shop.

In this chapter, we will cover all the things you need to customize a Magento theme. We will see how we can customize the templates, CSS, JavaScript, translations, and more.

Exploring the default Magento 2 themes

When Magento 2 is installed, there are two themes available. You have the **Luma** theme that you can see in the sample data, and you have the **Blank** theme that is developed as a starting point to customize your theme.

Log in to the backend and open the design configuration. We can find this in **Stores | Configuration | Design**.

How to do it...

The following instructions describe how we can configure the theme settings for a Magento 2 store:

1. When you look at the theme settings on the configuration page, we see that the **Magento Luma** theme is selected in the **Design Theme** section. Select the **Magento Blank** option in the dropdown, save the configuration, and reload the frontend. You should see something like the following screenshot:

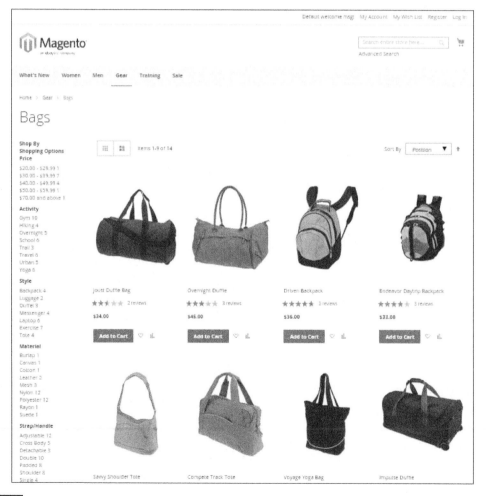

2. We have now configured the Magento Blank theme for the store. The Magento Blank theme is the default theme where the Magento Luma theme will extend from.

3. Open the page **Content | Themes** in the backend and you will see an overview of the available themes in Magento. When Magento 2 is installed without modules, the following themes are available:

   ❑ Magento Blank (used as the default theme)

   ❑ Magento Luma (used in the sample data store)

4. When clicking on **Magento Luma**, we will see the details of the theme like the following screenshot:

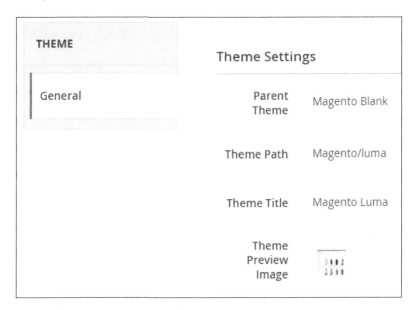

5. We see that the **Parent Theme** is **Magento Blank**. This means that this theme will extend the **Magento Blank** theme.

6. In the backend, open the page **Content | Schedule**. When clicking the **Add Design Change** button, we can configure a design change with a from and to date.

How it works...

In Magento 2 the concept of themes is much easier than in Magento 1. There are no packages any more, and no skins.

In Magento 2, a theme can have a parent theme and that's all. When a theme has a parent theme, it will inherit everything from that parent theme except you can override it in your theme. This means that if your theme is empty, all the settings of the parent theme will be used.

Like in Magento 1, you can override the theme settings in different ways such as the following:

- By a User Agent Exception on the **Stores | Configuration | Design page**
- By a scheduled theme setting on the **Content | Schedule** page
- On a specific CMS page (can be configured on the **Design** section of a CMS edit page)
- On a specific product detail page (this can be configured on the **Design** section of a product edit page)
- On a specific category page (this can be configured on the **Custom Design** step of a category)

Creating a Magento 2 theme

We will start customizing the look and feel of the shop by creating a custom theme. The purpose of a custom theme is that we don't have to modify the core files delivered by Magento.

Getting ready

Open your Magento webroot in your favorite IDE. We will create a theme and, for this, we will work in the `app/design/frontend` folder.

Before you start, disable the full-page cache because this will save you a lot of trouble. You can do this in the backend on the page **System | Cache Management**. Click on the **Flush Magento Cache** button after you have disabled the **Full page caching**.

How to do it...

The following procedure shows you which actions are required to create a custom theme:

1. For our theme, we will create a vendor namespace. We can do this by creating the folder `app/design/frontend/Packt`.

A theme namespace is always written in `CamelCase` such as `Magento`, `Packt`.

2. In that namespace, we will create a theme called `cookbook`. First, create the folder `app/design/frontend/Packt/cookbook`.

A theme is always written in small letters such as `luma`, `cookbook`, `blank`.

3. To register the theme, we have to create the file with the following content:

```php
<?php

\Magento\Framework\Component\ComponentRegistrar::register(
    \Magento\Framework\Component\ComponentRegistrar::THEME,
    'frontend/Packt/cookbook',
    __DIR__
);
```

4. At this point, we have to create a `theme` configuration file. We can do this by creating the file `app/design/frontend/Packt/cookbook/theme.xml` with the following content:

```xml
<theme xmlns:xsi="http://www.w3.org/2001/XMLSchema-
instance" xsi:noNamespaceSchemaLocation="urn:magento:
framework:Config/etc/theme.xsd">
    <title>Packt Cookbook</title>
    <parent>Magento/blank</parent>
</theme>
```

5. It is also possible to add a preview image to the theme. In the `theme` folder, create a media folder in the `theme` folder and add an image of your choice that we want to use as a preview.

6. To set the preview image, we have to add the highlighted XML configuration to the `theme.xml` file:

```xml
...
    <title>Packt Cookbook</title>
    <parent>Magento/blank</parent>
    <media>
        <preview_image>media/preview.png</preview_image>
    </media>
</theme>
```

7. Clear the cache and run the `composer install` to register the theme.

8. To test whether the theme exists, navigate to the page **Content | Themes** in the Magento backend. You should see the theme in the list. When we click on the theme, we can see the details that we have configured in the `theme.xml` file.

9. The last step is to configure the theme. Go to the page **Stores | Configuration | Design** and configure the theme like the following screenshot:

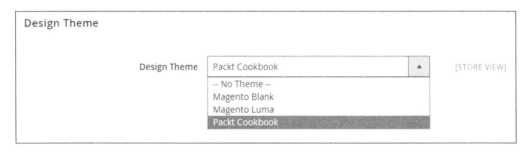

10. Flush the cache and reload the frontend. Your shop will now have the look and feel of the Blank theme.

 If you want to uninstall a theme, you can use the command `php bin/ magento theme:uninstall`.

How it works...

We have just created an empty theme that inherits everything from the Magento base theme. When we want to change stuff on the theme, we can do it in this theme without overriding the core.

When we want to customize some aspects of the theme, we can copy a file from the `Magento/Blank` theme and paste it in our theme. When copying a file, the directory structure needs to be the same as the structure of the parent theme.

 Changing code in the Magento core will also work, but this is *not recommended*. When you want to upgrade your store, all the core files will be overwritten and then all your changes will be lost.

We created a `theme.xml` file in our theme where we have set the default settings of the theme such as the name and parent theme. Magento will store this data in the theme table of the database.

 All the XML configurations will be cached by Magento. So when the caches are enabled and you change something in the `config` files, make sure you clean and flush the caches. You can also disable the caches when developing. You can clean the cache using the command `php bin/ magento cache:clean` or you can do it in the backend.

There's more...

In Magento, it is possible to enable template hints in the frontend. When this is enabled, containers will be shown around blocks of HTML with the reference to the file and class that is loaded.

To enable this, navigate to **Stores | Configuration | Advanced | Developer** and change the configuration scope dropdown to **Main Website** like the following screenshot:

In the **Debug** section, you can enable the hints by setting the dropdown values to `Yes` for the following fields: **Template Path Hints** and **Add Block Names to Hints**.

When this is done, reload your frontend and you will see red borders around each block of HTML.

Customizing the HTML output

You can customize a theme in two ways. We can only change some styles to make a shop look different. The second way is to customize the HTML output, which is what we will cover in this recipe.

It is very common to want to change some stuff on the HTML structure to make your shop look unique.

Getting ready

Make sure you have the theme installed and configured like we have done in the previous recipe.

If you don't have the theme installed, you can install the start files for this recipe.

How to do it...

In the next steps, we will change the logo, change a template, and we will add extra blocks to the footer:

1. First we will change the logo. If you look at the frontend of the webshop, you will see that the default Magento logo is used. This is an **SVG** image but what if I have a **PNG** image? Create a `logo.png` file in the folder `app/design/frontend/Packt/cookbook/web/images`. If this folder doesn't exist, create one.

2. The second step is to create a layout configuration file in the folder `app/design/frontend/Packt/cookbook/Magento_Theme/layout`.

3. In that folder, create a `default.xml` configuration with the following content:

```xml
<?xml version="1.0"?>
<page xmlns:xsi="http://www.w3.org/2001/XMLSchema-instance"
xsi:noNamespaceSchemaLocation="urn:magento:framework:View/
Layout/etc/page_configuration.xsd">
    <body>
        <referenceBlock name="logo">
            <action method="setLogoFile">
                <argument name="logo_file"
                xsi:type="string">
                images/logo.png</argument>
            </action>
        </referenceBlock>
        <referenceBlock name="logo" remove="true" />
    </body>
</page>
```

4. Flush the cache and reload the frontend. You should see that the logo is changed to the specified file.

5. Next we will change the toolbar on the category pages. In the frontend, navigate to a category page with products such as **Women | Tops**.

6. To change the output of a category page, we have to override the template. To know what template is used, we can enable the template hints. Enabling the template hints is described in the *There's more* section of the previous recipe *Creating a Magento 2 theme*.

7. With the template hints enabled, we see the template located in `app/code//Magento/Catalog/view/frontend/templates/product/list.phtml`. To override this template, copy and paste that file in `app/design/frontend/Packt/cookbook/Magento_Catalog/templates/product/`. If that folder doesn't exist, create it.

8. Clean the cache and reload the page. In the template hints, you will see that the file we just copied is used instead of the default one.

 If you don't see any changes to the frontend, you have to flush the Magento cache. Also disable the full-page cache when developing.

9. In this file, we can change what we want without overriding the core.

10. At last, we will add an extra menu with links in the footer. For this, we need to edit the file: `app/design/frontend/Packt/cookbook/Magento_Theme/layout/default.xml`.

11. Paste the following highlighted code in that XML file:

```
...
            </action>
        </referenceBlock>
        <referenceBlock name="footer">
            <block
            class="Magento\Framework\View\Element\Html
            \Links" name="footer_links_account" after=
            "footer_links">
                <arguments>
                    <argument name="css_class"
                    xsi:type="string">footer links
                    </argument>
                </arguments>
                <block
                class="Magento\Framework\View\Element\Html
                \Link\Current" name="my-account-link">
                    <arguments>
                        <argument name="label"
                        xsi:type="string">My account
                        </argument>
                        <argument name="path"
                        xsi:type="string">
                        customer/account</argument>
                    </arguments>
                </block>
                <block
                class="Magento\Framework\View\Element
                \Html\Link\Current" name="my-cart-link">
                    <arguments>
                        <argument name="label"
                        xsi:type="string">My cart
                        </argument>
```

```
                    <argument name="path"
                    xsi:type="string">
                    checkout/cart</argument>
                </arguments>
            </block>
        </block>
    </referenceBlock>
</body>
</page>
```

12. You have to paste the highlighted code as a child of the `<body>` tag.

13. Clean the cache and reload the frontend. You should now see an extra column in the footer with two links in it.

14. To end this recipe, we will add a link to the menu we have just created but that menu item is only visible on the cart page. To realize this, we have to add the file `app/design/frontend/Packt/cookbook/Magento_Theme/layout/checkout_cart_index.xml`.

15. In that file, add the following content:

```
<?xml version="1.0"?>
<page xmlns:xsi="http://www.w3.org/2001/XMLSchema-instance"
layout="1column" xsi:noNamespaceSchemaLocation="urn:magento:framew
ork:View/
Layout/etc/page_configuration.xsd">
    <body>
        <referenceContainer name="footer_links_account">
            <block class="Magento\Framework\View\Element\
            Html\Link\Current" name="checkout-link">
                <arguments>
                    <argument name="label" xsi:type="string">Go to
checkout</argument>
                    <argument name="path"
xsi:type="string">checkout/onepage</argument>
                </arguments>
            </block>
        </referenceContainer>
    </body>
</page>
```

16. Clean the cache and go to the cart page. You will see that there is an extra link in the menu.

How it works...

With the template hints on, we see that a lot of HTML blocks are used to build the page. All these blocks are configured in the layout XML files.

Every block in the page is from a specific type. This type is the class that is used to generate the block. The block class contains functions that could be called in the template by calling the `$block` variable.

In the layout XML files, the type of the block is specified with the class attribute.

For changing the logo file, we have changed a parameter of the block class that is used for the logo. With the XML configuration in the `default.xml` page, we have modified the `logo_file` parameter of that class for all pages. Every block has a name and by using the `<referenceBlock name="block_name">` tag, we can modify the contents of the block. We can modify page arguments like we have done with the logo or we can add child blocks like we have done with the extra footer menu.

The extra footer menu is a new block that we have specified as a child of the footer block. In the footer menu block, we have specified the links that are also implemented as a block.

We add the new block in the `default.xml` file. This means that the configuration is loaded on all pages.

If you want to add a configuration that is only for a specific page, you have to put that configuration in a different file. The name of the file is the layout handle that is used such as `checkout_cart_index` for the cart page.

Adding extra files to the theme

In the previous recipe, we learned how we can make structural changes to the HTML output. However an HTML output is not a completed website. With JavaScript and CSS, we can theme the HTML output.

Getting ready

We will learn how we can add CSS and JavaScript files to our theme. This is a common case when integrating an external JavaScript plugin. To do this, we have to work in the `theme` folder that we created in the recipe *Creating a Magento 2 theme* earlier in this chapter.

How to do it...

The following steps describe how we can add extra files to a theme:

1. Open the frontend and open the HTML source of a page, and have a look at the `<head>` section. We see that the included JS and CSS files are located in the `pub/static` map.

2. If we want to add an extra CSS file we have to configure that in the layout XML files. Open or create the file `app/design/frontend/Packt/cookbook/Magento_Theme/layout/default_head_blocks.xml`.

3. In that file add the following content:

```xml
<?xml version="1.0"?>
<page xmlns:xsi="http://www.w3.org/2001/XMLSchema-instance" xsi:no
NamespaceSchemaLocation="urn:magento:framework:View/
Layout/etc/page_configuration.xsd">
    <head>
        <css src="css/cookbook.css" />
    </head>
</page>
```

4. Create the file `app/design/frontend/Packt/cookbook/web/css/cookbook.css` and add the following content in it:

```css
body {
    background-color:#dcdcdc;
}
```

5. Clean the cache and reload the frontend. You will see that the background color is changed to light gray and that the `cookbook.css` file is included in the `<head>` section.

> In the next recipe, we will see how we can generate CSS using the LESS pre-processor in Magento 2. This method is recommended when you want to add a 3rd party CSS such as the CSS of a jQuery plugin.

6. The next thing is to add a JavaScript file to the `<head>` section. This works the same way as with the CSS file.

7. Open the file `app/design/frontend/Packt/cookbook/Magento_Theme/layout/default_head_blocks.xml` and add the highlighted code as a child of the `<head>` tag:

```
<head>
    <css src="css/cookbook.css" />
    <script src="js/cookbook.js" />
</head>
```

8. Create the file `cookbook.js` in the folder `app/design/frontend/Packt/cookbook/web/js/`.

9. Clean the cache and reload the source of the frontend. You will see that the `cookbook.js` file is added in the `<head>`.

How it works...

Like in the previous recipe, we did some layout XML configurations to add the CSS and JavaScript file. In the configuration file `default_head_blocks.xml`, we added XML configurations to add a CSS file and a JS file.

When rendering the HTML output, Magento will look for all `<head>` configuration entries and will generate a list of CSS and JS files.

We created the CSS and JavaScript files in the `theme` folder. But if we look at the HTML source, we see that Magento loads the file from a different location. The files are loaded from the `pub/static` folder.

Magento builds a symbolic link from the pub folder to the web folder in the theme. When we have static files such as CSS, JavaScript, images, web fonts, and more, we have to place these files in the web folder of the theme.

There's more...

In this recipe we learned how we can add **CSS** and **JavaScript** files to the HTML head, but with the same system we can also add meta link and title tags to the head. The following code snippet shows you how this works. This is an example of the `default_head_blocks.xml`:

```
<?xml version="1.0"?>
<page xmlns:xsi="http://www.w3.org/2001/XMLSchema-instance" xsi:no
NamespaceSchemaLocation="../../../../../../../lib/internal/Magento/
Framework/View/Layout/etc/page_configuration.xsd">
    <head>
```

```
        <css src="css/cookbook.css" />
        <script src="js/cookbook.js" />
        <link rel="publisher" src="https://www.packtpub.com/" />
        <meta name="author" content="Packt Publishing" />
    </head>
</page>
```

The `<title>` configuration is missing in this configuration. How to change a page title is explained in the recipe *Changing a page title* in this chapter.

 If you want to explore which configurations are possible in a particular XML file, have a look at the XSD file that is declared at the top of the file and you will see which configurations you can use in your `config` file.

Working with LESS

In Magento 1, the CSS of a Magento theme was stored in one big **CSS** file (the `styles.css`) but in Magento 2, it is completely different. The big CSS file has been replaced by a collection of **LESS** files.

LESS is a language that is used to generate CSS. CSS is very static. You can't use functions, variables, nesting, and so on but with LESS, you can.

Magento has a LESS pre-processor that generates a CSS file from the LESS files in the theme.

Getting ready

Open your favorite IDE and navigate to the `theme` folder of the `Packt/cookbook` theme that we have created in the previous recipes.

Access to a command line is also useful to work with **Grunt**.

How to do it...

The following steps describe how we can change the layout, such as how Magento 2 does it:

1. Copy the file `app/design/frontend/Magento/blank/web/css/source/_theme.less` to the folder `app/design/frontend/Packt/cookbook/web/css/source/_theme.less`.

If you installed Magento 2 using composer, you have to copy the `_theme. less` file from the folder `vendor/magento/theme-frontend-blank/ web/css/source/`.

2. In that file, add the following content:

```
@cookbook_primary_color: #FECA5C;
@cookbook_dark_color: #373C40;

@text__color: @cookbook_dark_color;

@navigation__background: @cookbook_primary_color;

@button-primary__background: @cookbook_primary_color;
@button-primary__border: 1px solid @cookbook_dark_color;
@button-primary__color: @cookbook_dark_color;
```

3. Reload the page. Normally you will see no layout changes because we have to clear the pre-generated file. Remove the following folders with pre-generated CSS:

   ❏ `rm -rf pub/static/*`

   ❏ `rm -rf var/view_preprocessed`

   Also don't forget to flush the cache before rendering the page.

4. Reload the page and your page will look like the following screenshot. The load time of the page is a bit longer because the CSS needs to be generated:

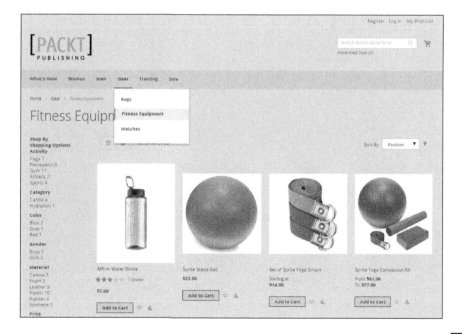

> If you get a page without styling, an error occurred when rendering the CSS file. If this happens, flush the cache and remove the folders again, as described in step 3.
>
> Another thing that can happen is that the `pub` and `var` folders do not have enough file permissions.

5. When we want to add some CSS entries to the header, we have to copy the file `app/design/frontend/Magento/blank/Magento_Theme/web/css/source/_module.less` to `app/design/frontend/Packt/cookbook/Magento_Theme/web/css/source/_module.less`.

6. Add the following highlighted code in that file around line 293. This will give the top menu a darker color:

```
. . .
.page-header {
    border: 0;
    margin-bottom: 0;
    .panel.wrapper {
        background-color: @cookbook_dark_color;
        li {
            a {
                color: @color-white;
            }
        }
        border-bottom: 1px solid @secondary__color;
    }
    .header.panel {
        padding-top: @indent__s;
        padding-bottom: @indent__s;
        &:extend(.abs-add-clearfix-desktop all);
    }
    .switcher {
        display: inline-block;
    }
}
. . .
```

7. Clean the cache and remove the folders `pub/static/*` and `var/view_preprocessed`, and reload the page. You will see that the top bar is now in a dark color.

How it works...

When working with LESS, there are a few ways of doing it. The goal is to avoid duplicate CSS code that is loaded in the browser.

First, we did some styling by changing some variables that are defined by Magento. The purpose of the `theme.less` file in the `web/css/source` directory is to override the default variables of the Magento theme. The LESS compiler converts the right values to the right CSS entries.

If you want to know which variables are available, have a look in the folder `lib/web/css/source/lib/variables`. In this folder, the variables of the default Magento components are initialized. One folder above in the `web/css/source/lib`, the CSS structure of these components is defined.

The second thing we did was to override a theme LESS file from the `Magento_Theme` module. We copied the original file to our theme. This means that the file of our theme is loaded instead of the default theme.

This process is called the **fallback mechanism**. When a file is loaded, Magento will look for it in the following order:

▸ `Theme` folder (`app/design/frontend/<Vendor>/<Theme>/web/css`)

▸ `Parent` theme folders (`app/design/frontend/<Vendor>/<Theme>/web/css`)

▸ `Module` folder (`app/code/<Vendor>/<Module>/view/frontend/web/css`)

 If you installed Magento 2 using composer, the default and Luma theme of Magento are in the `vendor/magento` folder.

When there is a change in a LESS file, we have to clear two folders. The first one is the `var/view_preprocessed` folder. In this folder, all the particular LESS files are merged in a large file.

That large file will be compiled in the folder `pub/static/frontend`. So that's the reason why we had to clear both the folders.

When Magento loads files from the `pub/static/frontend` folder that doesn't exist, Magento will look in its core folders to make those files available in this folder. For CSS files, Magento will start the generation of them. For other files such as images, Magento will create `symlinks` to the source file.

Changing files in the `pub` folder is not a good idea because you have to do it in the `app` folder and regenerate the files in `pub`.

It is also possible to use the JavaScript compiler. In the backend, you can enable it on the page **Stores | Configuration | Advanced | Developer | Front-end development workflow**.

There's more...

When working in LESS, it is not convenient to always clear the contents of the `pub/static` and `var/view_preprocessed` folders when testing the result of a change.

For normal LESS, you can install a LESS watcher, but with the modular architecture of Magento, we can use the JavaScript task runner Grunt.

With Grunt, we can configure a watcher for our theme. When there is a change in a LESS file, Grunt will regenerate the public file following the rules of Magento.

To use Grunt, we first have to install nodejs and `grunt-cli`. We can do this with the following commands (on a Ubuntu server):

- `sudo apt-get update`
- `apt-get install nodejs`
- `sudo apt-get install npm`
- `sudo npm install -g grunt-cli`

When Grunt is installed, we can configure it for our demo shop. Open your terminal and change to the Magento project root. In this directory, run the following commands:

- `npm install grunt --save-dev`
- `npm install`
- `npm update`
- `npm install grunt-contrib-less`

 These installation instructions are tested on an Ubuntu Server. If you want to install this on other operating systems, you can find more information on the following URL: `http://gruntjs.com/installing-grunt`.

Add your theme by adding the following configuration to the file `dev/tools/grunt/configs/themes.js`:

```
cookbook: {
    area: 'frontend',
    name: 'Packt/cookbook',
    locale: 'en_US',
    files: [
        'css/styles-m',
        'css/styles-l'
    ],
    dsl: 'less'
},
```

When running the command `grunt exec:cookbook`, the files will be generated for the cookbook theme.

When running `grunt watch`, these files will automatically be generated after a file change.

Changing a page title

Changing a page title helps you to improve the **SEO** of your website. For product pages, we can manage that with the backend but on other pages, such as the contact page, we can't do that.

In this recipe, we will change the page title of the contact page that is available at the `/contact` path.

How to do it...

To change the page title of the contact page, have a look at the following steps:

1. Go to the contact page in the frontend. This is available at the path `/contact`.

2. You see that the page title is set to **Contact Us**. We will change this to **Give us a message**.

3. Create the file `contact_index_index.xml` in the folder `app/design/frontend/Packt/cookbook/Magento_Contact/layout`. If that folder doesn't exist, create it.

4. In the `contact_index_index.xml` file, paste the following content:

```xml
<?xml version="1.0"?>
<page xmlns:xsi="http://www.w3.org/2001/XMLSchema-instance"
layout="1column" xsi:noNamespaceSchemaLocation="urn:magento:framew
ork:View/
Layout/etc/page_configuration.xsd">
    <head>
        <title>Give us a message!</title>
    </head>
</page>
```

5. Clean the cache and reload the frontend. You will see that the page title is changed to **Give us a message!**.

How it works...

The `<title>` and other tags in the head are generated in the class `lib/internal/Magento/Framework/Page/Config/Renderer.php`. When you look for the `renderTitle()` function, you see the following code:

```php
public function renderTitle()
{
    return '<title>' . $this->pageConfig->getTitle()->get() . '</title>' . "\n";
}
```

This function looks in the `pageConfig` for a title tag. The `pageConfig` looks in the `<head>` tag of the XML configuration file.

For other types of pages, such as a product detail page where we can set the title in the backend, the `pageConfig` values will be overwritten after loading the layout XML configuration. But for the contact page, this is not the case.

Working with translations

Magento has the ability to run a store in multiple languages. Every store view has a language, and Magento has a system to translate the interface into that particular language.

Getting ready

Open the backend and go to the store configuration at **Stores | Configuration | General**. We will configure the French language for the default store view.

How to do it...

The following steps show how we can translate the interface of Magento in a specific language:

1. First, we will configure the default language of the store view. In the backend, go to **Stores | Configuration | General** and change the locale to the preferred value. In Magento, the following language packs are installed:

   ❏ en_US—English (United States)

   ❏ de_DE—German (Germany)

   ❏ es_ES—Spanish (Spain)

   ❏ fr_FR—French (France)

   ❏ nl_NL—Dutch (Netherlands)

   ❏ pt_BR—Portuguese (Brazil)

   ❏ zh_CN—Chinese (China)

   This recipe works with a shop in the French language.

2. When cleaning the cache and reloading the frontend, you will see that the interface texts are translated into French.

3. When you want to translate existing strings, we can do this by the Inline Translation tool and we can do it in the theme. We can enable the Inline Translation tool in the backend on the page **Stores | Configuration | Advanced | Developer | Translate Inline**.

4. Reload the frontend and you will see red frames around each interface text. When hovering over a frame, an icon will appear. Click on it and a pop-up window will be shown with the translation form:

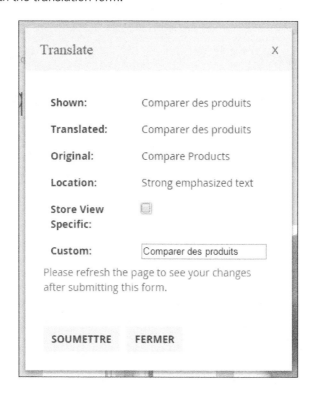

5. When submitting this form (by clicking **SOUMETTRE**), and after clearing the cache, you will see that the value you entered in this form is used.

6. The second way of translating the interface is to use a theme translation. For adding custom translations for a theme, we have to create the following file: `app/design/frontend/Packt/cookbook/i18n/fr_FR.csv`.

7. When we want to translate the string **Panier** on the shopping cart page, we have to know the original string. You can find the original string in the Inline Translation popup or in the templates:

   The original string for Panier is Shopping Cart. When we add the following line in the CSV file we have just created, the string will be translated to that value Shopping Cart, Votre panier.

8. Clean the cache and reload the shopping cart page. You will see that the title is changed from **Panier** to **Votre panier**.

How it works...

Magento has a powerful translate function. To make a string translatable through that function, we have to use the following syntax:

```
__('Translatable string')
```

When using this syntax, the following fallback mechanism will be used:

- ► First, Magento will look in the database table `translation`. This table is used to save the values translated with Inline Translation.

- ► If the string is not found in the `translation` table, Magento will look for it in the theme. It will search to see whether the string is present in the file `app/design/frontend/<VendorName>/<ThemeName>/i18n/<locale>.csv`.

- ► The last fallback is the translation files of the modules. These are located in `i18n/<locale.csv` of the module.

- ► If no matching string is found, the translate function will return the original string that is passed as an argument to the translate function.

Adding widgets to the layout

Magento has a set of predefined widgets that you can configure and show on the different pages. With the Magento widget interface, we can configure different widgets on different pages.

Getting ready

We will add a block of products on the content area of the homepage. Go to the backend and navigate to **Content | Widgets**.

How to do it...

In the following steps, we will configure a widget for the category pages:

1. Click on the button **Add Widget**.
2. In the form, set the following values:
    - ❏ **Type**: Catalog Products List
    - ❏ **Design Theme**: Packt cookbook

3. Click **continue** and the following screen shows up:

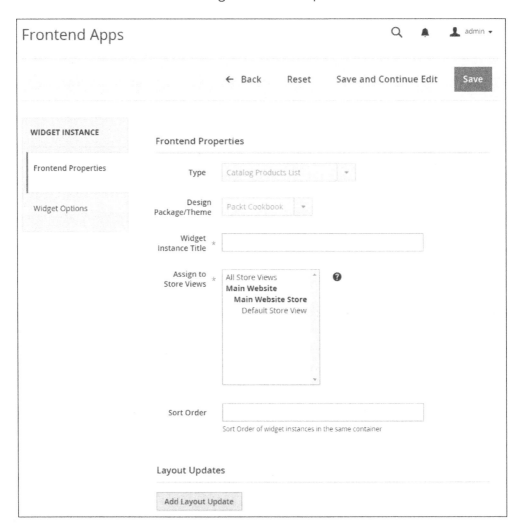

4. Complete the **Storefront Properties** tab with the following values:

- ❏ **Widget Instance Title**: Widget-home-products
- ❏ This is the title of the widget in the backend. A structural name is easy when working with a lot of widgets
- ❏ **Assign to Store Views**: All Store Views

5. Complete the **Widget Options** tab with the following values:

   ❑ **Title**: Featured products

   ❑ **Number of Products to Display**: 10

   ❑ **Conditions**: Choose a specific category like the following screenshot:

6. Save the widget by clicking **Save and Continue Edit**. The widget instance is now saved but nothing will show up in the frontend because there is no layout update set.

7. We have to create a layout update before the widget will show up in the frontend. On the widget page, open the **Frontend Properties** and complete the **Layout Updates** section as follows:

8. Clear the cache and reload the home page. You will see a list with products from the configured category.

How it works...

In the `Main Content Area`, a new block is added to the frontend. Like any other block in the frontend, this block has a block class and a template similar to other blocks.

The only difference is that this block is not generated by an XML file but by an XML layout instruction in the database.

The widget interface will generate a layout XML that is stored in the database. The block class and template are similar to other blocks in the XML files.

Customizing email templates

Magento has a lot of functionality that sends emails on particular actions, such as a new order, customer information, newsletter, and many more.

When customizing the look and feel of your website, it is nice that your email templates have the same look and feel.

In this recipe, we will learn how we can do this. We will customize the new account email and we will learn how we can edit the generic header and footer of the transactional emails.

Getting ready

We will customize email templates. To test this, make sure your development environment can send emails.

Like the previous recipes, we will build the code further on the things that we have done in the previous recipes. If you don't have the complete code, you can install the start files for this recipe.

How to do it...

The following steps show how we can customize the email templates without overriding the standard templates:

1. The email templates are located in the view folder of each module. If we want to change the new account email, we have to copy the original file to your theme. Copy the file `app/code/Magento/Customer/view/email/account_new.html` and paste this in the folder `app/design/frontend/Packt/cookbook/Magento_Customer/email/`.

 If you installed Magento with composer, you have to copy the file `vendor/magento/module-customer/view/frontend/email/account_new.html`.

2. When opening the new file, you can modify the content of the email in any way you want. We can use the following variables to make the file dynamic:

    ❑ `{{store url='<path>'}}` The URL of the store. You can also give a path between the quotes.

    ❑ `{{var customer.<field>}}` The customer object. After the dot, you can specify the attribute of the customer object.

- ❑ `{{var store.<field>}}` The store object where the email is sent from.
- ❑ `{{config path='<config path>'}}` A value of the configuration table `core_config_data`.

3. Save the file and create a new account in the frontend with your email address. You will receive an email of a new account. If you open it, you will see that the variables are replaced by the information of Magento.

4. When we look in the template, we see that an email header is included in the template. If we want to change the header, we have to copy the file `app/code/Magento/Email/view/frontend/email/header.html` to the folder `app/design/frontend/Packt/cookbook/Magento_Email/email/`.

5. To modify the footer, we have to copy the `app/code/Magento/Email/view/frontend/email/footer.html` file to the same folder.

 If you installed Magento with composer, you can find the header and footer files in the folder `vendor/magento/module-email/view/frontend/email/`.

How it works...

When an email is sent in Magento, the general email function is used. This function sends an email with the right template and email headers such as subject, sender.

The email function needs a template and that template is configured in the configuration XML files and uses a file from the email folder.

When an email template is configured through the configuration XML, it is also possible to overwrite this email template in the backend. This can be managed on the page **Marketing | Email Templates**.

New in Magento 2 is the ability to work with a header and footer template that is used in all the transactional emails. In the older versions of Magento 1, this was not possible and when you wanted to change something in the email header, you had to edit all the email template files.

Also new in Magento 2 is that you don't have an email template for each locale. With the `{{trans "Your string to translate"}}` code, you can use the Magento translation files to make your emails multilingual.

These two features make it a lot easier to develop the transactional emails in Magento 2.

Email templates are now part of a module. In the `view/<area>/email` folder are the email templates stored. To modify a template, you can copy the file and paste it in the `<module name>/email` folder in the theme.

4
Creating a Module

In this chapter, we will cover the following recipes:

- ▸ Creating the module files
- ▸ Creating a controller
- ▸ Adding layout updates
- ▸ Adding a translation file
- ▸ Adding a block of new products
- ▸ Adding an interceptor
- ▸ Adding a console command

Introduction

When you look in the `app/code` folder (the core of Magento), you see the modular architecture. Every concept in the e-commerce flow is stored in a module. The Magento application is a combination of all these modules.

One of the advantages of a modular architecture is the extendibility. It is easy to add modules that add to or modify the native behavior of Magento.

In this chapter, we will create a module with the most important things you need to know when writing code in Magento.

Creating the module files

When creating a module, the first step is to create the files and folders to register the module. At the end of this recipe, we will have a registered module but without functionality.

In the next recipes, we will add extra features to that module.

Getting ready

Open the root folder of your Magento 2 website. The `app/code/` folder is the folder where all the module development needs to be done.

Access to a command line is also recommended because Magento 2 has a built-in console tool with a lot of commands that we can use during the development.

How to do it...

In the following steps, we will create the required files to register a Magento module:

1. We will create a `HelloWorld` module in the Packt namespace. In your Magento root, create the following folders:

   - `app/code/Packt`
   - `app/code/Packt/HelloWorld`
   - `app/code/Packt/HelloWorld/etc`

2. In the `etc` folder of the module, create a file called `module.xml` with the following content:

```
<?xml version="1.0"?>
<config xmlns:xsi="http://www.w3.org/2001/XMLSchema-
instance" xsi:noNamespaceSchemaLocation=
"urn:magento:framework:Module/etc/module.xsd">
    <module name="Packt_HelloWorld" setup_version="2.0.0">
        <sequence>
            <module name="Magento_Catalog"/>
        </sequence>
    </module>
</config>
```

> In Magento 2, there are **XML Style Definition** (**XSD**) files that describes the structure of the configuration XML files. In the `<config>` tag, the correct XSD file is configured.

3. To register the module, we have to create a `registration.php` file in the `app/code/Packt/HelloWorld/` folder with the following content:

```php
<?php

\Magento\Framework\Component\ComponentRegistrar::register(
    \Magento\Framework\Component\ComponentRegistrar::
    MODULE,
    'Packt_HelloWorld',
    __DIR__
);
```

4. Open your terminal and go to the Magento directory. In this directory, run the following commands:

- `composer install`
- `php bin/magento cache:clean`
- `php bin/magento setup:upgrade`

5. When everything is OK, you can see the name of the module in the output of the last command.

6. To test that the module is installed, open the backend and navigate to **Stores | Configuration | Advanced | Advanced**, and check that the module is present in the list. Ensure that you have cleaned the Magento caches.

How it works...

Module development in Magento 2 is much easier than in Magento 1. The concept of code pools is gone, everything is stored in a single folder (code, translations, templates, CSS, and more). These things make it a lot easier to develop and maintain a Magento module.

To initialize, we have to create the folders and the `module.xml` file in the `etc` folder of the module. In the `module.xml` file, we initialize the `Packt_HelloWorld` name, the version number, and the sequence.

When we created the module files, we executed the `setup:upgrade` command. By running this command, we will run the install or upgrade procedure of all the modules. In this process, a lot of generated classes are created in the `var/generation` folder.

We used the `bin/magento` tool for cleaning the cache and running the upgrade scripts. This tool was introduced in Magento 2 and is a replacement of third-party tools from Magento 1 (such as `n98magerun` and `wiz`).

When running the `php bin/magento` command, you can see a list of all available commands. It is easy to add your own commands in a module.

Creating a controller

In your Magento root, create the following folders: We will add an extra page that we can use for several purposes.

Getting ready

We build further on the `Packt_HelloWorld` module that we created in the previous recipe. Ensure that you have this module in your Magento instance. Also, ensure that the full page cache is disabled when you are developing. You can disable this in the backend by navigating to **System | Cache Management**.

How to do it...

The following steps show how to add extra pages using controllers and controller actions:

1. Create the following folders:

    ❑ `app/code/Packt/HelloWorld/etc/frontend`

    ❑ `app/code/Packt/HelloWorld/Controller`

    ❑ `app/code/Packt/HelloWorld/Controller/Index`

2. In the `app/code/Packt/HelloWorld/etc/frontend` folder, create a `routes.xml` file with the following content:

    ```xml
    <?xml version="1.0"?>
    <config xmlns:xsi="http://www.w3.org/2001/XMLSchema-
    instance" xsi:noNamespaceSchemaLocation=
    "urn:magento:framework:App/etc/routes.xsd">
        <router id="standard">
            <route id="helloworld" frontName="helloworld">
                <module name="Packt_HelloWorld" />
            </route>
        </router>
    </config>
    ```

3. In the last folder, that is, `app/code/Packt/HelloWorld/Controller/Index`, create the `Index.php` file with the following content:

    ```php
    <?php
    namespace Packt\HelloWorld\Controller\Index;

    class Index extends \Magento\Framework\App\Action\Action
    {
    ```

```
/**
 * Index action
 *
 * @return $this
 */
public function execute()
{


}
}
```

4. Clean the cache using the `php bin/magento cache:clean` command.

5. Open your browser and navigate to the `/helloworld` URL of the shop. You will see a white page. This is normal because the controller action is empty.

6. To load the layout of the shop, add the following code in the `index.php` file:

```
/** @var \Magento\Framework\View\Result\PageFactory  */
protected $resultPageFactory;

public function __construct(
    \Magento\Framework\App\Action\Context $context,
    \Magento\Framework\View\Result\PageFactory
    $resultPageFactory
) {
    $this->resultPageFactory = $resultPageFactory;
    parent::__construct($context);
}

public function execute()
{
    $resultPage = $this->resultPageFactory->create();
    return $resultPage;
}
```

 If you still see a white page, the page is cached. You have to flush the cache using the `php bin/magento cache:flush` command. It is recommended that you disable the Full Page Cache, as explained in the beginning of this recipe.

7. We will now create an extra action that redirects us to the `HelloWorld` page and create the `app/code/Packt/HelloWorld/Controller/Index/Redirect.php` file.

8. In this file, add the following content:

```php
<?php
namespace Packt\HelloWorld\Controller\Index;

class Redirect extends \Magento\Framework\App\Action\Action
{
    public function execute()
    {
        $this->_redirect('helloworld');
    }
}
```

9. Clean the cache and go to the URL `/helloworld/index/redirect`. We will be redirected to the index action.

10. We can also change the content of the `execute()` method to `$this->_forward('index')`. We will see the same output but the URL doesn't change in the browser bar.

How it works...

All pages in Magento are executed by controller actions. All the controllers are placed in modules, and each controller can have multiple controller actions. This gives us the following structure of the URL: `<modulename or frontname>/<controllerName>/<actionName>`.

When you compare the controller part with Magento 1, a lot of things have been changed and made easier.

In Magento 2, every controller action is written in a separate class. This class extends the `Magento\Framework\App\Action\Action` class. The controller is the folder where the actions are placed.

 It is also possible that the controller is in a separate class, but this is only done when there are generic functions that the actions will use. A good example can be found in the `ProductController` of the `Magento_Catalog` module.

In a controller action, the `execute()` method is used to start the rendering of the page. When we have nothing in this method, the page will have an empty output (blank screen).

If we want to render the layout, we will initialize the `resultPageFactory` instance in the `__construct()` method of the controller. This factory class is used to start the layout rendering of the page.

The second controller action we created was one that does a redirect to another page. When calling the `_redirect()` method in a controller action, a `301` redirect will be returned to the given URL.

The `_forward()` method does likely the same, but this internally forwards the action to another controller. This means that the output of another controller action will be rendered on the page but the URL won't change. This method is used to translate an SEO-friendly URL (such as a product URL) to the right controller action with the right parameters.

There's more...

When things are not working as you expect, you can use the following tips to make it work:

- Clean the cache. You can do this using the `php bin/magento cache:clean` command.
- Flush the cache. You can do this using the `php bin/magento cache:flush` command.
- Remove the `var/generation` folder. Sometimes, the the generated classes in this folder needs to be regenerated.

Adding layout updates

In the previous recipe, we created a page without content. In this recipe, we will modify the content of that page with layout updates.

With layout updates, we can arrange the structure of the page as we have seen in the *Customizing the HTML output* recipe of *Chapter 3*, *Theming*. But here, we will see how we can do that in a module.

Getting ready

This recipe builds further on the previous recipe. You need the install the module that we created in the previous recipes of this chapter.

How to do it...

In the next steps, we will see how we can modify the block layout with our module:

1. Create the `app/code/Packt/HelloWorld/view/frontend/layout` folder.

2. In this folder, create a file called `default.xml` with the following content:

```xml
<?xml version="1.0"?>
<page xmlns:xsi="http://www.w3.org/2001/XMLSchema-instance"
xsi:noNamespaceSchemaLocation="urn:magento:framework:View/
Layout/etc/page_configuration.xsd">
    <body>
        <referenceBlock name="footer_links">
            <block class="Magento\Framework\View\Element\
            Html\Link\Current" name="helloworld-link">
                <arguments>
                    <argument name="label" translate="true"
                    xsi:type="string">Helloworld
                    landing</argument>
                    <argument name="path"
                    xsi:type="string">helloworld/
                    index/index</argument>
                </arguments>
            </block>
        </referenceBlock>
    </body>
</page>
```

3. Clean the cache using the `php bin/magento cache:clean` command and reload the frontend. In the footer, you will see an extra link leading to the page that we created in the previous recipe.

4. The layout update we just created is applied to all pages. If we want updates on the `helloworld` index page, we have to create the `app/code/Packt/HelloWorld/view/frontend/layout/helloworld_index_index.xml` file.

5. In this file, paste the following content:

```xml
<?xml version="1.0"?>
<page xmlns:xsi="http://www.w3.org/2001/XMLSchema-instance"
layout="2columns-left" xsi:noNamespaceSchemaLocation=
"urn:magento:framework:View/Layout/etc/
page_configuration.xsd">
    <head>
        <title>Helloworld Landingspage</title>
    </head>
    <body>
        <remove name="wishlist_sidebar" />
    </body>
</page>
```

6. We also need to register the page. For this, create the `app/code/Packt/HelloWorld/etc/frontend/page_types.xml` file with the following content:

```xml
<?xml version="1.0"?>
<page_types xmlns:xsi="http://www.w3.org/2001/XMLSchema-instance"
xsi:noNamespaceSchemaLocation=
"urn:magento:framework:View/Layout/etc/page_types.xsd">
    <type id="helloworld_index_index" label="HelloWorld
    landing page"/>
</page_types>
```

7. Clean the cache and reload the `/helloworld` page. You will see that the title is similar to what we configured in the XML file and the wishlist block is not present in the left-hand side column.

8. To finish this recipe, we will add a custom template with a custom `Block` class. Create the `app/code/Packt/HelloWorld/Block/Landingspage.php` file with the following content:

```php
<?php
namespace Packt\HelloWorld\Block;

use Magento\Framework\View\Element\Template;

class Landingspage extends Template
{
    public function getLandingsUrl()
    {
        return $this->getUrl('helloworld');
    }

    public function getRedirectUrl()
    {
        return $this->getUrl('helloworld/index/redirect');
    }
}
```

9. Now, we have to create the template where we will call the method from the `Landingspage` class. Create the `app/code/Packt/HelloWorld/view/frontend/templates/landingspage.phtml` file with the following content:

```html
<h2>Hello World</h2>
<p>
    <a href="<?php echo $block->getLandingsUrl(); ?>">Go to
    landings URL</a>
</p>
<p>
    <a href="<?php echo $block->getRedirectUrl(); ?>">Go to
    redirect URL</a>
</p>
```

10. As the last step, we have to add the block with our layout XML. Add the following configuration to the `app/code/Packt/HelloWorld/view/frontend/layout/helloworld_index_index.xml` file as a child of the `<body>` tag:

```
<referenceContainer name="content">
    <block class="Packt\HelloWorld\Block\Landingspage"
    name="landingsblock" template="Packt_HelloWorld::
    landingspage.phtml" />
</referenceContainer>
```

11. Clean the cache and reload the `/helloworld` URL. You will see something like the following:

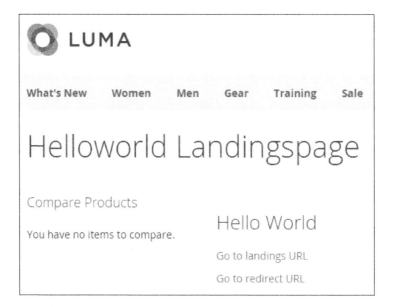

How it works...

Layout updates can be placed in modules and themes. In the *Customizing the HTML* output of *Chapter 3, Theming*, we explained how to layout updates work in Magento themes, but it is also possible to do the same principle in a module.

Every `Magento 2` folder has a `view` folder. In the `view` folder, all the stuff to render the page is stored, such as LESS (CSS), JavaScript, templates, and layout files.

In the view folder, we can have the following subfolders:

- adminhtml
- base
- frontend

As the name suggests, the adminhtml folder is used for the Magento backend, the frontend folder is used for the frontend, and the base folder is used for both (frontend and backend).

In these folders, the following structure is the internal folder structure that is used:

- layout (for layout update XML files)
- templates (for .phtml templates)
- web (for static files, such as LESS, JavaScript, and images)

In the layout folder, we can place layout XML files. For every layout handle, we can apply layout updates in a separate file.

We have placed a layout file for the default handle (these instructions are loaded on all pages). Every page also has its own handle in the structure <module front name>_<controllername>_<actionname>. For the helloworld landingspage, is this helloworld_index_index file. In the helloworld_index_index.xml file, we have placed the layout instructions of that page. The default handle, default.xml, is loaded on all pages.

In that file, we created a layout instruction that defines a custom block with template on a page. The landingspage.phtml template of the Packt_HelloWorld module is used to render the output. With the $block variable, we can call the methods of the Packt\HelloWorld\Block\Landingspage class.

> In Magento 1, we used the $this command to call methods from the block class. In Magento 2, we will use the $block variable for this.

The guideline is to use the .phtml files for the rendering of the HTML output. These files may not contain a log of th ePHP code. The PHP code is written in the block files and the HTML code in the .phtml files. In the .phtml files, we can call methods from the block class.

Adding a translation file

Magento is made to run in multiple languages. This means that the interface and content needs to be translatable in the configured languages.

In this recipe, you will learn how to make the strings in our module translatable in different languages.

Getting ready

We will create translation files for the module that we created in the previous recipes of this chapter. Ensure that you have the code in your Magento instance.

How to do it...

The following procedure demonstrates how we can manage translations in our module:

1. To make a test translation, we can create a test translation in the template file that we created in the previous recipe. Add the following code at the end of the file `app/code/Packt/HelloWorld/view/frontend/templates/landingspage.phtml`:

```
<p>
    <?php echo __('Test translation') ?>
</p>
```

2. Go to the `/helloworld` page and you will see that the text `Test translation` is added on the page.

3. To translate this string, we have to create the `app/code/Packt/HelloWorld/i18n` folder.

4. In this folder, create the `en_US.csv` file.

5. Add the following line in the CSV file:

```
"Test translation","Translation to test"
```

6. Clean the cache and reload the page. If the language of your shop is set to `English (United States)`, you will see that the output is set to `Translation to test`.

7. If we want, for example, a French translation, we have to create the `fr_FR.csv` file with the following content:

```
"Test translation","Test traduction"
```

8. Change the language of the store to `French`, clean the cache, and you will see the French translation.

If you want to know all the translations of a module, you can run the `php bin/magento i18n:collect-phrases app/code/<Vendor name>/<Module name>` command and you will get a CSV list of all the translations.

How it works...

When calling the `__('translate string')` function, Magento will search for a translation for that string in the current language. Magento will look for the strings in the following order:

▸ The database `translation` table

▸ The theme translation files (`app/design/fronted/<Package>/<theme>/i18n/<locale_code>.csv`)

▸ The module translation files (`app/code/<Vendor>/<Module>/i18n/<locale_code>.csv`)

When a string is found, Magento doesn't look further for other matching strings. If no matching string is found for the current language, Magento will return the string that is present in the first parameter of the translate function (that is, the untranslated string).

The implementation of translations in Magento 2 is much easier than in Magento 1. Everything is stored in the module folder, and you don't have to add configuration XML instructions to the module where you can do mistakes with.

Also, the translate function has now been moved to a global function. You don't need a helper class to call the `__()` function. The `__()` function is implemented as a global function that is available everywhere in the application.

Adding a block of new products

In the previous recipes, we prepared the module for the real work. We added the most common features to the module so that we can easily extend it with the new functionality.

In this recipe, we will create a block of new products to the page we created in the previous recipes.

Getting ready

In our module, we will create a block that will load a product collection. This product collection will be used in the template, which will show the newest products of the shop.

Ensure that you have the module of the previous recipe installed.

How to do it...

The following steps demonstrate how to start with adding the block with new products:

1. To create the block class, we have to create the `Newproducts.php` file in the `app/code/Packt/HelloWorld/Block/` folder.

2. Add the following content to that file:

```php
<?php
namespace Packt\HelloWorld\Block;

use Magento\Framework\View\Element\Template;

class Newproducts extends Template
{

}
```

3. Create a template in the module folder. We can do this by creating the `newproducts.phtml` file in the `app/code/Packt/HelloWorld/view/frontend/templates/` folder.

4. Add some HTML content to that template file such as `<h2>New Products</h2>`.

5. To add the block to the page, we have to create a layout update. In the `app/code/Packt/HelloWorld/view/frontend/layout/helloworld_index_index.xml` file, add the following code as a child of `<referenceContainer name="content">`:

```xml
<block class="Packt\HelloWorld\Block\Newproducts"
name="new_products" template="Packt_HelloWorld::
newproducts.phtml"/>
```

6. Clean the cache and reload the `/helloworld` page. You will see that the **New Products** title is visible.

7. Create a constructor in the block class that initializes the product collection factory. We can do this by adding the following code in that class (the `app/code/Packt/HelloWorld/Block/Newproducts.php` file):

```php
private $_productCollectionFactory;

public function __construct(
    Template\Context $context,
    \Magento\Catalog\Model\ResourceModel\Product\
    CollectionFactory $productCollectionFactory,
    array $data = [])
{
```

```
    parent::__construct($context, $data);

    $this->_productCollectionFactory = $productCollectionFactory;
}
```

8. Create the `getProducts()` method in the same block class. This method will return the five latest products of the shop. The code for the `getProducts()` method will look as follows:

```
public function getProducts() {
    $collection = $this->_productCollectionFactory->create();

    $collection
        ->addAttributeToSelect('*')
        ->setOrder('created_at')
        ->setPageSize(5);

    return $collection;
}
```

9. The last step is to call the method in the template and generate an HTML file for it. The code of the template is as follows:

```
<h2>New products</h2>

<ul>
<?php foreach ($block->getProducts() as $product): ?>
    <li><?php echo $product->getName() ?></li>
<?php endforeach; ?>
</ul>
```

10. Reload the `/helloworld` page and you will see a list with the names of the latest products.

How it works...

What we have done in this recipe is a basic extension of Magento. We added a custom block that uses the Magento framework to render the content.

We created a block class that has the `getProducts()` method. This method returns the latest five products of the webshop. In this method, we created a query that uses the Magento collections. With Magento collections, we can get data from the database. A collection builds a SQL query in the background.

The purpose of collections is that there is an easy interface to get the right entities. A product is not stored in one database table because it uses the **Entity Attribute Value** system (**EAV**). The Magento collections generate an SQL query that returns the values of that tables. This saves us the programming of very complex SQL queries.

To work with the collections, we used the `CollectionFactory` product to work with the collection functions. We initialized this class in the constructor and used it in the `getProducts()` method.

When we run the `create()` function on `CollectionFactory`, a product collection will be returned. It is like doing a collection using the `getCollection()` method on a Magento model, but because this method is deprecated, we have to use `CollectionFactory`.

Adding an interceptor

One of the major things that has changed in Magento 2 is that there is no `Mage` class. To replace this, all objects are passed to the classes with dependency injection.

Dependency injection is a powerful tool that adds a lot of flexibility to add or change behavior in Magento.

Getting ready

To explore the possibilities of dependency injection of Magento 2, we need the module that we created in the previous recipes.

How to do it...

The following steps describe how we can modify the behavior of some classes, which is a new concept in Magento 2 that replaces the rewriting of classes in Magento 1:

1. Create the `app/code/Packt/HelloWorld/etc/di.xml` file and paste the following content in it:

```xml
<?xml version="1.0"?>
<config xmlns:xsi="http://www.w3.org/2001/XMLSchema-instance"
xsi:noNamespaceSchemaLocation=
"urn:magento:framework:ObjectManager/etc/config.xsd">
    <type name="Magento\Catalog\Model\Product">
        <plugin name="Packt_HelloWorld::productName"
        type="Packt\HelloWorld\Plugin\Catalog\
        ProductAround" sortOrder="1" />
    </type>
</config>
```

The letters di in the di.xml file stands for Dependency Injection.

2. Create a plugin class by creating the app/code/Packt/HelloWorld/Plugin/ Catalog/ProductAround.php file with the following content:

```php
<?php
namespace Packt\HelloWorld\Plugin\Catalog;

use Magento\Catalog\Model\Product;

class ProductAround
{
    public function aroundGetName($interceptedInput)
    {
        return "Name of product";
    }
}
```

 It is highly recommended that you use around in the method name because you can also write interceptors that are executed before or after a method.

3. Clean the caches and regenerate the classes by removing the var/generation folder.

4. Reload a product page and you will see that every product name is changed to **Name of product**.

5. To undo this, comment the <type> tag and contents of the di.xml file and regenerate the classes by removing the var/generation folder. Also, don't forget to clean the cache.

6. Reload the product page and you will see the normal product names.

How it works...

In this recipe, we added a dependency injection into the Magento\Catalog\Model\ Product class. We did an override of an existing method in Magento.

With interception, we can execute the code before, after, and around any method of a class. This gives a lot of possibilities to add behavior to Magento.

In the di.xml file, we initialized a plugin that could override methods of the Magento\ Catalog\Model\Product class.

The overrides are done in the `Packt\HelloWorld\Plugin\Catalog\ProductAround` class. In this class, we did a modification of the `getName()` method of the original class using the `aroundGetName()` method.

To test our code, we had to create the generated classes. We can do this by removing the `var/generation` folder or by running the `php bin/magento setup:di:compile` command. The cache also needs to be cleaned because we changed things in the configuration XML files.

This command creates generated classes that will be placed in the `var/generation` folder. Without generating the classes, the configuration in the `di.xml` file will not load. This is also the reason why you have to do this when installing or upgrading a new module.

Dependency injection replaces the class rewrite system in Magento 1. With dependency injection, you can intercept every method that is called in a class. With the rewrite system of Magento 1, you could not do this with abstract classes.

It is also possible to execute code before and after a method is called.

See also

A lot of things are possible with Dependency Injection. For more information how it is integrated in Magento, you can read the documentation on the Magento site:

`http://devdocs.magento.com/guides/v2.0/extension-dev-guide/depend-inj.html.`

 More information about the dependency injection design pattern can be found on the following URL:

`https://en.wikipedia.org/wiki/Dependency_injection.`

Adding a console command

Another new thing in Magento 2 is the built-in command-line tool. In this chapter, we used this tool to clean the cache, for example.

Within a module, it is possible to extend this tool with custom commands, and this is the thing that we will do in this recipe.

Getting ready

This recipe will build further on the module that we have created in this chapter. If you don't have the code, you can install the starter files.

How to do it...

In the next steps, we will create a simple console command that will print some output to the console. Using this principle, you can create your own commands to automate some tasks:

1. For a custom console command, we have to add the following configuration in the `di.xml` file of the module. Paste the following code in that file as child of the `<config>` tag:

```
<type name="Magento\Framework\Console\CommandList">
    <arguments>
        <argument name="commands" xsi:type="array">
            <item name="helloWorldCommand"
            xsi:type="object">Packt\HelloWorld\Console\
            Command\HelloWorldCommand</item>
        </argument>
    </arguments>
</type>
```

2. Next, we will create the `app/code/Packt/HelloWorld/Console/Command/HelloWorldCommand.php` file with the following content:

```php
<?php

namespace Packt\HelloWorld\Console\Command;

use Symfony\Component\Console\Command\Command;
use Symfony\Component\Console\Input\InputInterface;
use Symfony\Component\Console\Output\OutputInterface;
use Symfony\Component\Console\Input\InputOption;

class HelloWorldCommand extends Command
{

}
```

3. In the previous step, we created the class for the command. To initialize the command, we have to add the following content to it:

```php
const INPUT_KEY_EXTENDED = 'extended';

protected function configure()
{
    $options = [
        new InputOption(
            self::INPUT_KEY_EXTENDED,
            null,
```

```
            InputOption::VALUE_NONE,
            'Get extended info'
        ),
    ];
    $this->setName('helloworld:info')
        ->setDescription('Get info about installation')
        ->setDefinition($options);
    parent::configure();
}


protected function execute(InputInterface $input,
OutputInterface $output)
{
    $output->writeln('<error>' . 'writeln surrounded by
    error tag' . '</error>');
    $output->writeln('<comment>' . 'writeln surrounded by
    comment tag' . '</comment>');
    $output->writeln('<info>' . 'writeln surrounded by info
    tag' . '</info>');
    $output->writeln('<question>' . 'writeln surrounded by
    question tag' . '</question>');
    $output->writeln('writeln with normal output');

    if ($input->getOption(self::INPUT_KEY_EXTENDED)) {
        $output->writeln('');
        $output->writeln('<info>'.'Extended parameter is
        given'.'</info>');
    }

    $output->writeln('');
}
```

4. Clean the cache, remove the `var/generation` folder, and run the `php bin/ magento` command. You will see that the `helloworld:info` command will be in the list.

5. When you run the command, you will see the following output:

6. When you run the command with the `extended` parameter, you will see some extra output. To do this, we have to run the command as follows:

```
php bin/magento helloworld:info --extended
```

How it works...

To register the console class to the command list, we had to create an extra argument for the `Magento\Framework\Console\CommandList` class in the `di.xml` file. In this file, we refer to the `Packt\HelloWorld\Console\Command\HelloWorldCommand` class for our custom command.

In the `configure()` method, we registered the name of the command, the description, and the other options. In this case, we initialized an optional input option.

The `execute()` method is made to execute the command. The `$input` parameter contains the input of the command, such as the options and arguments. With the `$output` parameter, we can modify the output of the command. This parameter is used to write output to the console with the `write()` and `writeln()` methods.

In this recipe, we worked with some colors to style the console output. The text between the error, comment, information, and question tags will be rendered in a different color, as we have seen in this recipe.

We also had an optional parameter called extended. To get the value of this parameter, we can use the `getOption()` method of the `$input` parameter. When the parameter is set without value, it will return `true`. If the parameter isn't set, it will return `false`. If a text is given to the parameter, it will return the text.

See also...

The Magento console is built using the **Symfony console** component. More information about how to use the Symfony console can be found at the following URL:

```
http://symfony.com/doc/current/components/console/introduction.html
```

5

Databases and Modules

In this chapter, we will cover:

- ▸ Registering database connections
- ▸ Creating an install and upgrade script
- ▸ Creating a flat table with models
- ▸ Working with Magento collections
- ▸ Programmatically adding product attributes
- ▸ Repairing the database

Introduction

In the previous chapter, we learned how to create a module and how we can do some basic stuff.

In this recipe, we will learn how we can integrate a module with the database of Magento. For this, we need the Magento module that we have created in *Chapter 4, Creating a Module*.

We will learn how we can run queries, add our own entities, and automate the installation of configurations in the database.

Creating an install and upgrade script

In some cases, you need to update the database to finish your work. Common cases are an extra column to a table, a new product attribute, or a setting.

If you have a development, staging, and production environment, you have to make sure that the right updates are done when deploying to these environments.

Magento has a way to automatically trigger the execution of certain scripts for an update. That's the thing we will learn in this recipe. Common things to automate are settings in the **Store** | **Configuration** page in the backend.

Getting ready

We will create a new module where we will add an install and upgrade script. We will also use the command line to run the scripts.

In Magento 2, the principle of installing and upgrading scripts is the same as in Magento 1 but some things have changed in the way of working. In this recipe, we will see how it works to save some data in the database with an install script.

How to do it...

The following steps describe how we can create an automated script:

1. Create a new module called `Packt_SEO`. We can do this by creating the file `app/code/Packt/SEO/etc/module.xml` with the following content:

```xml
<?xml version="1.0"?>
<config xmlns:xsi="http://www.w3.org/2001/XMLSchema-
instance" xsi:noNamespaceSchemaLocation=
"urn:magento:framework:Module/etc/module.xsd">
  <module name="Packt_SEO" setup_version="2.0.0">
  <sequence>
  <module name="Magento_Backend"/>
  </sequence>
  </module>
</config>
```

2. Next, create a file called `registration.php` in the folder app/code/Packt/SEO/ with the following content:

```php
<?php

\Magento\Framework\Component\ComponentRegistrar::register(
    \Magento\Framework\Component\ComponentRegistrar::
    MODULE,
    'Packt_SEO',
    __DIR__
);
```

3. The following step is to create the install script. We can do this by creating the file app/code/Packt/SEO/Setup/InstallData.php with the following content:

```php
<?php

namespace Packt\SEO\Setup;

use Magento\Framework\Setup\InstallDataInterface;
use Magento\Framework\Setup\ModuleContextInterface;
use Magento\Framework\Setup\ModuleDataSetupInterface;

class InstallData implements InstallDataInterface {
  protected $resourceConfig;

  public function __construct
  (\Magento\Config\Model\ResourceModel\Config $resourceConfig) {
    $this->resourceConfig = $resourceConfig;
  }

  public function install(ModuleDataSetupInterface $setup,
  ModuleContextInterface $context) {
    $setup->startSetup();

    $this->resourceConfig->saveConfig(
      'catalog/seo/category_canonical_tag',
      true,
      \Magento\Config\Block\System\Config\
      Form::SCOPE_DEFAULT,
      0
    );
```

```
        $this->resourceConfig->saveConfig(
          'catalog/seo/product_canonical_tag',
          true,
          \Magento\Config\Block\System\Config\
          Form::SCOPE_DEFAULT,
          0
        );

        $setup->endSetup();
      }
    }
```

4. When we want to run the script, we have to install the module. We can do this by running the following command:

   php bin/magento setup:upgrade

 The previous script will enable the canonical tags on the product and category pages.

5. If we want to add a new script to the existing module, we have to create an upgrade script. We can do this by creating the file app/code/Packt/SEO/Setup/ UpgradeData.php with the following content:

```
<?php
namespace Packt\SEO\Setup;

use Magento\Framework\Setup\UpgradeDataInterface;
use Magento\Framework\Setup\ModuleContextInterface;
use Magento\Framework\Setup\ModuleDataSetupInterface;

class UpgradeData implements UpgradeDataInterface {
  protected $resourceConfig;

  public function __construct
  (\Magento\Config\Model\ResourceModel\Config
  $resourceConfig) {
    $this->resourceConfig = $resourceConfig;
  }

  public function upgrade(ModuleDataSetupInterface $setup,
  ModuleContextInterface $context) {
    if (version_compare($context->getVersion(),
    '2.0.1') < 0) {
      $this->resourceConfig->saveConfig(
        'web/cookie/cookie_lifetime',
```

```
            '7200',
            \Magento\Config\Block\System\Config\
            Form::SCOPE_DEFAULT,
            0
        );
    }
    }
}
```

6. This script will run for version `2.0.1` so we have to configure our module to that version. We can do this by raising the version number in the file `app/code/Packt/ SEO/etc/module.xml` in the `setup_version` attribute. The file will have the following content:

```
<?xml version="1.0"?>
<config xmlns:xsi="http://www.w3.org/2001/XMLSchema-
instance" xsi:noNamespaceSchemaLocation=
"urn:magento:framework:Module/etc/module.xsd">
  <module name="Packt_SEO" setup_version="2.0.1">
  <sequence>
  <module name="Magento_Backend"/>
  </sequence>
  </module>
</config>
```

7. To run the script, we have to run the same command `php bin/magento setup:upgrade`.

8. When the upgrade script has finished, look at the page **Stores | Configuration | Web | Default Cookie Settings** and you will see that the lifetime has the value **7200**.

How it works...

Every Magento module has a version number that is stored in the `module.xml` file. When we look in the database table `setup_module`, we see the version numbers of every module.

When running the command `php bin/magento setup:upgrade`, Magento will check, for every module, the version number in the `module.xml` file and the database table `setup_module`.

 If you want to re-run an install or upgrade script, you can delete or change the version number of the module in the table `setup_module`.

If a module is not in the list, the `InstallData.php` script will be executed. After that, the `UpgradeData.php` script is always executed.

With an `if` statement, we can manage what things need to be executed in a specific upgrade.

In the database table `setup_module`, we see the following three columns:

- ▸ `module` (the name of the module)
- ▸ `schema_version` (the installed schema script)
- ▸ `data_version` (the installed data script)

There are two different types of install scripts. A schema install and a data install. A schema install is used to install database structures such as new tables, columns, and relations.

A data install or upgrade is used to add data to the database such as a setting, page, category, stores, and many more.

All the schema scripts are executed before the data upgrade scripts will start. This means that we can use the Magento models in the data scripts. This is not always possible in a schema script because it could be that the database structure is not completely installed when running your script.

In the scripts, we used the `resourceConfig` object to save configuration parameters. With this code, data is updated in the configuration pages that you can find in the backend at **Stores | Configuration**.

The values of these pages are saved in the table `core_config_data`.

Creating a flat table with models

When you want to save data in a module, you may want to store that in a custom entity. That entity needs a database table and a model that talks with that database table.

We will create a subscriptions entity where we can store subscriptions.

Getting ready

In this recipe, we will extend the module of *Chapter 4, Creating a Module*, with an entity with a database table. Make sure you have the starter files for this recipe installed.

How to do it...

In the next steps, we will learn how we can add entities to an existing module:

1. When installing a new entity, we have to create a resource model. We can do this by creating the file `app/code/Packt/HelloWorld/Model/ResourceModel/Subscription.php` with the following content:

```php
<?php
namespace Packt\HelloWorld\Model\ResourceModel;

class Subscription extends
\Magento\Framework\Model\ResourceModel\Db\AbstractDb {
  public function _construct() {
    $this->_init('packt_helloworld_subscription',
    'subscription_id');
  }
}
```

2. The second step is to create the table with a schema upgrade script. We have to create the script `app/code/Packt/HelloWorld/Setup/UpgradeSchema.php` with the following content:

```php
<?php

namespacePackt\HelloWorld\Setup;

use Magento\Framework\Setup\UpgradeSchemaInterface;
use Magento\Framework\Setup\ModuleContextInterface;
use Magento\Framework\Setup\SchemaSetupInterface;

classUpgradeSchema implements UpgradeSchemaInterface {
public function upgrade(SchemaSetupInterface $setup,
ModuleContextInterface $context) {
  if (version_compare($context->getVersion(), '2.0.1') < 0)
  {
    $installer = $setup;

    $installer->startSetup();
    $connection = $installer->getConnection();

    //Install new database table
    $table = $installer->getConnection()->newTable(
      $installer->getTable('packt_helloworld_subscription')
    )->addColumn(
```

```
                    'subscription_id',
                    \Magento\Framework\DB\Ddl\Table::TYPE_INTEGER,
                    null,[
                      'identity' => true,
                      'unsigned' => true,
                      'nullable' => false,
                      'primary' => true
                    ],
                    'Subscription Id'
                )->addColumn(
                    'created_at',
                    \Magento\Framework\DB\Ddl\Table::TYPE_TIMESTAMP,
                    null,[
                      'nullable' => false,
                      'default' =>
                      \Magento\Framework\DB\Ddl\Table::TIMESTAMP_INIT
                    ],
                    'Created at'
                )->addColumn(
                    'updated_at',
                    \Magento\Framework\DB\Ddl\Table::TYPE_TIMESTAMP,
                    null,
                    [],
                    'Updated at'
                )->addColumn(
                    'firstname',
                    \Magento\Framework\DB\Ddl\Table::TYPE_TEXT,
                    64,
                    ['nullable' => false],
                    'First name'
                )->addColumn(
                    'lastname',
                    \Magento\Framework\DB\Ddl\Table::TYPE_TEXT,
                    64,
                    ['nullable' => false],
                    'Last name'
                )->addColumn(
                    'email',
                    \Magento\Framework\DB\Ddl\Table::TYPE_TEXT,
                    255,
```

```
        ['nullable' => false],
        'Email address'
    )->addColumn(
        'status',
        \Magento\Framework\DB\Ddl\Table::TYPE_TEXT,
        255,[
            'nullable' => false,
            'default' => 'pending',
        ],
        'Status'
    )->addColumn(
        'message',
        \Magento\Framework\DB\Ddl\Table::TYPE_TEXT,
        '64k',[
            'unsigned' => true,
            'nullable' => false
        ],
        'Subscription notes'
    )->addIndex(
        $installer->getIdxName
        ('packt_helloworld_subscription', ['email']),
        ['email']
    )->setComment(
        'Cron Schedule'
    );

    $installer->getConnection()->createTable($table);

    $installer->endSetup();
    }
}
```

3. Raise the module version number in the file `app/code/Packt/HelloWorld/etc/module.xml` to `2.0.1`.

4. Run the following command to execute the upgrade script:

php bin/magento setup:upgrade

5. Check that the table is installed in the database. We can do this by running the query `describe packt_helloworld_subscription;` on a MySQL command line. This will give the following output:

```
mysql> describe packt_helloworld_subscription;
+-----------------+-------------------+------+-----+-------------------+----------------+
| Field           | Type              | Null | Key | Default           | Extra          |
+-----------------+-------------------+------+-----+-------------------+----------------+
| subscription_id | int(10) unsigned  | NO   | PRI | NULL              | auto_increment |
| created_at      | timestamp         | NO   |     | CURRENT_TIMESTAMP |                |
| updated_at      | timestamp         | YES  |     | NULL              |                |
| firstname       | varchar(64)       | NO   |     | NULL              |                |
| lastname        | varchar(64)       | NO   |     | NULL              |                |
| email           | varchar(255)      | NO   | MUL | NULL              |                |
| status          | varchar(255)      | NO   |     | pending           |                |
| message         | text              | NO   |     | NULL              |                |
+-----------------+-------------------+------+-----+-------------------+----------------+
8 rows in set (0.01 sec)
```

6. The next part is to create a model that interacts with the database table. To create a model, we have to create the file `app/code/Packt/HelloWorld/Model/Subscription.php` with the following content:

```php
<?php

namespacePackt\HelloWorld\Model;

class Subscription extends
\Magento\Framework\Model\AbstractModel {
constSTATUS_PENDING = 'pending';

constSTATUS_APPROVED = 'approved';

constSTATUS_DECLINED = 'declined';

public function __construct(
  \Magento\Framework\Model\Context $context,
  \Magento\Framework\Registry $registry,
  \Magento\Framework\Model\ResourceModel\AbstractResource
  $resource = null,
  \Magento\Framework\Data\Collection\AbstractDb
  $resourceCollection = null,
array $data = []
  ) {
```

```
  parent::__construct($context, $registry, $resource,
  $resourceCollection, $data);
}

public function _construct() {
  $this->_init
  ('Packt\HelloWorld\Model\ResourceModel\Subscription');
}
}
```

7. The last class that we have to create is the collection class. Create the file `app/code/Packt/HelloWorld/Model/ResourceModel/Subscription/Collection.php` with the following content:

```php
<?php

namespacePackt\HelloWorld\Model\ResourceModel\Subscription;

/**
 * Subscription Collection
 */
class Collection extends
\Magento\Framework\Model\ResourceModel\Db\Collection\
AbstractCollection {
  /**
   * Initialize resource collection
   *
   * @return void
   */
  public function _construct() {
    $this->_init('Packt\HelloWorld\Model\Subscription',
    'Packt\HelloWorld\Model\ResourceModel\Subscription');
  }
}
```

8. All the files are in the right place to start a test. To perform a simple test, we can create a controller action in the `IndexController` of the `HelloWorld` module that we have created in the previous recipe. Add the file `app/code/Packt/HelloWorld/Controller/Index/Subscription.php` with the following content:

```php
<?php
namespace Packt\HelloWorld\Controller\Index;
```

```
class Subscription extends
\Magento\Framework\App\Action\Action {
  public function execute() {
    $subscription = $this->_objectManager-
    >create('Packt\HelloWorld\Model\Subscription');

    $subscription->setFirstname('John');
    $subscription->setLastname('Doe');
    $subscription->setEmail('john.doe@example.com');
    $subscription->setMessage('A short message to test');

    $subscription->save();

    $this->getResponse()->setBody('success');
  }
}
```

9. Open the browser and go to the URL `/helloworld/index/subscription` of your Magento. When you see the word **success**, this will mean that a new subscription is added to the database table.

10. When you look in your database and run the query `select * from packt_helloworld_subscription;`, we will see the following output:

How it works...

When we work with the previous setup of entities, the Magento ORM makes the link between the entity and the database. All the SQL queries, security, and more are managed by the ORM.

The first step we did was to create a resource model. A resource model is used for the link between the model and the database. This class is initialized by specifying the database table and the primary key of that table.

The second part was to create a script that automatically creates a database table. A database table is created with the schema installer. Because this module was already installed, we had to create an upgrade script and we had to raise the version number.

The third step was the creation of the model. In a model, a lot of business logic is available in functions and variables. An important thing to mention is the initialization of the resource model that is done in the `_construct()` method of the model.

The last part to finish the model setup was to create the collection class. This class is responsible for allowing us to work with Magento collections in our model. The principle of collections is explained in the next recipe *Working with Magento collections*.

To test the model, we created a `test()` method in a controller action. To load a Magento entity, we have to use the `ObjectManager` interface. In a controller action, this interface is available in the variable `_objectManager`.

> In the controller action, we used the object manager to get the model and save a record to the table. This was just for debugging purposes. In the real world, the controller is used for controller actions such as redirects, adding messages, rendering the page, and more. The save of an entity is mostly done in a separate model but, for simplicity, we did it in the controller.

To create a Magento entity, we have to use the `create()` method of the object manager. The parameter is a string with the namespace and class name of the entity such as the following:

```
$this->_objectManager->create('Packt\HelloWorld\Model\Subscription');
```

With our Magento entity, we can use the following methods to interact with the database:

- `load($entityId)`
- `save()`
- `delete()`

All these methods are implemented in the `\Magento\Framework\Model\AbstractModel` class. All the entities that use the Magento ORM framework will extend this class.

Working with Magento collections

When you want to retrieve a set of entities of the same type, we usually use a query to get the data of a table.

But in Magento not every entity is stored in a single table and that means that a very complex query is required to get the data. A generic system/language to create queries for Magento entities was the solution.

For this solution, Magento has created a system called **collections**. A collection is a set of entities of the same type where you can add filters to it to customize your result.

In this recipe, we will see what we can do with Magento collections.

Getting ready

For this recipe, it is required to have the `Packt_HelloWorld` module installed with the code of the previous recipe *Creating a flat table with models*.

How to do it...

The next examples show the possibilities of working with Magento collections:

1. Create a `Collection` controller action by creating the file `app/code/Packt/HelloWorld/Controller/Index/Collection.php` with the following content:

```php
<?php
namespace Packt\HelloWorld\Controller\Index;

class Collection extends
\Magento\Framework\App\Action\Action {
  public function execute() {


  }
}
```

2. Paste the following code in the `execute()` method of that class:

```php
public function execute() {
  $productCollection = $this->_objectManager
  ->create
  ('Magento\Catalog\Model\ResourceModel\Product\
  Collection')
  ->setPageSize(10,1);
```

```
$output = '';

foreach ($productCollection as $product) {
  $output .= \Zend_Debug::dump($product->debug(), null,
  false);
}

$this->getResponse()->setBody($output);
}
```

3. When loading the page /helloworld/index/collection, we see a dump of the first 10 products like the following array:

```
array(9) {
  ["entity_id"]=>
  string(1) "1"
  ["attribute_set_id"]=>
  string(2) "15"
  ["type_id"]=>
  string(6) "simple"
  ["sku"]=>
  string(7) "24-MB01"
  ["has_options"]=>
  string(1) "0"
  ["required_options"]=>
  string(1) "0"
  ["created_at"]=>
  string(19) "2015-07-16 12:36:24"
  ["updated_at"]=>
  string(19) "2015-07-16 12:36:24"
  ["is_salable"]=>
  string(1) "1"
}
```

4. When we look at the array, we see no product attributes in the dump. To add an attribute to a collection, we have to use the method addAttributeToSelect('<attribute_code>'). Add the following code in the execute() method and we will see the name, price, and image of the products:

```
public function execute() {
  $productCollection = $this->_objectManager
  ->create('Magento\Catalog\Model\ResourceModel\
  Product\Collection')
  ->addAttributeToSelect([
    'name',
    'price',
```

```
      'image',
  ])
  ->setPageSize(10,1);

  $output = '';

  foreach ($productCollection as $product) {
    $output .= \Zend_Debug::dump($product->debug(), null,
    false);
  }

  $this->getResponse()->setBody($output);
}
```

5. When reloading the page, we will see an array of each product with the three attributes in it like the following code:

```
array(12) {
  ["entity_id"] =>string(1) "2"
  ["attribute_set_id"] =>string(2) "15"
  ["type_id"] =>string(6) "simple"
  ["sku"] =>string(7) "24-MB04"
  ["has_options"] =>string(1) "0"
  ["required_options"] =>string(1) "0"
  ["created_at"] =>string(19) "2015-07-16 12:36:25"
  ["updated_at"] =>string(19) "2015-07-16 12:36:25"
  ["name"] =>string(20) "Strive Shoulder Pack"
  ["image"] =>string(33) "/sample_data/m/b/mb04-black-
  0.jpg"
  ["price"] =>string(7) "32.0000"
  ["is_salable"] =>string(1) "1"
}
```

6. We will now create a filter on the product collection with the addAttributeToFilter() method. The next code shows how you can filter the products with the name **Overnight Duffle**:

```
public function execute() {
  $productCollection = $this->_objectManager
  ->create('Magento\Catalog\Model\ResourceModel\
  Product\Collection')
  ->addAttributeToSelect([
    'name',
    'price',
    'image',
  ])
```

```
  ->addAttributeToFilter('name', 'Overnight Duffle');

  $output = '';

  foreach ($productCollection as $product) {
    $output .= \Zend_Debug::dump($product->debug(), null,
    false);
  }

  $this->getResponse()->setBody($output);
}
```

 The code in this statement will create a WHERE name = 'Overnight Duffle' statement to the query, so all the items where the name is **Overnight Duffle** will be returned.

7. With the addAttributeToFilter() method, we can do more. The following code shows you how you can create a WHERE entity_id IN (159, 160, 161) statement:

```
public function execute() {
  $productCollection = $this->_objectManager
  ->create('Magento\Catalog\Model\ResourceModel\
  Product\Collection')
  ->addAttributeToSelect([
    'name',
    'price',
    'image',
  ])
  ->addAttributeToFilter('entity_id', array(
    'in' => array(159, 160, 161)
  ));

  $output = '';

  foreach ($productCollection as $product) {
    $output .= \Zend_Debug::dump($product->debug(), null,
    false);
  }

  $this->getResponse()->setBody($output);
}
```

8. The next filter that we will use is the `like` filter. Add the following code to make a query with the `WHERE name LIKE '%Sport%'` statement:

```
public function execute() {
  $productCollection = $this->_objectManager
  ->create('Magento\Catalog\Model\ResourceModel\
  Product\Collection')
  ->addAttributeToSelect([
    'name',
    'price',
    'image',
  ])
  ->addAttributeToFilter('name', array(
    'like' => '%Sport%'
  ));

  $output = '';

  foreach ($productCollection as $product) {
    $output .= \Zend_Debug::dump($product->debug(), null,
    false);
  }

  $this->getResponse()->setBody($output);
}
```

9. When the queries become more complex, sometimes it is nice to know what SQL query will be generated to get the collection. To print the SQL query, which is used for a collection, we can use the following line of code:

```
$productCollection->getSelect()->__toString();
```

10. When we add the following code, we can see the query for the previous collection:

```
public function execute() {
  $productCollection = $this->_objectManager
  ->create('Magento\Catalog\Model\ResourceModel\
  Product\Collection')
  ->addAttributeToSelect([
    'name',
    'price',
    'image',
  ])
  ->addAttributeToFilter('name', array(
    'like' => '%Sport%'
  ));
```

```
$output = $productCollection->getSelect()->__toString();

$this->getResponse()->setBody($output);
}
```

11. This code will output the following SQL query:

```
SELECT
    e.*,
IF(at_name.value_id> 0, at_name.value,
at_name_default.value) AS `name`
FROM catalog_product_entity` AS e
    INNER JOIN catalog_product_entity_varchar AS
`at_name_default
        ON (at_name_default.entity_id = e.entity_id)
        AND (at_name_default.attribute_id = '69')
        AND at_name_default.store_id = 0
    LEFT JOIN catalog_product_entity_varchar AS at_name
        ON (at_name.entity_id = e.entity_id)
        AND (at_name.attribute_id = '69')
        AND (at_name.store_id = 1)
WHERE (IF(at_name.value_id> 0, at_name.value,
at_name_default.value) LIKE '%Sport%')
```

12. When you run the previous query in an SQL prompt such as phpMyAdmin, we can see the response with all the attributes that are used for the product collection.

13. With the previous code examples, we can only read data from the database. By using the setDataToAll() method, we can update some attributes for all the entities in the collection. Use the next code to update all the prices in the collection:

```
public function execute() {
  $productCollection = $this->_objectManager
  ->create('Magento\Catalog\Model\ResourceModel\
  Product\Collection')
  ->addAttributeToSelect([
    'name',
    'price',
    'image',
  ])
  ->addAttributeToFilter('entity_id', array(
    'in' => array(159, 160, 161)
  ));
```

```
$output = '';

$productCollection->setDataToAll('price', 20);

foreach ($productCollection as $product) {
  $output .= \Zend_Debug::dump($product->debug(), null,
  false);
}

$this->getResponse()->setBody($output);
}
```

14. When you use the `setDataToAll()` method, nothing will be changed in the database until you have called the `save()` method. Add the following code after the `setDataToAll()` method to save the collection:

```
$productCollection->save();
```

How it works...

When we want a collection of Magento entities, we can do this by calling the `collection` class of the model. This class is located in the resource model folder of a module (`Model/ResourceModel/<Model name>/Collection.php`).

To get a collection, we can use the `getCollection()` method of a model. When we use that method, an instance of the collection class is returned. A better way is to directly call the collection class like we did in this recipe.

A collection class always extends from the `\Magento\Framework\Data\Collection` class, which gives access to all the methods to work with collections. The result of a collection is always returned as an iterable object so we can loop through the objects in the collection.

When working with collections, we have two types of collections. The collections working with flat entities, and the collections working with EAV entities (such as products).

The difference between a flat and an EAV collection is that, with a flat collection, all the fields of the table are included in the collection. With an EAV collection, we have to use the method `addAttributeToSelect()` to include the EAV attributes that we want in our collection.

This is because EAV data is stored in multiple tables for a single entity. For a product, the values of every type of attribute are stored in a different table (the `catalog_product_entity_*` tables).

With the `addAttributeToFilter()` method, we can create conditions on the SQL statement. With flat collections, we can also use the `addFieldToFilter()` method.

For this recipe, we used the `\Zend_Debug::dump()` method to create dumps of our objects. We use this method because this adds `<pre>` tags around the dump so we can easily read it in a browser.

In that `dump` statement, we set the third parameter to `false`. This means that this method will return the data instead of printing it. To correctly add a response to a controller, we need to use the `$this->getResponse()->setData()` method at the end of the controller action.

Programmatically adding product attributes

In the recipe *Creating an install and upgrade script*, we learned how we can automate the execution of database changes.

In these install scripts, we can also add attributes to products, as we will learn in this recipe.

Getting ready

We will work further on the `Packt_HelloWorld` module that we have created in the previous recipes. Make sure you have the module installed.

How to do it...

The following steps describe the procedure to create an upgrade script that adds a product attribute to all products:

1. The module `Packt_HelloWorld` is already installed in our system so we have to create an upgrade script. Create the file `UpgradeData.php` in the folder `app/code/Packt/HelloWorld/Setup`. Add the following content in that file:

```php
<?php
namespace Packt\HelloWorld\Setup;

use Magento\Framework\Setup\UpgradeDataInterface;
use Magento\Framework\Setup\ModuleContextInterface;
use Magento\Framework\Setup\ModuleDataSetupInterface;

class UpgradeData implements UpgradeDataInterface {
  protected $categorySetupFactory;
```

```
public function __construct
(\Magento\Catalog\Setup\CategorySetupFactory
$categorySetupFactory) {
  $this->categorySetupFactory = $categorySetupFactory;
}

public function upgrade(ModuleDataSetupInterface $setup,
ModuleContextInterface $context) {
  if (version_compare($context->getVersion(), '2.0.2') <
  0) {
    $categorySetup = $this->categorySetupFactory-
    >create(['setup' => $setup]);

    $entityTypeId = $categorySetup-
    >getEntityTypeId
    (\Magento\Catalog\Model\Product::ENTITY);

    $categorySetup->addAttribute($entityTypeId,
    'helloworld_label', array(
      'type' => 'varchar',
      'label' => 'HeloWorld label',
      'input' => 'text',
      'required' => false,
      'visible_on_front' => true,
      'apply_to' =>
      'simple,configurable,virtual,bundle,downloadable',
      'unique' => false,
      'group' => 'HelloWorld'
    ));
  }
 }
}
```

2. Update the version number in the `module.xml` file. Open the file `app/code/Packt/HelloWorld/etc/module.xml` and change the `setup_version` attribute of the `<module>` tag to `2.0.2`. This file will look as follows:

```xml
<?xml version="1.0"?>
<config xmlns:xsi="http://www.w3.org/2001/XMLSchema-
instance" xsi:noNamespaceSchemaLocation=
"urn:magento:framework:Module/etc/module.xsd">
  <module name="Packt_HelloWorld" setup_version="2.0.2">
    <sequence>
      <module name="Magento_Catalog"/>
    </sequence>
  </module>
</config>
```

3. Run the command `php bin/magento setup:upgrade` in your command line to run the upgrade scripts.

4. Log in to the backend and look for a product. You will see that the attribute is added to the **HelloWorld** tab like in the following screenshot:

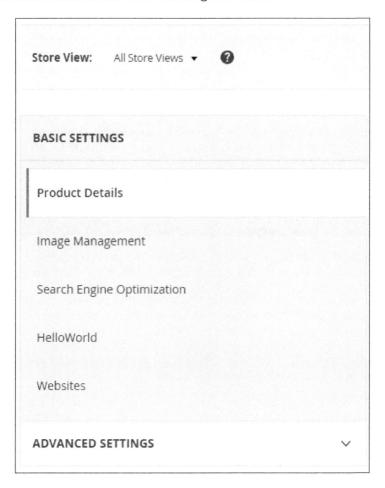

The first version of Magento 2 has an issue that the product edit page will not load correctly after adding a new attribute. If the product edit page doesn't load correctly, you have to save the product template (attribute set) of the product manually. After saving this, the page will load correctly.

How it works...

Installing a `product` attribute is done in the data install or upgrade scripts. In that script, we use the `categorySetup` class to add the attributes. In this class, the `addAttribute()` method is available for adding attributes.

The `addAttribute()` method will create an EAV attribute that will be stored in the table `eav_attribute`. Every EAV attribute is from a specific entity type. That's the reason why we have retrieved the entity type with the method `$categorySetup->getEntityTypeId(\ Magento\Catalog\Model\Product::ENTITY);`.

For a product, some information of the attribute (such as the `visible_on_front, used_in_product_listing,` and more) is stored in a separate table. This table is the `catalog_eav_attribute` table where all the extended information of the catalog attributes is saved. With the `attribute_id` parameter, every row is related to an EAV attribute from the table `eav_attribute`.

Repairing the database

Sometimes, it can happen that your Magento database is broken or corrupt. This can be caused by various reasons such as a hack or a server crash. When the database is broken, everyone wants to repair it as quickly as possible.

Common examples of a corrupt database are missing tables or columns after running an unsaved query, or missing relations after an import of a dump without the relations.

Magento has a database repair tool that compares database A with database B and this tool can fix the missing structures between them.

In this recipe, we will make our database corrupt and we will repair it with the repair tool.

Getting ready

To prepare yourselves, download the database repair tool from the Magento site at `http://www.magentocommerce.com` and place the PHP file in your webroot.

How to do it...

The next steps show you how you can break your database and how to fix it using the database repair tool:

1. Create a backup of your existing Magento 2 database.

2. Create a new empty database that we will use as the reference database. Let's say we call it `magento2_dev_repair`.

3. Configure Magento to use this empty database in the `app/etc/env.php` file.

4. Run the command `php bin/magento setupsetupsetup:upgrade` in the Magento root. This will install an empty Magento in the database.

5. Make your original database corrupt. You can do this by running the following queries that remove a foreign key and a table:

   ```
   ALTER TABLE store DROP FOREIGN KEY
   STORE_WEBSITE_ID_STORE_WEBSITE_WEBSITE_ID;

   DROP TABLE catalog_product_index_price;
   ```

6. Browse to the repair tool in your browser, and configure your original and reference database as shown in the following screenshot:

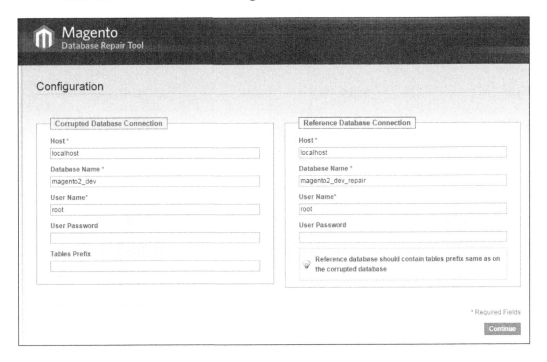

7. Submit the form and the script will repair your database. On the next page, you will see what changes are made to your original database.

8. Switch the database back to the original one in `app/etc/env.php`, flush the cache, and your store is back up and running.

How it works...

The database repair tool of Magento compares the structure of two databases with each other and will fix the differences.

We created an empty database where we installed a new empty Magento with the install scripts. This database was used as the reference database.

In the database repair tool, we entered the original database as the corrupted database.

The tool will compare the structure of the reference database with the corrupted database. When the comparisons are done, the tool will make the structure of the corrupted database the same as the structure of the reference database.

When this is done, all broken structures (such as missing relations, tables, columns, and more) are fixed in the corrupted database.

The compare tool only fixes structural issues with your database. If you miss some of your data, this is not the right tool to get it back.

6
Magento Backend

In this chapter, we will cover:

- ▸ Registering a backend controller
- ▸ Extending the menu
- ▸ Adding an ACL
- ▸ Adding configuration parameters
- ▸ Creating a grid of a database table
- ▸ Working with backend components
- ▸ Adding customer attributes
- ▸ Working with source models

Introduction

For a store owner, the backend is the interface to manage everything in their store. It is very important for everything to be secured against visitors with bad intentions. The backend of a standard Magento installation is extendible in many ways (like the frontend), so everyone can extend it with custom pages, configuration, roles, and so on.

By following the best practices of Magento, all security risks are managed by Magento like the access for anonymous users.

The recipes in this chapter describe the most common ways in which you can extend your backend using the best practices of Magento 2.

Registering a backend controller

The first thing that we will learn is how to extend the backend with a custom controller action. We need a controller that is secured so that only logged-in backend users can see the contents of this page.

A backend controller is required when you want to add an extra page to the backend of Magento. This is mostly the case when you are working with a custom form or overview that you need for your module.

Getting ready

For development purposes, it is recommended that we remove the secret key (the hash in the URL) from the admin URLs. You can configure this in **Stores** | **Configuration** | **Advanced** | **Admin** | **Security**. Change the configuration as shown in the following screenshot:

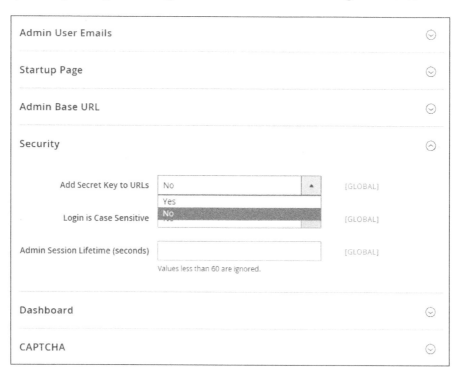

How to do it...

When you want to add an extra page to your backend, you have to follow these steps:

1. Create the file `routes.xml` in the folder `app/code/Packt/HelloWorld/etc/adminhtml` with the following content:

```xml
<?xml version="1.0"?>
<config xmlns:xsi="http://www.w3.org/2001/XMLSchema-
instance" xsi:noNamespaceSchemaLocation=
"urn:magento:framework:App/etc/routes.xsd">
    <router id="admin">
        <route id="helloworld" frontName="helloworld">
            <module name="Packt_HelloWorld"
            before="Magento_Backend" />
        </route>
    </router>
</config>
```

2. In the folder `app/code/Packt/HelloWorld/Controller/Adminhtml/Index`, create a file called `Index.php` with the following content:

```php
<?php
namespace Packt\HelloWorld\Controller\Adminhtml\Index;

use Magento\Backend\App\Action\Context;
use Magento\Framework\View\Result\PageFactory;

class Index extends \Magento\Backend\App\Action
{
    protected $resultPageFactory;

    public function __construct(
        Context $context,
        PageFactory $resultPageFactory
    ) {
        parent::__construct($context);
        $this->resultPageFactory = $resultPageFactory;
    }

    public function execute()
    {

    }
}
```

Make sure that your controller action extends from the `\Magento\Backend\App\Action` class. This will cover the access for authorized users.

3. Clean the cache using the command `php bin/magento cache:clean` and navigate to the URL `/admin/helloworld/index`. You will see a white page, which is normal because the action is empty.

4. When you add the following code in the `execute()` function of that class, you will see that the backend interface is there with an empty page:

```
public function execute()
{
    $resultPage = $this->resultPageFactory->create();

    return $resultPage;
}
```

How it works...

Backend controllers work similar to frontend controllers. The main difference between them is that a backend controller action will extend from the class `\Magento\Backend\App\Action` where a frontend controller will extend from the class `\Magento\Framework\App\Action\Action`.

The class where the backend action extends from manages all the security so that the page is only accessible for authenticated backend users.

The route for the backend controller is initialized in the `routes.xml` file for `adminhtml`. In this file, the route name is configured for the `Packt_HelloWorld` module. We called this route `helloworld`.

The controller action files are placed in the `Adminhtml` subfolder of the `Controller` folder of the module. Magento knows that it has to look in the `Adminhtml` folder for backend controllers and actions.

In the configuration, we disabled the secret keys to the admin URLs so it is easy to debug new URLs. The structure of a backend URL is likely the same as in the frontend. The only difference is that backend controller actions always start with the `adminhtml` prefix. When this prefix is `admin`, the URLs will have the following structure:

```
<path_to_backend>/<route_name>/<controller_name>/<action_name>
```

Extending the menu

In the previous recipe, we added a new page to the backend, but it is important that you are able to easily navigate to your custom pages. Not everyone knows the URL, and if the secret keys are enabled for the administrator URLs, it is likely impossible to build a correct URL because you have to know the key.

Getting ready

This recipe builds further on the previous one. Make sure you have the code of the previous recipe installed.

How to do it...

The following steps describe how we can add extra menu items to the **Admin** menu:

1. First we have to think about where we will get an extra menu item in the **Admin** menu. For this tutorial, we will add an extra item in the **Marketing** menu. For this we need to know the ID of the marketing menu.

2. Create the file `app/code/Packt/HelloWorld/etc/adminhtml/menu.xml` with the following content:

```xml
<?xml version="1.0"?>
<config xmlns:xsi="http://www.w3.org/2001/XMLSchema-
instance" xsi:noNamespaceSchemaLocation=
"urn:magento:module:Magento_Backend:etc/menu.xsd">
    <menu>
        <add
            id="Packt_HelloWorld::helloworld"
            title="HelloWorld"
            module="Packt_HelloWorld"
            sortOrder="50"
            parent="Magento_Backend::marketing"
            resource="Packt_HelloWorld::helloworld"
        />
        <add
            id="Packt_HelloWorld::index"
            title="Helloworld Index"
            module="Packt_HelloWorld"
            sortOrder="55"
            parent="Packt_HelloWorld::helloworld"
            action="helloworld/index/"
            resource="Packt_HelloWorld::index"
        />
    </menu>
</config>
```

3. Clean the cache and reload the backend. When opening the marketing menu, you will see that there is a **HelloWorld** group with a link, like in the following screenshot:

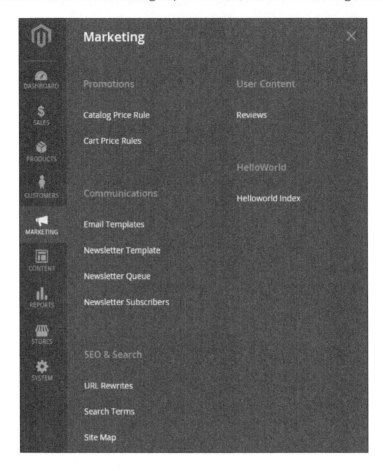

4. To change the position of the links, we can play with the `sortOrder` attribute of the configuration.

How it works...

The Admin menu of Magento is based on all the `menu.xml` files of all the modules. The standard menu contains the following root items:

- **Dashboard**
- **Sales**
- **Products**
- **Customers**
- **Marketing**
- **Content**
- **Reports**
- **Stores**
- **System**

All these items are defined in the file `app/code/Magento/Backend/etc/adminhtml/menu.xml`, so if you need an identifier of the root items, you have to look in that file. If a link is not configured in that file, you have to look in the `menu.xml` files of the other modules, such as `catalog`, `customer`, and `reports`.

We added an item to the menu with a custom `menu.xml` file. In that file, we configured two statements that add a menu item. The first one is used to configure the `HelloWorld` heading of the menu. This item has no action attribute, and the parent is `Magento_Backend::marketing` (the ID of the parent menu item). The second one is used to configure the link. In the action attribute, the URL is configured. The parent attribute is the ID of the `HelloWorld` heading (`Packt_HelloWorld::helloworld`).

An `<add />` statement can have the following attributes:

- `id`: The identifier of the menu item
- `title`: The title of the menu item
- `module`: The module that the menu item will refer to
- `sortOrder`: The sequence by which all the menu items will be ordered
- `parent`: The parent menu item
- `action`: If the item contains a link, this is the URL leading to the controller action
- `resource`: The identifier of the ACL resource explained in the recipe *Adding an ACL*

Adding an ACL

In the previous recipes of this chapter, we created a backend controller action that is accessible using the admin menu. However, when you want to configure a custom admin role, you can't restrict the access to this page for a specific role. In this recipe, we will create an **Access Control List** (**ACL**) for the backend page and create a role with restricted permissions so an admin user can only view a restricted set of pages.

Getting ready

Each admin user is a member of an admin role. These roles have access permissions that manage the access to certain pages in the backend.

In this recipe, we will add new permissions for the page we created in the previous recipes of this chapter. Make sure you have installed the files of the previous recipes.

How to do it...

The following steps describe how you can limit the access to a page for a role of users:

1. Open the backend and navigate to **System | Permissions | User Roles**. Click on the button **Add New Role** and open the **Role Resources** tab. You will see a tree with all the available ACLs in this Magento installation.

2. The second step is to add an extra ACL to that page. For this we need to create the file `app/code/Packt/HelloWorld/etc/acl.xml` with the following content:

```xml
<?xml version="1.0"?>
<config xmlns:xsi="http://www.w3.org/2001/XMLSchema-
instance" xsi:noNamespaceSchemaLocation=
"urn:magento:framework:Acl/etc/acl.xsd">
    <acl>
        <resources>
            <resource id="Magento_Backend::admin">
                <resource id="Magento_Backend::marketing">
                    <resource
                    id="Packt_HelloWorld::helloworld"
                    title="HelloWorld" sortOrder="60">
                        <resource
                        id="Packt_HelloWorld::
                        index" title="HelloWorld index" />
                    </resource>
                </resource>
            </resource>
        </resources>
    </acl>
</config>
```

3. Clean the cache and navigate to **System | Permissions | User Roles**, click on the **Add New Role** button, and open the **Role Resources** tab. When you search for `HelloWorld`, you will see that that the ACLs we have just created are in the list, as you can see in the following screenshot:

4. Submit this form to add a new role with the **HelloWorld index** checkbox checked. Let's say we call this role `Test HelloWorld`.

5. Create a new backend user in **System** | **Permissions** | **All Users**. Fill in the required fields and add the user to the role that we have just created, as shown in the following screenshot:

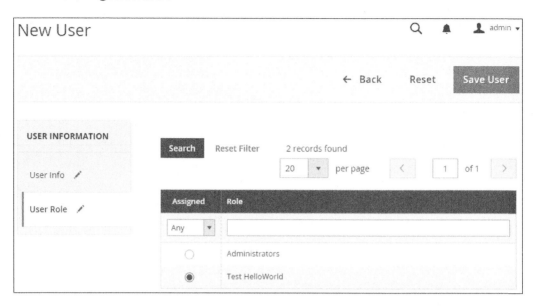

6. We have just created an ACL for the page that is available at `/admin/helloworld/index/index`. We have to add the following function to that controller so the controller action knows which ACL is active for that page. Open `app/code/Packt/HelloWorld/Controller/Adminhtml/Index/Index.php` and add the following function in class of that file:

```
protected function _isAllowed()
{
    return $this->_authorization-
    >isAllowed('Packt_HelloWorld::index');
}
```

7. Log into the backend with the new user and you will see that this user has only access to the pages that we have configured for the specific role of that user.

How it works...

With the Magento ACLs, it is possible to restrict the access of backend pages to a specific user role. For example, the product manager role can only access the products, categories, and promotion rules pages, and the logistic partner only has access to the order pages.

When you don't create the ACLs for custom pages, only the roles that have access to all the resources can access the pages. In most cases, this is the administrator. For other roles, it is not possible to access pages with no ACLs.

> In the Magento Community Editions, it is not possible to restrict the access to the data of a specific store. For example, a logistic partner can only see the orders of store 1. The ACL restrictions are only based on controller actions.

That's the reason that we have configured the ACLs in the `acl.xml` file of the module. In this file, we define new ACLs in a tree structure. These ACLs haves an identifier that is used to manage the access to the menu and controller page.

In the controller action, we have created an `_isAllowed()` function that checks the access to the given ACL.

In the `menu.xml` file of the module, the ACL for every menu item is configured in the resource attribute of the configurations (like the highlighted code shown here):

```
<add
    id="Packt_HelloWorld::helloworld"
    title="HelloWorld"
    module="Packt_HelloWorld"
    sortOrder="50"
    parent="Magento_Backend::marketing"
    resource="Packt_HelloWorld::helloworld"
/>
```

Adding configuration parameters

When you want to save some configuration parameters for your module, you can use the Magento configuration table to save your configuration in it. You can find all the configuration forms under **Stores | Configuration** in the Magento backend. In this recipe, we will add an extra page with some configuration parameters.

Getting ready

Like the previous recipes in this chapter, we will build further on the module that we have created in the previous recipes. Make sure you have the module files installed.

How to do it...

The following instructions describe what you have to do when you want to add some custom configuration parameters:

1. The system configuration is always configured in the `system.xml` file of the module. So create the file `app/code/Packt/HelloWorld/etc/adminhtml/system.xml` with the following content:

    ```xml
    <?xml version="1.0"?>
    <config xmlns:xsi="http://www.w3.org/2001/XMLSchema-
    instance" xsi:noNamespaceSchemaLocation=
    "urn:magento:module:Magento_Config:etc/system_file.xsd">
        <system>

        </system>
    </config>
    ```

2. To add a new tab to the configuration menu, we have to add the following configuration XML in the `system.xml` file. Paste the following code as a child of the `<system>` tag:

    ```xml
    <tab id="packt" translate="label" sortOrder="500">
        <label>Packt</label>
    </tab>
    ```

3. The next thing to do is to create an ACL for the new configuration page. Add the following configuration in the file `app/code/Packt/HelloWorld/etc/acl.xml`. Paste the following code as a child of the `<resource id="Magento_Backend::admin">` tag:

```
<resource id="Magento_Backend::stores">
    <resource id="Magento_Backend::stores_settings">
        <resource id="Magento_Config::config">
            <resource
            id="Packt_HelloWorld::config_helloworld"
            title="HelloWorld Section" />
        </resource>
    </resource>
</resource>
```

4. Clean the cache and open **System | Permissions | User Roles**. Click on the **Add New Role** button and open the **Role Resources** tab. If everything is OK, you will see **HelloWorld Section** in the list, like in the following screenshot:

5. When **HelloWorld Section** is in the list, it means that the ACL is added. Don't save the new role; this step was just to verify that the ACL settings are right.

6. With the right ACL settings installed, we can add the right code for a new Magento configuration page. Open the file `app/code/Packt/HelloWorld/etc/adminhtml/system.xml` and add the following code as a child of the `<system>` tag:

```
<section id="helloworld" translate="label" type="text"
sortOrder="100" showInDefault="1" showInWebsite="1"
showInStore="1">
    <label>HelloWorld</label>
    <tab>packt</tab>
    <resource>Packt_HelloWorld::config_helloworld
    </resource>
    <group id="hellopage" translate="label" type="text"
    sortOrder="1" showInDefault="1" showInWebsite="1"
    showInStore="1">
        <label>HelloWorld page settings</label>
        <field id="is_enabled" translate="label"
        type="select" sortOrder="10" showInDefault="1"
        showInWebsite="1" showInStore="1">
            <label>Is Enabled</label>
            <source_model>Magento\Config\Model\Config\
            Source\Yesno</source_model>
        </field>
        <field id="header_title" translate="label"
        type="text" sortOrder="20" showInDefault="1"
        showInWebsite="1" showInStore="1">
            <label>Header title</label>
        </field>
    </group>
</section>
```

7. Clean the cache and open **Stores | Configuration**. If everything went well, you will see the **PACKT** group in the menu. When you click on it, you will see the configuration fields **Is Enabled** and **Header title**, as shown in the following screenshot:

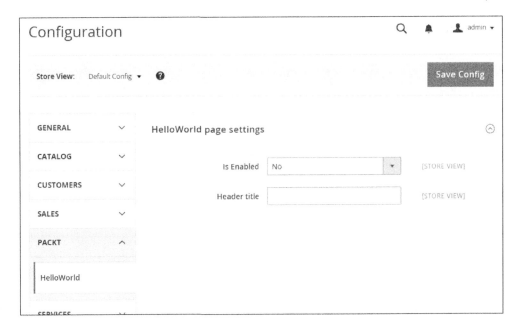

8. When we want to configure a default value for this field, we have to create the file app/code/Packt/HelloWorld/etc/config.xml with the following content:

```xml
<?xml version="1.0"?>
<config xmlns:xsi="http://www.w3.org/2001/XMLSchema-
instance" xsi:noNamespaceSchemaLocation=
"urn:magento:module:Magento_Store:etc/config.xsd">
    <default>
        <helloworld>
            <hellopage>
                <is_enabled>1</is_enabled>
                <header_title>HelloWorld
                title</header_title>
            </hellopage>
        </helloworld>
    </default>
</config>
```

9. Clean the cache and reload the configuration page. You will see that the default values are filled as specified in the config.xml file that we just created.

How it works...

All the values of the Magento configuration are specified in the `system.xml` file of the module. Magento reads each file and merges them together when building the configuration page.

The first thing we did was to create a tab in the menu of the configuration pages. The tab has an ID attribute that is used to link a section to a tab.

The second thing was to add a new page with configuration parameters. Because a new page requires access permissions, we had to create a new ACL for that page. We extended the `acl.xml` file with an ACL for the new configuration page.

After the ACL, we created the configuration to show the two configuration fields. The XML tree starts to define the section. A section is used to define a new configuration page. In this tutorial, we have created a section with the identifier `helloworld`.

Each section is divided into groups. These are the accordions that you can open and close on the configuration page. We created a group with the ID `hellopage`.

In a group, we can configure the configuration fields. In this recipe, we created two fields. The first field was a field with a dropdown to say whether it is enabled or not. The second one was a text field to configure the title.

With the `<source_model>` tag, we configured the values for the dropdown menu by specifying the class of the source model. More information about source models can be found in the recipe *Working with source models* in this chapter.

The last thing we did in this recipe was to provide some default values for the configuration parameters. The default values are set in the `config.xml` file of the module. In the `<default>` tag, you can specify a default value for a configuration parameter. Let's take a look at the following code snippet:

```
<section_id>
    <group_id>
        <field_id>Value</field_id>
    </group_id>
</section_id>
```

Make sure you replace `section_id`, `group_id` and `field_id` so it matches the configuration for your field.

Each section, group, and field has the attributes `showInDefault`, `showInWebsite`, and `showInStore`. With these attributes, you can specify that the configuration option is visible when configuring something for that scope.

In Magento, there are three levels of configuration scopes available. These scopes are used when you run multiple stores on the same Magento installation. The following configuration scopes are available in Magento:

- Global configuration (showInDefault)
- Website configuration (showInWebsite)
- Store view configuration (showInStore)

When you want to change the scope of the configuration page, you can use the **Store View** dropdown on the configuration page, as shown in the following screenshot:

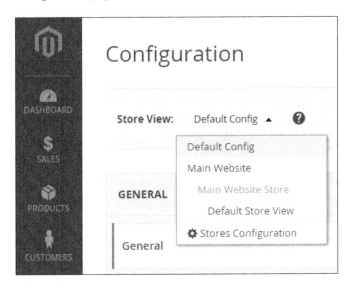

When you save the configuration form, the values are stored in the database table core_ config_data. When you open that table, you see the following columns:

- config_id: The configuration ID
- scope: By default, this is website or store
- scope_id: The ID of the website or store
- path: The configuration path
- value: The configuration value

The path column is the combination of the section id, group id, and field id columns. For the fields that we created in this recipe, the paths will be as shown here:

- helloworld/hellopage/is_enabled
- helloworld/hellopage/header_title

Creating a grid of a database table

In the previous chapter, we created a Magento entity that was linked to a database table. In this recipe, we will create a backend interface so that the backend users can see the data from this table in the backend.

Getting ready

Make sure you have the right files for this recipe installed in your Magento instance.

We will create an overview that will use the standard Magento backend grid widget. This widget is used for a lot of grids in the backend, such as the products, orders, CMS pages, and more.

How to do it...

Follow these steps to create backend grids:

1. When we want a new page, we need a controller with a controller action. So we need to add an ACL for that page. Open the file `app/code/Packt/HelloWorld/etc/acl.xml`, and add the following line of code as a child of the `<resource id="Packt_HelloWorld::helloworld" title="HelloWorld" sortOrder="60">` tag:

    ```
    <resource id="Packt_HelloWorld::subscription"
    title="HelloWorld subscription" />
    ```

2. We need some navigation to the new page. We can do this by creating a menu item for the page. Open `app/code/Packt/HelloWorld/etc/adminhtml/menu.xml` and add the following code as a child of the `<menu>` tag:

    ```
    <add
        id="Packt_HelloWorld::subscription"
        title="Subscriptions"
        module="Packt_HelloWorld"
        sortOrder="70"
        parent="Packt_HelloWorld::helloworld"
        action="helloworld/subscription/"
        resource="Packt_HelloWorld::subscription"
    />
    ```

3. As previously, we need to create the controller action. Create the file app/code/ Packt/HelloWorld/Controller/Adminhtml/Subscription/Index.php with the following content:

```php
<?php
namespace Packt\HelloWorld\Controller\Adminhtml\Subscription;

use Magento\Backend\App\Action\Context;
use Magento\Framework\View\Result\PageFactory;

class Index extends \Magento\Backend\App\Action
{
    protected $resultPageFactory;

    public function __construct(
        Context $context,
        PageFactory $resultPageFactory
    ) {
        parent::__construct($context);
        $this->resultPageFactory = $resultPageFactory;
    }

    public function execute()
    {
        $resultPage = $this->resultPageFactory->create();

        $resultPage-
        >setActiveMenu('Packt_HelloWorld::subscription');
        $resultPage->addBreadcrumb(__('HelloWorld'),
        __('HelloWorld'));
        $resultPage->addBreadcrumb(__('Manage
        Subscriptions'), __('Manage Subscriptions'));
        $resultPage->getConfig()->getTitle()-
        >prepend(__('Subscriptions'));

        return $resultPage;
    }

    protected function _isAllowed()
    {
        return $this->_authorization-
        >isAllowed('Packt_HelloWorld::subscription');
    }
}
```

4. Clean the cache and open the **Marketing** menu in the backend. You will see that there is a new menu item added under the **HelloWorld** section. When you click on the link **Subscriptions**, you will be redirected to the page that we have just created.

5. The backend page is now up and running. In the next steps, we will complete this recipe by adding a grid on this page.

6. To add a grid, we have to add the grid container block. To create this block, we have to create the file app/code/Packt/HelloWorld/Block/Adminhtml/Subscription.php with the following content:

```php
<?php

namespace Packt\HelloWorld\Block\Adminhtml;

class Subscription extends
\Magento\Backend\Block\Widget\Grid\Container
{
    protected function _construct()
    {
        $this->_blockGroup = 'Packt_HelloWorld';
        $this->_controller = 'adminhtml_subscription';

        parent::_construct();
    }
}
```

7. In the grid container block, we have to add the grid block. For this, we need to create the file app/code/Packt/HelloWorld/Block/Adminhtml/Subscription/Grid.php with the following content:

```php
<?php

namespace Packt\HelloWorld\Block\Adminhtml\Subscription;

use Magento\Backend\Block\Widget\Grid as WidgetGrid;

class Grid extends
\Magento\Backend\Block\Widget\Grid\Extended
{
    /**
     * @var \Packt\HelloWorld\Model\Resource\Subscription\
     Collection
     */
    protected $_subscriptionCollection;
```

```
/**
 * @param \Magento\Backend\Block\Template\Context
 $context
 * @param \Magento\Backend\Helper\Data $backendHelper
 * @param \Packt\HelloWorld\Model\ResourceModel\
 Subscription\Collection $subscriptionCollection
 * @param array $data
 */
public function __construct(
    \Magento\Backend\Block\Template\Context $context,
    \Magento\Backend\Helper\Data $backendHelper,
    \Packt\HelloWorld\Model\ResourceModel\Subscription\
    Collection $subscriptionCollection,
    array $data = []
) {
    $this->_subscriptionCollection =
    $subscriptionCollection;
    parent::__construct($context, $backendHelper,
    $data);
    $this->setEmptyText(__('No Subscriptions Found'));
}


/**
 * Initialize the subscription collection
 *
 * @return WidgetGrid
 */
protected function _prepareCollection()
{
    $this->setCollection($this-
    >_subscriptionCollection);

    return parent::_prepareCollection();
}
}
```

8. The blocks are created, but we have to add them to the controller with a layout update. Create the file `app/code/Packt/HelloWorld/view/adminhtml/layout/helloworld_subscription_index.xml` with the following content to create the layout update:

```
<?xml version="1.0"?>
<page xmlns:xsi="http://www.w3.org/2001/XMLSchema-instance"
xsi:noNamespaceSchemaLocation="urn:magento:framework:View/
Layout/etc/page_configuration.xsd">
    <body>
```

```
        <referenceContainer name="content">
            <block class="Packt\HelloWorld\Block\Adminhtml\
            Subscription" name="adminhtml.block.helloworld.
            subscription.container">
                <block class="Packt\HelloWorld\Block\
                Adminhtml\Subscription\Grid"
                name="adminhtml.block.helloworld.
                subscription.grid" as="grid" />
            </block>
        </referenceContainer>
    </body>
</page>
```

9. Clean the cache and reload the **Subscriptions** page in the backend. You will see something like the following screenshot:

10. In the screenshot, we see the filter buttons of the grid, but if we want to show the grid, we need to define the columns. We can do this by adding the following function to the file `app/code/Packt/HelloWorld/Block/Adminhtml/Subscription/Grid.php`. Paste the function in the existing class.

```
/**
 * Prepare grid columns
 *
 * @return $this
 */
protected function _prepareColumns()
{
    $this->addColumn(
        'subscription_id',
        [
```

```
                        'header' => __('ID'),
                        'index' => 'subscription_id',
                    ]
                );
                $this->addColumn(
                    'firstname',
                    [
                        'header' => __('Firstname'),
                        'index' => 'firstname',
                    ]
                );

                $this->addColumn(
                    'lastname',
                    [
                        'header' => __('Lastname'),
                        'index' => 'lastname',
                    ]
                );

                $this->addColumn(
                    'email',
                    [
                        'header' => __('Email address'),
                        'index' => 'email',
                    ]
                );

                $this->addColumn(
                    'status',
                    [
                        'header' => __('Status'),
                        'index' => 'status',
                    ]
                );

                return $this;
            }
```

11. When you reload the page, you will see that a grid appears with the content of the database table.

12. When we want to decorate the status column to improve the visibility of the statuses, we have to create a `frame_callback` parameter. Add the `frame_callback` parameter to the `addColumn()` function of the status so it looks like this:

```
$this->addColumn(
    'status',
    [
        'header' => __('Status'),
        'index' => 'status',
        'frame_callback' => [$this, 'decorateStatus']
    ]
);
```

 Add the highlighted line of code.

13. `frame_callback` refers to the function `decorateStatus()`. Add the following function to the class that we're editing:

```
public function decorateStatus($value) {
    $class = '';

    switch ($value) {
        case 'pending':
            $class = 'grid-severity-minor';
            break;
        case 'approved':
            $class = 'grid-severity-notice';
            break;
        case 'declined':
        default:
            $class = 'grid-severity-critical';
            break;
    }

    return '<span class="' . $class . '"><span>' . $value . '</span></span>';
}
```

14. Reload the page, and you should have an output like that shown in the following screenshot:

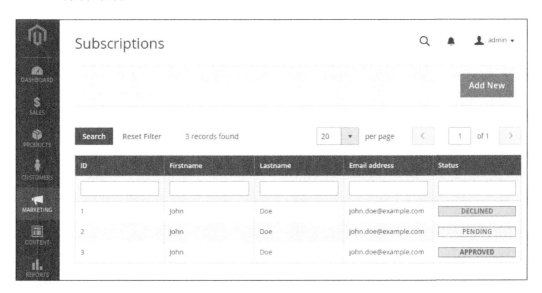

How it works...

The backend grid is one of the backend widgets that is available in Magento. Other widgets that are widely used are the forms to edit data or the tabbed menu on the left-hand side.

The grid widget is made to display the content of a collection in a grid. By using the grid widget of Magento, it is possible to sort and filter the columns that are visible in the grid. A pager is automatically included when you have a lot of data. This prevents out-of-memory exceptions when there are a large number of records in a collection.

A grid widget is always placed inside a grid container. We started this recipe by creating a container widget in which we will place a grid. The container widget is used to show the heading and buttons like the **Add New** button (which has currently no action). A grid container block always extends from the class `\Magento\Backend\Block\Widget\Grid\Container`.

In that container, we created a `Grid` block that is responsible for showing the grid. A grid block always extends from the class `\Magento\Backend\Block\Widget\Grid`. In this recipe, our class extends from `\Magento\Backend\Block\Widget\Grid\Extended`. This class adds the filters to the grid. A grid needs a collection. This collection is passed as a parameter in the `__construct()` method of the class. In the `_prepareCollection()` method, the collection is assigned to the class. A grid needs also a specification of the columns to be shown. The columns are specified in the `_prepareColumns()` function of that class. In that function, the `addColumn()` function is used to specify the columns.

The `addColumn()` function has two parameters. The first one is the identifier, and the second one is a key-value array with the specifications of the column. In this recipe, we used the following parameters:

> ▶ `header`: The name of the column
> ▶ `index`: The column in the database

The previous options are required, while the following ones are optional:

> ▶ `frame_callback` (A function call to render the value of a cell)
> ▶ `type` (This defines the filter widget like `number`, `datetime`, and `options`)
> ▶ `options` (This defines a source model when the type is `options`)

Working with backend components

The Magento backend exists with a lot of reusable components, such as a button, menus, forms, and more. When creating backend extensions, you can use these components to build you custom pages. In this recipe, we will create a page where we can play with the components available .

Getting ready

We will extend the existing `Packt_HelloWorld` module with a new page where we can play with the backend components.

How to do it...

In the following steps, we will create a page that uses some backend components:

1. We will make some tests in a new controller action. Create a file `app/code/Packt/HelloWorld/Controller/Adminhtml/Component/Index.php` with the following content:

```php
<?php
namespace Packt\HelloWorld\Controller\Adminhtml\Component;

use Magento\Backend\App\Action\Context;
use Magento\Framework\View\Result\PageFactory;

class Index extends \Magento\Backend\App\Action
{
    protected $resultPageFactory;

    public function __construct(
        Context $context,
        PageFactory $resultPageFactory
    ) {
        parent::__construct($context);
        $this->resultPageFactory = $resultPageFactory;
    }

    public function execute()
    {
        $resultPage = $this->resultPageFactory->create();

        $resultPage->setActiveMenu(
        'Packt_HelloWorld::component');
        $resultPage->addBreadcrumb(__('HelloWorld'),
        __('HelloWorld'));
        $resultPage->addBreadcrumb(__('Components'),
        __('Components'));
        $resultPage->getConfig()->getTitle()-
        >prepend(__('Components'));

        return $resultPage;
    }

    protected function _isAllowed()
    {
        return $this->_authorization-
        >isAllowed('Packt_HelloWorld::helloworld');
    }
}
```

2. Create a menu item for the page by adding the following XML in the file `app/code/Packt/HelloWorld/etc/adminhtml/menu.xml`. Paste the code as a child of the `<menu>` tag:

```
<add
    id="Packt_HelloWorld::component"
    title="Components"
    module="Packt_HelloWorld"
    sortOrder="80"
    parent="Packt_HelloWorld::helloworld"
    action="helloworld/component/"
    resource="Packt_HelloWorld::helloworld"
/>
```

3. Clean the cache and reload the backend. In the menu, you will see an item that leads to the component page that we have just created. This menu item is visible in the **Marketing** menu. When you open that page, we see an empty page.

4. To add some buttons to the page, we have to create the file `app/code/Packt/HelloWorld/view/adminhtml/templates/component/toolbar/buttons.phtml` with the following content:

```
<div class="page-actions">
    <div class="page-actions-inner">
        <div class="page-actions-buttons">
            <button
                class="action-primary"
                title="<?php echo __('Primary button') ?>">
                    <?php echo __('Primary button') ?>
            </button>
            <button
                class="action-secondary"
                title="<?php echo __('Secondary button') ?>">
                    <?php echo __('Secondary button') ?>
            </button>
            <button
                class="action-secondary back"
                title="<?php echo __('Back') ?>">
                    <?php echo __('Back') ?>
            </button>
        </div>
    </div>
</div>
```

5. To add this file to the components page, we have to add the file `app/code/Packt/HelloWorld/view/adminhtml/layout/helloworld_component_index.xml` with the following content:

```
<?xml version="1.0"?>
<page xmlns:xsi="http://www.w3.org/2001/XMLSchema-instance"
xsi:noNamespaceSchemaLocation="urn:magento:framework:View/
Layout/etc/page_configuration.xsd">
    <body>
        <referenceContainer name="page.main.actions">
            <block class="Magento\Backend\Block\Template"
            name="component_buttons" template=
            "Packt_HelloWorld::component/toolbar/
            buttons.phtml"/>
        </referenceContainer>
    </body>
</page>
```

6. Clean the cache and reload the page. You will now see something like in the following screenshot:

7. We will continue with adding the content of the page. The following code is an example of the possibilities for form components. Add it in the file `app/code/Packt/HelloWorld/view/adminhtml/templates/component/index.phtml`.

```
<div class="col-m-4">
    <fieldset class="fieldset admin__fieldset " id="theme">
        <div class="admin__field field" data-ui-id="theme-
        edit-tabs-tab-general-section-fieldset-element-
        form-field-theme-path">
            <label class="label admin__field-label">
            <span>Label</span></label>
            <div class="admin__field-control control">
                <div class="control-value">A value</div>
```

```
            </div>
        </div>

        <div class="admin__field field ">
            <label class="label admin__field-label" for=
            "test_input"><span>Test input</span></label>
            <div class="admin__field-control control">
                <input name="design[test_input]" id=
                "test_input" value="" title="Test input"
                type="text" class="input-text admin
                __control-text" />
            </div>
        </div>
    </fieldset>
</div>
```

8. To add this file to the page, add the following line of code to the file `app/code/Packt/HelloWorld/view/adminhtml/layout/helloworld_component_index.xml` as a child of the `<body>` tag:

```
<referenceContainer name="content">
    <block class="Magento\Backend\Block\Template"
    name="adminhtml.block.helloworld.component"
    template="Packt_HelloWorld::component/index.phtml" />
</referenceContainer>
```

9. Clean the cache and reload the page. You will see that a form appears on the screen.

 Magento also has a form API that generates the elements for you. This API is widely used for backend forms such as for the CMS pages (and many other forms).

10. The following code shows how to add a small data table to a page. Add it to the end of the file `app/code/Packt/HelloWorld/view/adminhtml/templates/component/index.phtml`.

```
<div class="col-m-4">
    <table class="admin__table-secondary">
        <tr>
            <th><?php echo __('First name') ?></th>
            <td>John</td>
```

```
        </tr>
        <tr>
            <th><?php echo __('Last name') ?></th>
            <td>Doe</td>
        </tr>
        <tr>
            <th><?php echo __('Email') ?></th>
            <td>john.doe@example.com</td>
        </tr>
        <tr>
            <th><?php echo __('Phone') ?></th>
            <td>000 000 000</td>
        </tr>
    </table>
</div>
```

11. Reload the page, and you will see a small table near the form.

How it works...

In this recipe, we created some HTML that is used to render backend components. The Magento backend is a combination of many of these components, such as the button bar, forms, tables, grids, and many more.

In the first steps, we created a controller action that uses an existing ACL. On this controller action, we placed a block that contains the buttons. The button bar is placed in the `page.main.actions` block. This block is the gray action bar that appears on many pages in the backend.

Later, we created a template that contains some backend components. The first one was a form with a `fieldset` element. This `fieldset` element contains a textbox, a label, and an on-off button.

The last thing we did was to create a small table with data in a new column. For these columns, we used the class `col-m-4`. By using this class, the `div` instance will have a width of four columns. The standard Magento backend is divided into 12 columns, so four columns is a third of the width of the backend page.

Adding customer attributes

In some cases, it could be that we need extra attributes for a customer like we did for products. Because a customer is an EAV object, it is possible to add attributes to it, but there is no interface for that in the Community Edition of Magento. When we want to do that, we need to install the attributes by code, and that's the thing that we will do in this recipe. We will add a new field `loyaltynumber` to the customer.

Getting ready

To add a customer attribute, we need to create an installation or upgrade script. In this recipe, we will create a new module that will install the attribute with the installation script so we don't need to install starter files in Magento.

How to do it...

In the following steps, we will create a small module that adds a customer attribute:

1. Create a module `Packt_CustomerAttribute` by creating a file `app/code/Packt/CustomerAttribute/etc/module.xml` with the following content:

   ```xml
   <?xml version="1.0"?>
   <config xmlns:xsi="http://www.w3.org/2001/XMLSchema-
   instance" xsi:noNamespaceSchemaLocation=
   "urn:magento:framework:Module/etc/module.xsd">
       <module name="Packt_CustomerAttribute"
       setup_version="2.0.0">
           <sequence>
               <module name="Magento_Customer"/>
           </sequence>
       </module>
   </config>
   ```

2. In `app/code/Packt/HelloWorld/`, create a file called `registration.php` with the following content:

   ```php
   <?php

   \Magento\Framework\Component\ComponentRegistrar::register(
       \Magento\Framework\Component\ComponentRegistrar::
       MODULE,
       'Packt_CustomerAttribute',
       __DIR__
   );
   ```

3. Create a data installation script by creating a file app/code/Packt/
   CustomerAttribute/Setup/InstallData.php with the following content:

```php
<?php
namespace Packt\CustomerAttribute\Setup;

use Magento\Framework\Setup\InstallDataInterface;
use Magento\Framework\Setup\ModuleContextInterface;
use Magento\Framework\Setup\ModuleDataSetupInterface;

class InstallData implements InstallDataInterface
{
    private $customerSetupFactory;

    public function __construct(\Magento\Customer\Setup\
    CustomerSetupFactory $customerSetupFactory)
    {
        $this->customerSetupFactory =
        $customerSetupFactory;
    }

    public function install(ModuleDataSetupInterface
    $setup, ModuleContextInterface $context)
    {
        /** @var CustomerSetup $customerSetup */
        $customerSetup = $this->customerSetupFactory-
        >create(['setup' => $setup]);

        $setup->startSetup();

        $customerSetup->addAttribute('customer',
        'loyaltynumber', [
            'label' => 'Loyaltynumber',
            'type' => 'static',
            'frontend_input' => 'text',
            'required' => false,
            'visible' => true,
            'position' => 105,
        ]);

        $loyaltyAttribute = $customerSetup->getEavConfig()-
        >getAttribute('customer', 'loyaltynumber');
```

```
$loyaltyAttribute->setData('used_in_forms',
['adminhtml_customer']);

$loyaltyAttribute->save();

$setup->endSetup();
    }
}
```

4. To add the attribute to the backend, we have to create a `ui_component` XML file. Create a file `app/code/Packt/CustomerAttribute/view/base/ui_component/customer_form.xml` with the following content:

```xml
<?xml version="1.0" encoding="UTF-8"?>
<form xmlns:xsi="http://www.w3.org/2001/XMLSchema-instance"
xsi:noNamespaceSchemaLocation="urn:magento:module:Magento_
Ui:etc/ui_configuration.xsd">
    <fieldset name="customer">
        <field name="loyaltynumber">
            <argument name="data" xsi:type="array">
                <item name="config" xsi:type="array">
                    <item name="dataType"
                    xsi:type="string">text</item>
                    <item name="formElement"
                    xsi:type="string">input</item>
                    <item name="source"
                    xsi:type="string">customer</item>
                </item>
            </argument>
        </field>
    </fieldset>
</form>
```

5. To install the attribute in the database, run the command `php bin/magento setup:upgrade`.

6. In the backend, create a new customer. You will see the **Loyaltynumber** attribute in the form like in the following screenshot:

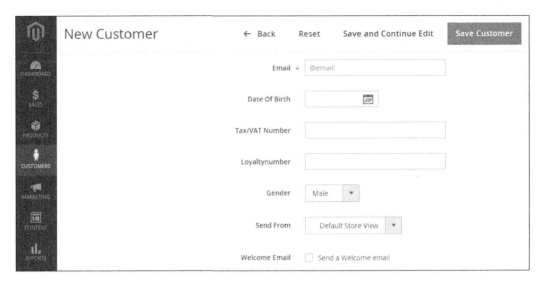

How it works...

We started to create a simple module with a data installation script like we did in *Chapter 4, Creating a Module*, and *Chapter 5, Databases and Modules*.

In the installation script, we placed some code that installs a customer attribute. This works in likely the same way as adding a product attribute. The main difference is the first parameter of the `addAttribute()` function.

To add a customer attribute, we have to place the value `customer` in that parameter. The options of the third parameter are also different when you compare it with a product.

The configuration of a customer attribute is saved in the following two tables:

- `eav_attribute`
- `customer_eav_attribute`

In the table `eav_attribute`, the generic data of the attribute, such as the entity type and the attribute code, is saved.

In the table `customer_eav_attribute`, the specific data for a customer attribute, such as the position and validation rules, is saved.

The attribute is added to the database with the `addAttribute()` function. To add the attribute to the customer form, we have to save that configuration in the database with the following code:

```
$loyaltyAttribute->setData('used_in_forms',
['adminhtml_customer']);
```

With the preceding code, the attribute will be linked to the `adminhtml_customer` form. This is the customer form of the backend.

Another required step is to add the attribute in the `ui_component` XML configuration. This configuration works like the layout XML files. This layout XML file works as a layout handle. When you look in the file `app/code/Magento/Customer/view/adminhtml/layout/customer_index_edit.xml`, you will see the following code that initializes the layout update of the `ui_component`:

```
<uiComponent name="customer_form"/>
```

With our custom `customer_form` UI component, we extended the fields of the customer entity.

Working with source models

Magento works with a lot of dropdown fields that you can select in the forms of the application. We can see dropdowns in the configuration, product, customer, and many more pages.

Magento has a system to set the options of the dropdown and multiselect fields. Magento uses a model that returns the values and labels to render the options of a dropdown or multiselect field. These models are called source models.

In this recipe, we will see which source models Magento uses and how we can create a custom source model for a custom configuration field.

Getting ready

In this recipe, we will extend the `Packt_HelloWorld` module that we created in the previous recipes. Make sure you have the right version installed for this recipe.

How to do it...

The following steps describe how you can create your custom source models for your custom form fields:

1. First we will create an extra field in the system configuration to run some tests. The following code adds a new field to the `HelloWorld` configuration page. Add it to the file `app/code/Packt/HelloWorld/etc/adminhtml/system.xml` as a child of the `<group id="hellopage" translate="label" type="text" sortOrder="1" showInDefault="1" showInWebsite="1" showInStore="1">` tag.

   ```
   <field id="source_model_test" translate="label" type="text"
   sortOrder="30" showInDefault="1" showInWebsite="1"
   showInStore="1">
       <label>Source model test</label>
   </field>
   ```

2. In the backend, open **Stores | Configuration | Packt | HelloWorld**. You will see a new text field called **Source model test**.

3. If we want to change that field to a dropdown, we have to change the `type` attribute to `select` like in the following code snippet:

   ```
   <field id="source_model_test" translate="label"
   type="select" sortOrder="30" showInDefault="1"
   showInWebsite="1" showInStore="1">
       <label>Source model test</label>
   </field>
   ```

4. Clean the cache and reload the page. You will now see a field with an empty dropdown.

5. To add options to the dropdown, we have to specify a source model. We can do this by adding the `<source_model>` tag as in the following code:

   ```
   <field id="source_model_test" translate="label"
   type="select" sortOrder="30" showInDefault="1"
   showInWebsite="1" showInStore="1">
       <label>Source model test</label>
       <source_model>Magento\Config\Model\Config\Source\Locale
       </source_model>
   </field>
   ```

6. If we want to create a custom source model, we have to create a custom model class. Create a file `app/code/Packt/HelloWorld/Model/Config/Source/Relation.php` with the following content:

```php
<?php

namespace Packt\HelloWorld\Model\Config\Source;

class Relation implements
\Magento\Framework\Option\ArrayInterface
{
    public function toOptionArray()
    {
        return [
            [
                'value' => null,
                'label' => __('--Please Select--')
            ],
            [
                'value' => 'bronze',
                'label' => __('Bronze')
            ],
            [
                'value' => 'silver',
                'label' => __('Silver')
            ],
            [
                'value' => 'gold',
                'label' => __('Gold')
            ],
        ];
    }
}
```

7. To assign the previously created source model to the test configuration field, we have to change the line `<source_model>` in the `system.xml` file. Change it to the following:

```xml
<source_model>Packt\HelloWorld\Model\Config\Source\Relation
</source_model>
```

8. Clean your cache and you will see that the options of the field are changed based on the output from the source model. You can see this in the following screenshot:

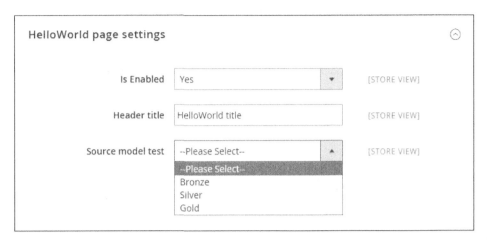

How it works...

A source model is a model instance with a `toOptionArray()` function. This function returns an array with all the items of the source array. This array has the following format:

```
[
    'value' => '0',
    'label' => 'Label option 0'
],
[
    'value' => '1',
    'label' => 'Label option 1'
]
```

The `value` key is the value of the `<option>` element in the dropdown list. The `label` key is the text that appears in the dropdown list.

In this recipe, we configured a source model for a configuration field. We can also use source models in the following cases:

- ▸ A product attribute in the backend
- ▸ A customer attribute in the backend
- ▸ Dropdown filters in backend grids
- ▸ Magento forms in the frontend and backend (like the country dropdown at checkout and so on)

The configuration of the source model is mostly done in the XML configuration of the field. For EAV fields, the information of the source model is stored in the attribute configuration, which is stored in the database.

When a dropdown field or multiselect field is saved, it is always saved in a single field of the database. If a field is a dropdown, the value will be stored for that field. When the field is a multiselect field, a comma-separated list of the selected values will be saved in that field.

7
Event Handlers and Cronjobs

In this chapter, we will cover the following topics:

- ▸ Understanding event types
- ▸ Creating your own event
- ▸ Adding an event observer
- ▸ Introducing cronjobs
- ▸ Creating and testing a new cronjob

Introduction

In the Magento application, there are a lot of events that happen when visitors are browsing through your website. The visitor can add something to the cart, log in, create an order, and do a lot more.

Magento has an event system that fires events when some actions happens in your shop. With a configuration, it is possible to execute some code when an event occurs. It's like hooking into a click event in JavaScript.

The observer design pattern is used to implement the event handling system. When an event is triggered, Magento looks for event observers that hook into that event and execute the right method that is configured for that event handler.

Another similar system in Magento is a **cronjob**. In the configuration, you can create a cronjob that will be executed on a specific timestamp. When it is the right time, Magento will execute the code that is configured for that cronjob.

In this chapter, we will explore the possibilities of using these two systems (Event handlers and cronjobs).

Understanding event types

Working with event types is better than overwriting a function with dependency injection. When analyzing a process, it is good to think about how you can solve your problem. It is better to execute extra code instead of rewriting the standard functions of Magento.

With events, it is possible to execute code when something happens, but before we can do that, we have to know which events are available, when they are dispatched, and which parameters are available.

Getting ready

In this recipe, we will debug the events that are fired in Magento. Ensure that you have access to the command line because we will debug using the Magento log files.

How to do it...

The following steps describe how we can create a list from the dispatched events in a Magento request:

1. Magento events are dispatched using the `dispatch()` method of the `eventManager` interface. When we want to debug this function, we have to modify the `Magento\Framework\Event\Manager` class. The first thing to do is to enable the logger interface. Create the `$_logger` variable in the `lib/internal/Magento/Framework/Event/Manager.php` file, as shown by the highlighted code.

```
. . .
protected $_eventConfig;

/**
 * Logger interface
 * @var \Psr\Log\LoggerInterface $logger
 */
protected $_logger;

/**
 * @param InvokerInterface $invoker
 * @param ConfigInterface $eventConfig
 */
public function __construct(InvokerInterface $invoker,
ConfigInterface $eventConfig) {
  $this->_invoker = $invoker;
. . .
```

If you have installed Magento with composer, you will have to edit the `vendor/magento/framework/Event/Manager.php` file.

2. Add the logger interface to the constructor and initialize the parameter that we have just created. Replace the constructor of that class with the following code:

```
/**
 * @param InvokerInterface $invoker
 * @param ConfigInterface $eventConfig
 * @param \Psr\Log\LoggerInterface $logger
 */
public function __construct(InvokerInterface $invoker,
ConfigInterface $eventConfig, \Psr\Log\LoggerInterface
$logger) {
  $this->_invoker = $invoker;
  $this->_eventConfig = $eventConfig;
  $this->_logger = $logger;
}
```

3. In the same class, go to the `dispatch()` function. In the first line, we will add a log statement to print the event name in the log file when an event is fired. Add the highlighted line of code to that function:

```
public function dispatch($eventName, array $data = []) {
  $this->_logger->debug($eventName);
  \Magento\Framework\Profiler::start('EVENT:' . $eventName,
  ['group' => 'EVENT', 'name' => $eventName]);
  foreach ($this->_eventConfig->getObservers($eventName) as
  $observerConfig) {
    $event = new \Magento\Framework\Event($data);
    $event->setName($eventName);

    $wrapper = new Observer();
    $wrapper->setData(array_merge(['event' => $event],
    $data));

    \Magento\Framework\Profiler::start('OBSERVER:' .
    $observerConfig['name']);
  ...
```

4. Take a look at the log file that you can find in the `var/log/debug.log` folder. Using the tail `-f` command, you can see what text will be added to that file. In your Magento installation, change the directory to `Magento` root and run the following command:

```
tail -f var/log/debug.log
```

5. When you load a page, you will see a lot of output in the log file as shown in the following screenshot. These are all the events that are dispatched when loading a page:

```
~/magento2$ tail -f var/log/debug.log

:31] main.DEBUG: core_collection_abstract_load_before {"is_exception":false} []
:31] main.DEBUG: store_collection_load_before {"is_exception":false} []
:31] main.DEBUG: core_collection_abstract_load_after {"is_exception":false} []
:31] main.DEBUG: store_collection_load_after {"is_exception":false} []
:31] main.DEBUG: core_collection_abstract_load_before {"is_exception":false} []
:31] main.DEBUG: core_collection_abstract_load_after {"is_exception":false} []
:31] main.DEBUG: core_collection_abstract_load_before {"is_exception":false} []
:31] main.DEBUG: core_collection_abstract_load_after {"is_exception":false} []
:31] main.DEBUG: core_app_init_current_store_after {"is_exception":false} []
:31] main.DEBUG: customer_session_init {"is_exception":false} []
:31] main.DEBUG: model_load_before {"is_exception":false} []
:31] main.DEBUG: theme_load_before {"is_exception":false} []
:31] main.DEBUG: model_load_after {"is_exception":false} []
:31] main.DEBUG: theme_load_after {"is_exception":false} []
:31] main.DEBUG: controller_action_predispatch {"is_exception":false} []
:31] main.DEBUG: controller_action_predispatch_catalog {"is_exception":false} []
```

6. Enough debugging for now. It is time to revert the `lib/internal/Magento/Framework/Event/Manager.php` file. Undo your changes, or if you use Git, you can use the `git checkout lib/internal/Magento/Framework/Event/Manager.php` command to undo the local changes in that file.

How it works...

In this recipe, we used the Magento debug logger to print the names of the fired events. This is an alternative for printing the names directly in the browser. The main advantage of this method is that the debug messages doesn't affect the output of your browser.

If you are aware about the system of Magento 1, you will notice that logging in Magento 2 is changed. In Magento 1, we had the `Mage::log()` function, but this function doesn't exist in Magento 2. In Magento 2, we have to use the logger interface that we initialize in the constructor of a class.

To debug the event names, we used the debug() function of the logger interface that writes a message to the var/log/debug.log file. In the logger interface, the following functions are available:

- ▸ alert()
- ▸ critical()
- ▸ debug()
- ▸ emergency()
- ▸ error()
- ▸ info()
- ▸ log()
- ▸ notice()
- ▸ warning()

The debug() function writes to the var/log/debug.log file, and the exception() function writes to the var/log/exception.log file. The other functions write to var/log/system.log.

We placed the log statement in the dispatch() function of the lib/internal/Magento/Framework/Event/Manager.php class. This function is called every time an event is dispatched. By logging the name, we can see all the events that are called in a Magento request.

On all these events, we can write hooks that execute the code when an event is dispatched. As you can see, this function doesn't return something to the parent, so it is not possible to send data back to the initiator of the event. However, you can modify the objects that are sent with the event.

For debugging purposes, we modified a core class of Magento. At the end, we reverted the class to the original code. Modifying the core of Magento is not recommended, but for debugging, you can do it if you revert your code when the debugging is done.

See also

Magento 2 is currently new and does not have a lot of documentation, but you can find more information about some of the available events in Magento 2 at http://cyrillschumacher.com/magento2-list-of-all-dispatched-events/.

Creating your own event

When we create our own event, we have to dispatch it with a custom name. In this recipe, you will learn how events are dispatched and what we can do with parameters that are sent with the event.

Getting ready

We will create an event that is fired when a visitor opens the `/helloworld/index/event` page.

The code in this recipe builds further on the `Packt_HelloWorld` module that we created in *Chapter 4*, *Creating a Module*, *Chapter 5*, *Databases and Modules* and *Chapter 6*, *Magento Backend*. Ensure that you have installed the start files.

How to do it...

The following steps describe how we can dispatch our own event:

1. First, we will create the event page. For this, we need a controller action. Create the `app/code/Packt/HelloWorld/Controller/Index/Event.php` file with the following content:

```php
<?php
namespace Packt\HelloWorld\Controller\Index;

class Event extends \Magento\Framework\App\Action\Action {
  /** @var \Magento\Framework\View\Result\PageFactory  */
  protected $resultPageFactory;

  public function __construct(
    \Magento\Framework\App\Action\Context $context,
    \Magento\Framework\View\Result\PageFactory
    $resultPageFactory
  ) {
    $this->resultPageFactory = $resultPageFactory;
    parent::__construct($context);
  }

  public function execute() {
    $resultPage = $this->resultPageFactory->create();
    return $resultPage;
  }
}
```

2. Clean the cache and navigate to the `/helloworld/index/event` page. You will see a Magento page without any content.

3. When we want to dispatch an event on the pageview, we have to add the highlighted code in the `execute()` action:

```
public function execute() {
  $resultPage = $this->resultPageFactory->create();

  $this->_eventManager->dispatch('helloworld_register_visit');

  return $resultPage;
}
```

4. It is also possible to send some parameters with the event. We will send a product and category with the event. To send the event, we have to pass the following key-value array to the event:

```
public function execute() {
  $resultPage = $this->resultPageFactory->create();

  $parameters = [
    'product' => $this->_objectManager-
    >create('Magento\Catalog\Model\Product')->load(50),
    'category' => $this->_objectManager-
    >create('Magento\Catalog\Model\Product')->load(10),
  ];

  $this->_eventManager-
  >dispatch('helloworld_register_visit', $parameters);

  return $resultPage;
}
```

 Ensure that the product ID and category ID exists in your installation. If not, you can choose another ID that exists in your installation.

How it works...

The `dispatch()` function of the `eventManager` method fires an event in Magento. The event manager is created in the construct of the `controller` class (in this example, it is the controller action) and stored in the `$_eventManager` variable. This is an instance of the `\Magento\Framework\Event\ManagerInterface` class.

When this function is fired, Magento will look into the configuration to see which event listeners are watching for that event. If there are matching listeners, Magento will execute the code of the observer.

Adding an event observer

If you read the previous recipe, you know how to fire an event using the `dispatch()` function. In this recipe, you will learn how to execute some code when an event is dispatched and what we can do with it.

Getting ready

In this recipe, we will add two event observers. The first one will catch the event that we created in the previous recipe. The second event listener (observer) will hook into the `add to cart` action of a product.

In this recipe, we will work further on the `Packt_HelloWorld` module from the previous recipes. Ensure that you have the right code files installed for this recipe.

How to do it...

In this tutorial, you will discover how to listen for an event and execute your code by performing these steps:

1. When we want to add an event observer for the `helloworld_register_visit` event, we have to add the following configuration to the `app/code/Packt/HelloWorld/etc/events.xml` file with the following content:

    ```xml
    <?xml version="1.0"?>
    <config xmlns:xsi="http://www.w3.org/2001/XMLSchema-
    instance" xsi:noNamespaceSchemaLocation=
    "urn:magento:framework:Event/etc/events.xsd">
      <event name="helloworld_register_visit">
        <observer name="register_helloworld_visit"
        instance="Packt\HelloWorld\Observer\
        RegisterVisitObserver" />
      </event>
    </config>
    ```

2. The configuration of the previous file executes the `registerVisit()` function in the `Packt\HelloWorld\Observer\RegisterVisitObserver` class. To create this class, we have to add the `app/code/Packt/HelloWorld/Model/Observer.php` file with the following content:

```php
<?php

namespace Packt\HelloWorld\Observer;

use Magento\Framework\Event\ObserverInterface;

class RegisterVisitObserver implements ObserverInterface
{
    /** @var \Psr\Log\LoggerInterface $logger */
    protected $logger;

    public function __construct(\Psr\Log\LoggerInterface
    $logger)
    {
        $this->logger = $logger;
    }

    public function execute(\Magento\Framework\Event\
    Observer $observer)
    {
        $this->logger->debug('Registered');
    }
}
```

3. Now, it is time to test our event. Clean the cache and open your terminal and execute the `tail -f var/log/debug.log` command in your Magento root. When you load the `/helloworld/index/event` page, you will see that the `Registered` message appears in the log file.

4. Let's look at the parameters that are sent with the event. These parameters are stored in the `$observer` variable that is passed to the `execute()` method. Add the following code to this method to debug the product and category that is passed to that event:

```php
public function execute(\Magento\Framework\Event\Observer
$observer)
{
    $product = $observer->getProduct();
    $category = $observer->getCategory();

    $this->logger->debug(print_r($product->debug(), true));
    $this->logger->debug(print_r($category->debug(), true));
}
```

5. When you reload the `/helloworld/index/event` page, you will see that a dump of products and categories appears in the log file.

 When nothing appears in your log file, it is possible that your full page cache is active. If this is so, you can disable it and flush the cache after disabling it. You can also flush the cache each time you are testing.

6. For the next part, we will hook into the `add to cart` event. When a user adds a product to the cart, we need to check that the quantity is odd. If not, we will have to show an error message that the product can't be added to the cart.

7. We can do this by creating an event observer for the `checkout_cart_product_add_after` event. To create an event listener for this event, add the following code in the `app/code/Packt/HelloWorld/etc/frontend/events.xml` file:

```xml
<?xml version="1.0"?>
<config xmlns:xsi="http://www.w3.org/2001/XMLSchema-instance"
xsi:noNamespaceSchemaLocation=
"urn:magento:framework:Event/etc/events.xsd">
    <event name="checkout_cart_product_add_after">
        <observer name="check_cart_qty" instance=
        "Packt\HelloWorld\Observer\CheckCartQtyObserver" />
    </event>
</config>
```

8. Create the `app/code/Packt/HelloWorld/Observer/CheckCartQtyObserver.php` file with the following content:

```php
<?php

namespace Packt\HelloWorld\Observer;

use Magento\Framework\Event\ObserverInterface;

class CheckCartQtyObserver implements ObserverInterface
{
    public function execute(\Magento\Framework\Event\
    Observer $observer)
    {
        if ($observer->getProduct()->getQty() %2 != 0) {
            //Odd qty
            throw new \Exception('Qty must be even');
        }
    }
}
```

9. Clean the cache and try to add something to the cart with an even and odd quantity. You will see that an error occurs when you add an odd quantity. When you add an even quantity.

How it works...

Event listeners are configured in the `events.xml` file. When we look at the structure of the XML file, we can say the following things about tags and attributes when we have the following code:

```xml
<?xml version="1.0"?>
<config xmlns:xsi="http://www.w3.org/2001/XMLSchema-instance"
xsi:noNamespaceSchemaLocation="urn:magento:framework:Event/etc/
events.xsd">
    <event name="checkout_cart_product_add_after">
        <observer name="check_cart_qty" instance=
        "Packt\HelloWorld\Observer\CheckCartQtyObserver" />
    </event>
</config>
```

The root tag is the `<config>` tag. This tag can have one or more `<event>` subtags.

The `<event>` subtag defines a new event observer. With the name attribute, we configure the name of the event that will be observed. In this recipe, we used the `checkout_cart_product_add_after` event to check the quantity. This event is dispatched in the `app/code/Magento/Checkout/Model/Cart.php` file.

The `<event>` tag can have one or more `<observer>` subtags. With this tag, we configure the event observer. The name attribute is the name of the observer. This name must be unique. The instance attribute is the class that will be called.

For the previous example, this means:

▸ The `checkout_cart_product_add_after` event will be observed

▸ The name of the observer is `check_cart_qty`

▸ The `execute()` method will be executed from the class `Packt\HelloWorld\Observer\CheckCartQtyObserver`

With an event observer, there is one object passed that contains an array of data that is sent with the event in the `dispatch()` function.

In the previous recipe, we dispatched an event called `helloworld_register_visit`. With that dispatch, we added a product and category to that event.

In this recipe, we extracted a product and category from the `$observer` parameter, which is the first argument of the observed event function.

Introducing cronjobs

Cronjobs, or scheduled tasks, are background processes that keep your Magento webshop running by automating some tasks. Some examples of cronjobs are as follows:

- Sending newsletters
- Recalculating catalog promotion rules
- Cleaning visitor logs
- Sending price and stock alert e-mails
- Updating currency rates

When the Magento cron is not configured correctly, you will see that some features of your Magento shop will not work as expected.

Getting ready

In this recipe, you will learn how you can configure cronjobs on the server and how you can verify that they are working. Open your SSH client and change to the Magento folder.

How to do it...

Using the following steps, we will configure cronjobs on the server:

1. The Magento cron needs to be executed on periodic timestamps, for example, every five minutes. To run the crons, the following command is used:

```
php bin/magento cron:run
```

 To avoid permission problems, you have to run this command as the user that Apache uses to serve HTTP requests. On a basic apache setup, this user is www-data, but this can be different on other setups.

2. When you execute the previous command, the cronjob table, cron_schedule, is updated with the recent cronjobs. When you run the following command in your database client, you can see the content of that table:

```
SELECT * FROM cron_schedule;
```

This query gives the following output:

schedule_id	job_code	status	messages	created_at	scheduled_at	executed_at	finished_at
17	sales_grid_order_async_insert	pending	NULL	2015-08-03 21:02:44	2015-08-03 21:02:00	NULL	NULL
18	sales_grid_order_invoice_async_insert	pending	NULL	2015-08-03 21:02:44	2015-08-03 21:02:00	NULL	NULL
19	sales_grid_order_shipment_async_insert	pending	NULL	2015-08-03 21:02:44	2015-08-03 21:02:00	NULL	NULL
20	sales_grid_order_creditmemo_async_insert	pending	NULL	2015-08-03 21:02:44	2015-08-03 21:02:00	NULL	NULL
21	sales_send_order_emails	pending	NULL	2015-08-03 21:02:44	2015-08-03 21:02:00	NULL	NULL
22	sales_send_order_invoice_emails	pending	NULL	2015-08-03 21:02:44	2015-08-03 21:02:00	NULL	NULL
23	sales_send_order_shipment_emails	pending	NULL	2015-08-03 21:02:44	2015-08-03 21:02:00	NULL	NULL
24	sales_send_order_creditmemo_emails	pending	NULL	2015-08-03 21:02:44	2015-08-03 21:02:00	NULL	NULL
25	newsletter_send_all	pending	NULL	2015-08-03 21:02:44	2015-08-03 21:05:00	NULL	NULL
26	captcha_delete_expired_images	pending	NULL	2015-08-03 21:02:44	2015-08-03 21:10:00	NULL	NULL
27	indexer_reindex_all_invalid	pending	NULL	2015-08-03 21:02:45	2015-08-03 21:02:00	NULL	NULL
28	indexer_update_all_views	pending	NULL	2015-08-03 21:02:45	2015-08-03 21:02:00	NULL	NULL

3. In the `scheduled_at` column, we can see when the cronjob is planned to run. Run the last command again after a minute. Magento will run the cronjobs where the `scheduled_at` time is in the past and the status is `pending`. The content of the `cron_schedule` table will look as follows:

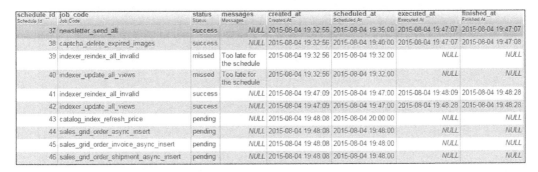

schedule_id	job_code	status	messages	created_at	scheduled_at	executed_at	finished_at
37	newsletter_send_all	success	NULL	2015-08-04 19:32:55	2015-08-04 19:35:00	2015-08-04 19:47:07	2015-08-04 19:47:07
38	captcha_delete_expired_images	success	NULL	2015-08-04 19:32:56	2015-08-04 19:40:00	2015-08-04 19:47:07	2015-08-04 19:47:08
39	indexer_reindex_all_invalid	missed	Too late for the schedule	2015-08-04 19:32:56	2015-08-04 19:32:00	NULL	NULL
40	indexer_update_all_views	missed	Too late for the schedule	2015-08-04 19:32:56	2015-08-04 19:32:00	NULL	NULL
41	indexer_reindex_all_invalid	success	NULL	2015-08-04 19:47:09	2015-08-04 19:47:00	2015-08-04 19:48:09	2015-08-04 19:48:28
42	indexer_update_all_views	success	NULL	2015-08-04 19:47:09	2015-08-04 19:47:00	2015-08-04 19:48:28	2015-08-04 19:48:28
43	catalog_index_refresh_price	pending	NULL	2015-08-04 19:48:08	2015-08-04 20:00:00	NULL	NULL
44	sales_grid_order_async_insert	pending	NULL	2015-08-04 19:48:08	2015-08-04 19:48:00	NULL	NULL
45	sales_grid_order_invoice_async_insert	pending	NULL	2015-08-04 19:48:08	2015-08-04 19:48:00	NULL	NULL
46	sales_grid_order_shipment_async_insert	pending	NULL	2015-08-04 19:48:08	2015-08-04 19:48:00	NULL	NULL

4. When we want to configure that the cron command will be executed every minute, we have to use the `crontab` file of the Linux server. First, switch to the `www` user of your project. For a standard Apache 2 webserver, it is `www-data`. We can change the user with the following command:

```
sudo su www-data
```

5. The next thing to do is to open the `crontab` file. We can do this by running the `crontab -e` command. This will open a file where we have to put the content, as shown in the following screenshot:

```
# Edit this file to introduce tasks to be run by cron.
#
# Each task to run has to be defined through a single line
# indicating with different fields when the task will be run
# and what command to run for the task
#
# To define the time you can provide concrete values for
# minute (m), hour (h), day of month (dom), month (mon),
# and day of week (dow) or use '*' in these fields (for 'any').#
# Notice that tasks will be started based on the cron's system
# daemon's notion of time and timezones.
#
# Output of the crontab jobs (including errors) is sent through
# email to the user the crontab file belongs to (unless redirected).
#
# For example, you can run a backup of all your user accounts
# at 5 a.m every week with:
# 0 5 * * 1 tar -zcf /var/backups/home.tgz /home/
#
# For more information see the manual pages of crontab(5) and cron(8)
#
# m h  dom mon dow   command
*/1 * * * * php /var/www/magento2/bin/magento cron:run &
```

6. Save the file and your cronjob will run after every minute.

How it works...

The Magento cron will be executed with the Magento 2 command-line tool. The command to run the cron (the `cron.sh` script in Magento 1) is as follows:

```
php bin/magento cron:run
```

This will start the Magento cron process. The `cron` command will execute the PHP code over the **Command Line Interface** (**CLI**). This means that the `php-cli` settings are used to execute the cronjobs instead of the apache PHP settings that are used by apache.

When the cron process is initialized, Magento looks at the `cron_schedule` table. Every scheduled cronjob with the `scheduled_at` field in the past and with the status `pending` will be executed. When a job starts, the `executed_at` field will be updated with the current timestamp and the status will be changed.

When a job is finished, the `finished_at` field is updated with the current timestamp. Also, the `status` will be updated. When the status is an error, the message field will be updated with the error message.

When the process is finished, Magento will create a queue for the next period. Based on the configuration files, Magento knows when it has to schedule each cronjob.

Creating and testing a new cronjob

In Magento 2, cronjobs are defined in the `crontab.xml` file of each module. Like every configuration in the Magento modules, the configuration of the cronjobs is easy to extend in custom modules. And that's what we will do in this recipe. We will create a new cronjob for our module.

Testing a cronjob is a bit tricky. You can wait while the cron will is executed, but in this recipe, we will see how we can trigger it for development purposes.

Getting ready

The workflow to create a new cronjob is mostly the same as working with event observers. We have to configure a new cronjob that will start a function in a configured class.

For the creation of a new cronjob, we will use the existing `Packt_HelloWorld` module. Make sure you have the latest version installed.

How to do it...

In the next steps, we will create the configuration for a new cronjob:

1. The first thing is to create the configuration file. Create the `app/code/Packt/HelloWorld/etc/crontab.xml` file with the following content:

```xml
<?xml version="1.0"?>
<config xmlns:xsi="http://www.w3.org/2001/XMLSchema-
instance" xsi:noNamespaceSchemaLocation=
"urn:magento:module:Magento_Cron:etc/crontab.xsd">
  <group id="default">
    <job name="helloworld_check_subscriptions"
    instance="Packt\HelloWorld\Model\Cron"
    method="checkSubscriptions">
    <schedule>* * * * *</schedule>
    </job>
  </group>
</config>
```

2. The next thing is to create the `cron` class with the function that will be executed. Create the `app/code/Packt/HelloWorld/Model/Cron.php` file with the following content:

```php
<?php
namespace Packt\HelloWorld\Model;
class Cron {
  /** @var \Psr\Log\LoggerInterface $logger */
  protected $logger;

  /** @var \Magento\Framework\ObjectManagerInterface */
  protected $objectManager;

  public function __construct(
    \Psr\Log\LoggerInterface $logger,
    \Magento\Framework\ObjectManagerInterface
    $objectManager
  ) {
    $this->logger = $logger;
    $this->objectManager = $objectManager;
  }

  public function checkSubscriptions() {
    $subscription = $this->objectManager-
    >create(''Packt\HelloWorld\Model\Subscription'');

    $subscription->setFirstname(''Cron'');
    $subscription->setLastname(''Job'');
    $subscription->setEmail(''cron.job@example.com'');
    $subscription->setMessage(!'Created from cron'');

    $subscription->save();

    $this->logger->debug(''Test subscription added'');
  }
}
```

3. When we want to test our cronjob, we can create a cron group to run the test with. To create a cron group, we have to create the `app/code/Packt/HelloWorld/etc/cron_groups.xml` file with the following content:

```xml
<?xml version="1.0"?>
<config xmlns:xsi="http://www.w3.org/2001/XMLSchema-
instance" xsi:noNamespaceSchemaLocation=
"urn:magento:module:Magento_Cron:etc/cron_groups.xsd">
  <group id="packt">
```

```
      <schedule_generate_every>1</schedule_generate_every>
      <schedule_ahead_for>4</schedule_ahead_for>
      <schedule_lifetime>2</schedule_lifetime>
      <history_cleanup_every>10</history_cleanup_every>
      <history_success_lifetime>60</history_success_lifetime>
      <history_failure_lifetime>600
      </history_failure_lifetime>
      <use_separate_process>1</use_separate_process>
   </group>
</config>
```

4. The next thing to do is to link the cronjob to the group. In the `app/code/Packt/HelloWorld/etc/crontab.xml` file, change the `id` attribute of the `<group>` tag to the following:

```
<group id="packt">
```

5. Clean the cache and run the following command:

```
php bin/magento cron:run --group="packt"
```

6. When you look at the contents of the `cron_schedule` table, you can see that a new pending job is added. The `job_code` instance of this is `helloworld_check_subscriptions` as we have configured in the `crontab.xml` file.

7. Run the same command again and the job will be executed. When you look into the `var/log/debug.log` file, you will see that the `Test subscription added` message is logged at the end of the file.

8. When we look at the subscriptions table in the backend of Magento (**Marketing | HelloWorld | Subscriptions**), we see that a new subscription with name **Cron Job** is added.

9. Now, we know that the cronjob is working. To finish it, we can add the job to the default group and schedule it in such a way that it runs every night at 2:30 a.m. For this, we have to change the highlighted lines of code from the `app/code/Packt/HelloWorld/etc/crontab.xml`:

```
<?xml version="1.0"?>
<config xmlns:xsi="http://www.w3.org/2001/XMLSchema-
instance" xsi:noNamespaceSchemaLocation=
"urn:magento:module:Magento_Cron:etc/crontab.xsd">
  <group id="default">
    <job name="helloworld_check_subscriptions"
    instance="Packt\HelloWorld\Model\Cron"
    method="checkSubscriptions">
    <schedule>30 2 * * *</schedule>
    </job>
  </group>
</config>
```

10. Clean the cache and your cron will run in the default group. The job will be scheduled for 2:30 a.m.

How it works...

Cronjobs are always configured in the `crontab.xml` file. Like in Magento 1, a cronjob has a name with a class and method that will be executed. For every cronjob, you have to give a schedule in the cron time format to specify the interval.

 The name of a cronjob is always written using lowercase and underscores.

Another new thing in Magento 2 is that you need to associate a cronjob to a group. A group is always specified in the `cron_groups.xml` file. By default, Magento 2 has the following cron groups:

 ▶ `default`
 ▶ `index`

In a cron group, you can specify settings for how crons will be handled in the `cron_schedule` table. You can make settings, such as the lifetime of errors, cleanup, and schedule. For the development group, we used a setting that always schedules a new cronjob when the previous cronjob is executed.

You have two advantages when you use a cron group for development stuff.

The first one is that you can use specific settings about the scheduling of the cronjob. The second one is that you can use the `cron` command to run only the cronjobs of a specific group.

With the `--group` parameter, you can specify the group for which the jobs need to be executed and scheduled. When this parameter is empty, all the groups will be executed and scheduled.

In every cronjob tag (the `<job>` tag), there is a `<schedule>` subtag. In this subtag, you can configure the interval of the cronjob. This configuration contains five parameters that represent the following configurations:

- ▸ Minute
- ▸ Hour
- ▸ Day
- ▸ Month
- ▸ Year

When you have a configuration like `0 10 * * *`, this means that this cron runs at minute 0, hour 10, all days, all months, all years. So the time at which this runs is at 10 a.m.

8
Creating a Shipping Module

In this chapter, we will cover:

- ▶ Initializing module configurations
- ▶ Writing an adapter model
- ▶ Extending the shipping method features
- ▶ Adding the module in the frontend

Introduction

Shipping the ordered products to the customers is one of the key parts of the e-commerce flow. In most cases, a store owner has a contract with a shipping handler, and every shipping handler has their own business rules.

In Magento 2, the following shipping handlers have an extension:

- ▶ DHL
- ▶ FedEx
- ▶ UPS
- ▶ USPS

If your handler is not on this list, check whether your shipping handler has a Magento module. If not, you can configure a standard shipping method or you can create your own shipping method, as you will learn to do in this chapter.

Initializing module configurations

In *Chapter 4, Creating a Module*, you learned how to create a custom module. In this recipe, we will create a new module where we will add the required settings for a shipping module.

In the later recipes of this chapter, we will extend this module with more shipping features.

Getting ready

Open your IDE with the Magento 2 project. We will also need the backend, where we will check some configurations.

How to do it...

The following steps describe how we can create the configuration for a shipping module:

1. First, we have to create the following folders:

    ❏   app/code/Packt/

    ❏   app/code/Packt/Shipme/

    ❏   app/code/Packt/Shipme/etc/

    ❏   app/code/Packt/Shipme/Model/

    ❏   app/code/Packt/Shipme/Model/Carrier/

2. Create a module.xml file in the app/code/Packt/Shipme/etc/ folder with the following content:

    ```xml
    <?xml version="1.0"?>
    <config xmlns:xsi="http://www.w3.org/2001/XMLSchema-
    instance" xsi:noNamespaceSchemaLocation=
    "urn:magento:framework:Module/etc/module.xsd">
      <module name="Packt_Shipme" setup_version="2.0.0">
        <sequence>
          <module name="Magento_Shipping"/>
        </sequence>
      </module>
    </config>
    ```

3. Create a `registration.php` file in the `app/code/Packt/Shipme/` folder with the following content:

```php
<?php

\Magento\Framework\Component\ComponentRegistrar::register(
  \Magento\Framework\Component\ComponentRegistrar::MODULE,
  'Packt_Shipme',
  __DIR__
);
```

4. With this file, we can install the module by running the `php bin/magento setup:upgrade` command.

5. To check that the module is active, open the backend and navigate to **Stores | Configuration | Advanced | Advanced** and check whether `Packt_Shipme` is in the list and is enabled.

6. At this point, the module is initialized and active. We can now create a `system.xml` file in the `app/code/Packt/Shipme/etc/adminhtml/` folder.

7. When the previous file is created, add the following content to it. This will create the shipping configuration parameters near all the other shipping methods:

```xml
<?xml version="1.0"?>
<config xmlns:xsi="http://www.w3.org/2001/XMLSchema-
instance" xsi:noNamespaceSchemaLocation=
"urn:magento:module:Magento_Config:etc/system_file.xsd">
  <system>
    <section id="carriers">
      <group id="shipme" translate="label" type="text"
      sortOrder="50" showInDefault="1" showInWebsite="1"
      showInStore="1">
        <label>Shipme</label>
        <field id="active" translate="label" type="select"
        sortOrder="10" showInDefault="1" showInWebsite="1"
        showInStore="0">
          <label>Enabled</label>
          <source_model>Magento\Config\Model\Config\Source\
          Yesno</source_model>
        </field>
        <field id="name" translate="label" type="text"
        sortOrder="20" showInDefault="1" showInWebsite="1"
        showInStore="1">
```

```
        <label>Method Name</label>
      </field>
      <field id="title" translate="label" type="text"
      sortOrder="20" showInDefault="1" showInWebsite="1"
      showInStore="1">
        <label>Method Title</label>
      </field>
    </group>
  </section>
  </system>
</config>
```

8. Next, we can configure some default settings. Create a `config.xml` file in the `app/code/Packt/Shipme/etc/` folder with the following content:

```
<?xml version="1.0"?>
<config xmlns:xsi="http://www.w3.org/2001/XMLSchema-
instance" xsi:noNamespaceSchemaLocation=
"urn:magento:module:Magento_Store:etc/config.xsd">
  <default>
    <carriers>
      <shipme>
        <model>Packt\Shipme\Model\Carrier\Shipme</model>
        <active>1</active>
        <name>Shipme Shipping</name>
        <title>Shipme Shipping</title>
      </shipme>
    </carriers>
  </default>
</config>
```

9. Clean the cache and navigate to **Stores | Configuration | Sales | Shipping Methods**. You will see that an extra group is added, as shown in the following screenshot:

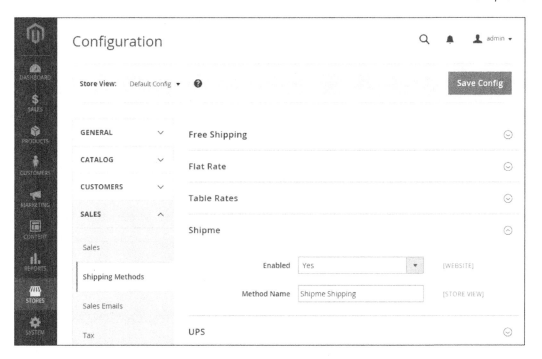

10. Now, when the configuration is working, we can extend the configuration with some extra values. Modify the `system.xml` file so that it looks as follows (the highlighted code is added in this step):

```xml
<?xml version="1.0"?>
<config xmlns:xsi="http://www.w3.org/2001/XMLSchema-
instance" xsi:noNamespaceSchemaLocation=
"urn:magento:module:Magento_Config:etc/system_file.xsd">
  <system>
    <section id="carriers">
      <group id="shipme" translate="label" type="text"
      sortOrder="50" showInDefault="1" showInWebsite="1"
      showInStore="1">
        <label>Shipme</label>
        <field id="active" translate="label" type="select"
        sortOrder="10" showInDefault="1" showInWebsite="1"
        showInStore="0">
```

```xml
    <label>Enabled</label>
    <source_model>Magento\Config\Model\Config\Source\
    Yesno</source_model>
</field>
<field id="name" translate="label" type="text"
sortOrder="20" showInDefault="1" showInWebsite="1"
showInStore="1">
    <label>Method Name</label>
</field>
<field id="title" translate="label" type="text"
sortOrder="20" showInDefault="1" showInWebsite="1"
showInStore="1">
    <label>Method Title</label>
</field>

<field id="express_enabled" translate="label"
type="select" sortOrder="30" showInDefault="1"
showInWebsite="1" showInStore="0">
    <label>Enable express</label>
    <source_model>Magento\Config\Model\Config\Source\
    Yesno</source_model>
</field>
<field id="express_title" translate="label" type="text"
sortOrder="40" showInDefault="1" showInWebsite="1"
showInStore="1">
    <label>Title express</label>
</field>
<field id="express_price" translate="label" type="text"
sortOrder="50" showInDefault="1" showInWebsite="1"
showInStore="1">
    <label>Price express</label>
</field>

<field id="business_enabled" translate="label"
type="select" sortOrder="60" showInDefault="1"
showInWebsite="1" showInStore="0">
    <label>Enable business</label>
    <source_model>Magento\Config\Model\Config\Source\
    Yesno</source_model>
</field>
<field id="business_title" translate="label"
type="text" sortOrder="70" showInDefault="1"
showInWebsite="1" showInStore="1">
    <label>Title business</label>
</field>
```

```
          <field id="business_price" translate="label"
          type="text" sortOrder="80" showInDefault="1"
          showInWebsite="1" showInStore="1">
            <label>Price business</label>
          </field>

          <field id="specificerrmsg" translate="label"
          type="textarea" sortOrder="90" showInDefault="1"
          showInWebsite="1" showInStore="1">
            <label>Displayed Error Message</label>
          </field>
        </group>
      </section>
    </system>
  </config>
```

11. To configure the default values, add the highlighted code into the `config.xml` file of the module:

```
<?xml version="1.0"?>
<config xmlns:xsi="http://www.w3.org/2001/XMLSchema-
instance" xsi:noNamespaceSchemaLocation=
"urn:magento:module:Magento_Store:etc/config.xsd">
  <default>
    <carriers>
      <shipme>
        <model>Packt\Shipme\Model\Carrier\Shipme</model>
        <active>1</active>
        <name>Shipme Shipping</name>
        <title>Shipme Shipping</title>

        <express_enabled>1</express_enabled>
        <express_title>Express delivery</express_title>
        <express_price>4</express_price>

        <business_enabled>1</business_enabled>
        <business_title>Business delivery</business_title>
        <business_price>5</business_price>

        <specificerrmsg>This shipping method is currently
        unavailable. If you would like to ship using this
        shipping method, please contact us.</specificerrmsg>
      </shipme>
    </carriers>
  </default>
</config>
```

12. Clean the cache and reload the shipping method configuration page in the backend. You will see that the extra fields are available under the **Shipme** section, as shown in the following screenshot:

How it works...

In the first steps of this recipe, we created the necessary files to initialize the module. To initialize a module, we need a `module.xml` file in the `etc` folder of the module.

In the `module.xml` file, we configured the name and version in the `<module>` tag. In the `<sequence>` subtag, we configured the dependencies of the module.

The `<sequence>` configuration checks whether the `Magento_Shipping` and `Magento_OfflineShipping` modules are active. Otherwise, the module cannot be installed.

When the module was installed, we extended the module with the configurations for a shipping method. All the Magento shipping methods are configurable on the **Shipping Methods** page in the configuration. So, to create an extra shipping method, we have to create an extra section on that page.

We created a shipping handler that has a **Method Name** option. In that handler, we created two shipping options: **express** and **business**. For those two options, we created the name, enabled, and price fields.

The configuration parameters are configured in the system.xml file of the module. For every configuration parameter, there is a default value. These values are configured in the config.xml file.

In this config.xml file, there is also a model configured. This is the adapter model that we will create in the next recipe, *Writing an adapter model*.

See also

In this recipe, we used the system.xml file of the module to create the configuration values. More information about configuration values is explained in the *Adding configuration parameters* recipe of *Chapter 6, Magento Backend*.

Writing an adapter model

In the previous recipe, we enabled a new module with the settings for a new shipping method. This was a preparation for the business part, which we will do in this recipe.

We will add a model with the business logic for the shipping method. The model is called an adapter class because Magento requires an adapter class for each shipping method.

The adapter class will be used for the following things:

- Making the shipping method available
- Calculating the shipping costs
- Setting the title in the frontend of the shipping methods

Getting ready

Ensure that you have installed the module that we created in the previous recipe because we need this for creating the adapter class.

How to do it...

The following steps describe how you can write an adapter class for a shipping method:

1. Create the app/code/Packt/Shipme/Model/Carrier/ folder if it doesn't already exist.

2. In this folder, create a file called `Shipme.php` with the following content:

```php
<?php
namespace Packt\Shipme\Model\Carrier;
use Magento\Shipping\Model\Rate\Result;
class Shipme extends \Magento\Shipping\Model\Carrier\
AbstractCarrier implements
\Magento\Shipping\Model\Carrier\CarrierInterface {
  protected $_code = 'shipme';

  /**
  * @var \Magento\Shipping\Model\Rate\ResultFactory
  */
  protected $_rateResultFactory;

  /**
  * @var \Magento\Quote\Model\Quote\Address\RateResult\
  MethodFactory
  */
  protected $_rateMethodFactory;

  public function __construct(
    \Magento\Framework\App\Config\ScopeConfigInterface
    $scopeConfig,
    \Magento\Quote\Model\Quote\Address\RateResult\
    ErrorFactory $rateErrorFactory,
    \Psr\Log\LoggerInterface $logger,
    \Magento\Shipping\Model\Rate\ResultFactory
    $rateResultFactory,
    \Magento\Quote\Model\Quote\Address\RateResult\
    MethodFactory $rateMethodFactory,
    array $data = []
  ) {
    $this->_rateResultFactory = $rateResultFactory;
    $this->_rateMethodFactory = $rateMethodFactory;
    parent::__construct($scopeConfig, $rateErrorFactory,
    $logger, $data);
  }

  public function collectRates
  (\Magento\Quote\Model\Quote\Address\RateRequest $request)
  {
```

```php
if (!$this->getConfigFlag('active')) {
  return false;
}

$result = $this->_rateResultFactory->create();

//Check if express method is enabled
if ($this->getConfigData('express_enabled')) {
  $method = $this->_rateMethodFactory->create();

  $method->setCarrier($this->_code);
  $method->setCarrierTitle($this-
  >getConfigData('name'));

  $method->setMethod('express');
  $method->setMethodTitle($this-
  >getConfigData('express_title'));

  $method->setPrice($this-
  >getConfigData('express_price'));
  $method->setCost($this-
  >getConfigData('express_price'));

  $result->append($method);
}

//Check if business method is enabled
if ($this->getConfigData('business_enabled')) {
  $method = $this->_rateMethodFactory->create();

  $method->setCarrier($this->_code);
  $method->setCarrierTitle($this-
  >getConfigData('name'));

  $method->setMethod('business');
  $method->setMethodTitle($this-
  >getConfigData('business_title'));

  $method->setPrice($this-
  >getConfigData('business_price'));
  $method->setCost($this-
  >getConfigData('business_price'));
```

```
        $result->append($method);
    }

    return $result;
}

public function getAllowedMethods() {
    return ['shipme' => $this->getConfigData('name')];
}
}
```

3. Save the file and clear the cache. Your adapter model is now created.

How it works...

The class that we created in this recipe handles all the business logic that is needed for the shipping method. Because this adapter class extends from the \Magento\Shipping\ Model\Carrier\AbstractCarrier class, we can overwrite some methods to customize the business logic of the standard class.

This class implements the \Magento\Shipping\Model\Carrier\CarrierInterface interface. When we look in this class, we see that the following methods must be available in the adapter class:

*   isTrackingAvailable()
*   getAllowedMethods()

These methods are set in the AbstractCarrier class—the class where the adapter model extends from. This means that the class is valid. In that class, there is also the isAvailable() method. In this method, there is decided that the shipping method is active or not. If you want, you can overwrite this method with your custom code.

The second and most important function is the collectRates() function. This function decides which methods are available and the shipping costs.

In Magento, a shipping method has a carrier. The carrier from the methods of this recipe is **Shipme**. Every carrier can have multiple methods, such as **Express** and **Business delivery**.

In the collectRates() function, we create a rateResult variable to which you can assign shipping methods. In this recipe, we added two methods to this: **Express** and **Business delivery**.

A method is created form the `rateMethodFactory` instance and this can have the following options:

- ▸ Carrier (shipme)
- ▸ Title of the carrier
- ▸ Method (code of the method)
- ▸ Method title
- ▸ Price
- ▸ Cost

When these options are set, the method is added to the `rateResult` instance using the `append()` function.

The next function that we used is the `getAllowedMethods()` function. In this function, we add the methods of the **Shipme** carrier to the allowed shipping methods.

Extending the shipping method features

Now that all the files are installed, we can add more features to the shipping method. In this recipe, we will add a country configuration and enable tracking codes for the shipping method.

Getting ready

Similar to all recipes in this chapter, we will build further on the module that we created in the previous recipes of this chapter. Ensure that you have the right files installed.

How to do it...

In the following steps, you will learn how we can enable tracking codes and country configurations for the shipping method:

1. Open the shipping adapter file, `app/code/Packt/Shipme/Model/Carrier/Shipme.php`.

2. Add the following function to that class to enable tracking codes:

```
public function isTrackingAvailable() {
  return true;
}
```

3. Next, we will enable the country-specific options. In the `app/code/Packt/Shipme/etc/adminhtml/system.xml` file, add the following content:

```
<field id="sallowspecific" translate="label" type="select"
sortOrder="100" showInDefault="1" showInWebsite="1"
showInStore="0">
  <label>Ship to Applicable Countries</label>
  <frontend_class>shipping-applicable-
  country</frontend_class>
  <source_model>Magento\Shipping\Model\Config\Source\
  Allspecificcountries</source_model>
</field>

<field id="specificcountry" translate="label"
type="multiselect" sortOrder="110" showInDefault="1"
showInWebsite="1" showInStore="0">
  <label>Ship to Specific Countries</label>
  <source_model>Magento\Directory\Model\Config\Source\
  Country</source_model>
  <can_be_empty>1</can_be_empty>
</field>
```

4. Clean the cache and open the configuration page of the shipping method. You will see that there are two new configuration options. When you change the value of the **Ship to Applicable Countries** field to **Specific Countries**, you can select from multiple countries, as you can see in the following screenshot:

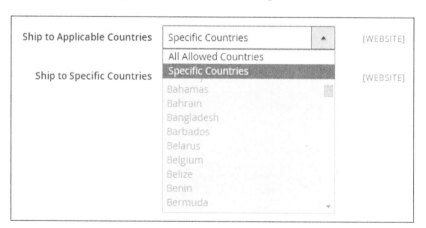

How it works...

In this recipe, we extended the shipping method with two new features. The first feature was to add the possibility to create tracking codes for the **Shipme** shipping method. We overwrote the `isTrackingAvailable()` function, which returns `false` by default. By overwriting this function and returning `true`, we enable the tracking codes.

The second thing that we did was to enable country-specific shipping. We added two fields with a standard naming convention. Using the following names for the two fields, Magento recognises the configuration for countries:

- `sallowspecific`
- `specificcountry`

When we enable this configuration in the backend, the shipping method is only available when the country of the shipping address is one of the selected countries in the **Ship to Specific Countries** configuration of the shipping method.

Adding the module in the frontend

In the previous recipes, we created configurations for a new shipping method. We have seen that we can configure this in the backend. Now, it is time to test the shipping method in the frontend. We will create a test order with the shipping method that we have created in this chapter.

Getting ready

We need the shipping module that we created in the previous recipes. Ensure you have the right files installed.

How to do it...

The following steps describe how the order flow works in Magento:

1. Log in to the backend.
2. Navigate to the configuration of the shipping method. You can find this by navigating to **Stores** | **Configuration** | **Sales** | **Shipping Methods** | **Shipme**.
3. Check whether all the values are correct for the **Shipme - Express** method. Ensure that everything is enabled.
4. Save the configuration.

5. In the frontend, add a product to the shopping cart and proceed to checkout.

 In *Chapter 7, Event Handlers and Cronjobs*, we created an event that checks whether the quantity is odd or even when adding something to the cart. When you get the **We can't add this item to your shopping cart right now.** message, you have to add an even quantity or you have to disable that code.

6. When you are on the checkout page, fill in the right data for the shipping address.

7. In the **Shipping Methods** section, the new methods will appear as shown in the following screenshot:

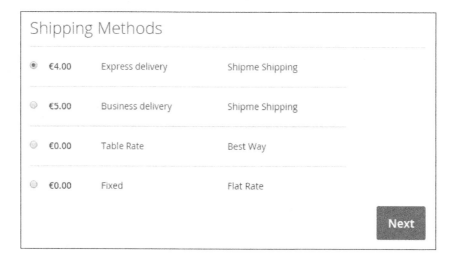

8. Select one of the **Shipme Shipping** methods and click on the **Next** button.

9. Check your payment information. Ensure that you have checked the **Check / Money order** method if there is more than one method available.

 If you don't see the **Check \ Money order** payment method, you have to enable it in the stores configuration.

10. Click on the **Place Order** button and your order will be created. You will see the order success page where you optionally can create an account for the website.

11. When you look into the backend by navigating to **Sales | Orders**, you can see the order that we have created. Click on the **View** link of that order and you will see all the details of that order.

12. To process the order, we can create an invoice for it to confirm that the order is paid. When you click on the **Invoice** button, you will be forwarded to the form where you can submit the invoice for that order.

13. When the invoice is saved, you will see that the status of the order is changed to **Processing**. To create a shipment for this order, we can click on the **Ship** button. You will see the following screen:

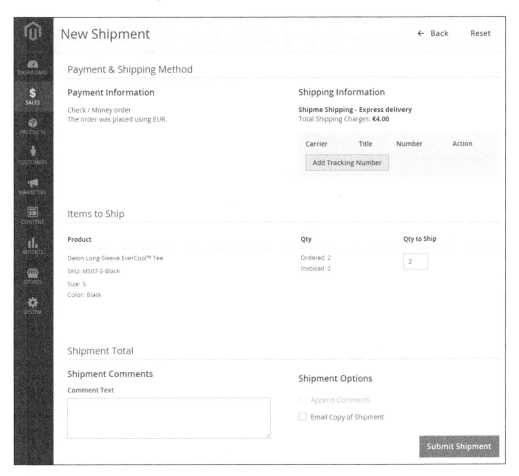

14. When you click on the **Add Tracking Number** button, you can create a tracking code for that shipment. In the **Carrier** dropdown, select the **Shipme Shipping** option and add a sample tracking code, such as **1234567890**.

15. When you click on the **Submit Shipment** button, your shipment is processed and the status of the order will change to **Complete**.

How it works...

In this recipe, we tested the shipping method that we created in this chapter. We placed an order with the new shipping method to check that everything works as expected.

When the order is placed, it is the task of the store owner to complete the order. The payment method of the order is **Check / Money order**. This means that the payment will happen later.

When the order is paid, you can set the paid amount by creating an invoice. The status will change from **Pending** to **Processing**. Processing means that the order is ready to be processed. When you look at the order totals on the order page, you see that **Total Paid** is the same as the **Grand Total** (if you have marked the invoice as paid).

When the order can be shipped, we can create a shipment of the order. All the shipping information can be stored in the shipment such as the tracking code(s), comments, status updates, and much more.

When there is an invoice and shipment for all the order items, the order is *Complete* in Magento. When the order is complete, it is always possible to create a **Credit Memo** receipt for special cases in the order flow (damaged shipping, a returning order, and so on).

9
Creating a Product Slider Widget

In this chapter, we will cover the following recipes:

- ▶ Creating an empty module
- ▶ Creating a widget configuration file
- ▶ Creating the block and template files
- ▶ Creating a custom configuration parameter
- ▶ Finalizing the theming

Introduction

The Magento widgets system is a graphical interface where you can configure blocks in the frontend. For every widget, there is a configuration page available where you can set the required values for that widget.

With a Magento widget, you can configure the layout instructions to show the widget at several places in the frontend.

In this chapter, we will create a new module in which we will create our own widget. We will create a product slider with the products of a category that we can configure in that widget.

When we are done with the technical part (configuration page, block class, template initialization), we can finish with its representation in the frontend. We will create a product list that we will style with a **jQuery** slider script.

Creating an empty module

As we did in the previous chapter and fully explained in *Chapter 4, Creating a Module*, we will create the required files to create an empty module that we will extend with widget configurations in further chapters. We will start with an empty Magento module that we will create in this recipe. We will create all the required files to initialize a new module that can be used for the creation of a widget.

Getting ready

We will create new module called `Packt_ProductSlider`. Open your IDE to add some code to it.

How to do it...

Using the following steps, we will create an empty module called `Packt_ProductSlider`:

1. Create the following folders in your Magento root:

    ❑ `app/code/Packt/`

    ❑ `app/code/Packt/ProductSlider/`

    ❑ `app/code/Packt/ProductSlider/etc/`

2. In the `app/code/Packt/ProductSlider/etc/` folder, create a file called `module.xml`.

3. In this file, paste the following code:

```xml
<?xml version="1.0"?>
<configxmlns:xsi="http://www.w3.org/2001/XMLSchema-instance"
xsi:noNamespaceSchemaLocation=
"urn:magento:framework:Module/etc/module.xsd">
  <module name="Packt_ProductSlider" setup_version="2.0.0">
    <sequence>
      <module name="Magento_Catalog"/>
      <module name="Magento_Widget"/>
    </sequence>
  </module>
</config>
```

4. In the `app/code/Packt/ProductSlider/` folder, create a `registration.php` file with the following content:

```php
<?php

\Magento\Framework\Component\ComponentRegistrar::register(
    \Magento\Framework\Component\ComponentRegistrar::MODULE,
    'Packt_ProductSlider',
    __DIR__
);
```

5. To install the module, run the following command:

   php bin/magento setup:upgrade

6. To check whether the module is installed, open the backend and navigate to the configuration page (**Stores | Configuration | Advanced | Advanced**). Check whether the `Packt_ProductSlider` module is in the list.

7. You can alternatively run the following command to get a list of all installed and enabled modules:

   php bin/magento module:status

How it works...

We have just created, installed, and enabled a new module called `Packt_ProductSlider`. To initialize a module, we need a `module.xml` file in the `etc` folder of the module.

In the `module.xml` file, we configured the name and version in the `<module>` tag. In the `<sequence>` subtag, we configured the dependencies of the module.

The `<sequence>` configuration checks whether the `Magento_Widget` and `Magento_Catalog` modules are active. Otherwise, the module cannot be installed.

Practically, this module does nothing, but we will extend this in the next recipes of this chapter.

Creating a widget configuration file

In this recipe, we will extend the features of the `Packt_ProductSlider` module with a widget configuration file. In this configuration file, we will declare a new widget or frontend app type.

For a new frontend app, we need to configure the following things:

▶ Name of the widget (used in the backend)

▶ Widget configuration parameters

▶ Widget block type

▶ Widget templates (the `.phtml` files)

Getting ready

We will extend the module that we created in the previous recipe with a widget configuration. Ensure that you have the right files installed.

How to do it...

Using the following steps, you can explore the purpose of a `widget.xml` configuration file:

1. Create the `app/code/Packt/ProductSlider/etc/widget.xml` file using the following code:

```
<?xml version="1.0" encoding="UTF-8"?>
<widgets xmlns:xsi="http://www.w3.org/2001/XMLSchema-
instance"
  xsi:noNamespaceSchemaLocation=
  "urn:magento:module:Magento_Widget:etc/widget.xsd">
  <widget
    id="category_product_slider"
    class="Magento\Catalog\Block\Product\List"
    is_email_compatible="false"
    placeholder_image="Magento_Widget::placeholder.gif">
    <label translate="true">Category product slider</label>
    <description translate="true">List of Products for a
    given category in a slider widget</description>
  </widget>
</widgets>
```

2. Clean the cache and check whether the configuration works. We can check this in two ways:

   1. The first method is to navigate to **Content | Widgets** in the backend. When you click on the **Add Widget** button, you can see the new widget type in the list, as shown in the following screenshot:

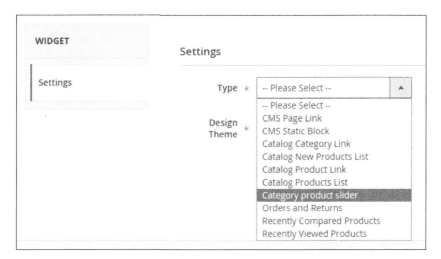

   2. The second way to test the widget types is to add a widget to a CMS page. Navigate to **Content | Elements | Pages** and click on the **Add New Page** button. In the **Content** tab, click on the highlighted button in the **WYSIWYG** editor, as shown in the following screenshot:

3. When clicking on that button, an overlay shows up where you can choose a widget. In the **Widget Type** dropdown, you can select **Category product slider** when the configuration is right.

4. Now that the widget works, it's time to add some configuration parameters to the widget. When we add the following highlighted code to the `widget.xml` file, we will create a parameter for the title:

```xml
<widget
  id="category_product_slider"
  class="Magento\Catalog\Block\Product\List"
  is_email_compatible="false"
  placeholder_image="Magento_Widget::placeholder.gif">
  <label translate="true">Category product slider</label>
  <description translate="true">List of Products for a
  given category in a slider widget</description>
  <parameters>
    <parameter name="title" xsi:type="text" required="true"
    visible="true">
      <label translate="true">Title (frontend)</label>
    </parameter>
  </parameters>
</widget>
```

5. Clean the cache and open the widget configuration page. We can do this by navigating to **Content | Elements | Widgets**. Click on the **Add Widget** button and choose the following configuration in the form:

    ❑ **Type**: **Category product slider**

    ❑ **Design Theme**: **Magento Luma** (the theme of your shop)

6. When you click on the **Continue** button, you will land on the widget configuration page. When you click on **Widget Options**, you will see the title parameter, as shown in the following screenshot:

7. When we want to show products for a category, we have to create a configuration field where we can set the category ID. When we want to add a text field where we can configure the right category ID, we need to add the highlighted code to the `widget.xml` file. The highlighted code needs to be pasted as the child of the `<parameters>` tag:

```
<parameters>
  <parameter name="title" xsi:type="text" required="true"
  visible="true">
    <label translate="true">Title (frontend)</label>
  </parameter>
  <parameter name="category_id" xsi:type="text" required="true"
  visible="true">
    <label translate="true">Category ID</label>
  </parameter>
</parameters>
```

8. Clean the cache and reload the frontend. You will see that a second textbox is added to the configuration page.

How it works...

The `widget.xml` file is used to define widget types in your Magento installation. All widget types are defined as child `<widget>` tags of the global `<widgets>` tag.

A widget type is declared in the `<widget>` tag and this element has the following three required attributes:

▶ `id` (the unique identifier of a widget)

▶ `class` (the `Block` class for the widget)

▶ `is_email_compatible` (the Boolean that the widget can be used in e-mail templates)

▶ `placeholder_image` (an image that is used when the widget is inserted in a *WYSIWYG* editor)

The widget type that we created in this recipe uses the `Magento\Catalog\Block\Product\List` block class. In Magento, this class is used to render all product lists, just like it is used on the category page.

In the child tags of the `<widget>` tag, we can configure the additional fields for the widget type.

With the `<name>` tag, we configured the name for the widget type that is displayed in the dropdown of the configuration page.

In the `<description>` tag, we can configure a description for the widget type. This description is shown when you insert a new widget in a CMS page.

Finally, we used the `<parameters>` tag to define the additional configuration parameters. In this recipe, we added `name` and `category_id` as text configuration fields.

Every configuration parameter is defined as a child `<parameter>` tag from the `<parameters>` tag. The `<parameter>` tag has the following attributes:

- ▸ `name` (the ID of the field)
- ▸ `xsi:type` (the type of the field, such as text, dropdown, and so on)
- ▸ `required` (can be set to `true` or `false`)
- ▸ `visible` (can be set to `true` or `false`)

Every `<parameter>` tag has a `<label>` subtag where you can configure the label of the field page.

Creating the block and template files

In the previous recipe, you learned how to configure an extra widget type to Magento. Now, it is time to display the widget.

We will extend the widget configuration with the option to select two different templates to render the widget in the frontend.

The second thing that we will do is create a custom `Block` class where we can write our own specific methods for the widget.

Getting ready

We will work further on the widget module that we created in the previous recipes. Ensure that you have the right code installed.

How to do it...

Using the following steps, you will learn how we can configure a custom `Block` class with custom templates for a widget instance:

1. The first thing that we will do is create the `Block` class for the widget. The `Block` class will extend `Magento\Catalog\Block\Product\List` class because we need the functionality of that class in our widget type. Create a file called `ProductSlider.php` in the `app/code/Packt/ProductSlider/Block/Catalog/Product/` folder.

2. Add the following content to that file:

```php
<?php

namespace Packt\ProductSlider\Block\Catalog\Product;

class ProductSlider extends
\Magento\Catalog\Block\Product\ListProduct {

}
```

3. Configure the widget configuration to use the `Block` class that we just created. Open the `app/code/Packt/ProductSlider/etc/widget.xml` file and change the class attribute as shown in the following highlighted code:

```xml
. . .
<widget
  id="category_product_slider"
  class="Packt\ProductSlider\Block\Catalog\Product\
  ProductSlider"
  is_email_compatible="false"
  placeholder_image="Magento_Widget::placeholder.gif">
  <label translate="true">Category product slider</label>
  <description translate="true">List of Products for a
  given category in a slider widget</description>
  <parameters>
. . .
```

4. Now when the `Block` class is created and configured, it is time to create templates for the block. For this widget, we will configure two templates. The first one will contain the image, price, and title of the products, and the second one is a simplified version that only shows the image and an **Add To Cart** button.

5. To store the templates, create the following folders:

   ❏ `app/code/Packt/ProductSlider/view/`

   ❏ `app/code/Packt/ProductSlider/view/frontend/`

   ❏ `app/code/Packt/ProductSlider/view/frontend/templates/`

   ❏ `app/code/Packt/ProductSlider/view/frontend/templates/product/`

   ❏ `app/code/Packt/ProductSlider/view/frontend/templates/product/slider/`

6. In the last folder, create the following files:
   - ❏ list.phtml
   - ❏ teaser.phtml

7. In the list.phtml file, add the following content:

```
<div class="block block-product-slider slider-list">
  <div class="block-title">
    <h2>List</h2>
  </div>
  <div class="block-content">
    Product slider
  </div>
</div>
```

8. In the teaser.phtml file, add the following content:

```
<div class="block block-product-slider slider-teaser">
  <div class="block-title">
    <h2>Teaser</h2>
  </div>
  <div class="block-content">
    Product slider
  </div>
</div>
```

9. Now when the files are created, we can create the configuration in the widget.xml file for the two templates. Add the following highlighted code to the widget.xml file. The code needs to be pasted as child of the <parameters> tag:

```
. . .
  </parameter>
  <parameter name="template" xsi:type="select" required="true"
  visible="true">
    <label translate="true">Template</label>
    <options>
      <option name="default" value="product/slider/list.phtml"
      selected="true">
        <label translate="true">Product list slider</label>
      </option>
      <option name="teaser" value=
      "product/slider/teaser.phtml">
        <label translate="true">Product teaser slider</label>
```

```
        </option>
      </options>
    </parameter>
  </parameters>
  . . .
```

10. Clean the cache and go to the widget configuration page. When you click on the **Add Layout Update** button, you can see the two configured templates, as shown in the following screenshot:

11. When you complete the form with the layout update as shown, the widget template will appear on the home page.

 Ensure that you have cleaned the cache and configured the widget for the right theme and storeview.

12. The last thing that we will do is create a loop that shows the name of the products. Add the following code to the `list.phtml` file:

```php
<?php $productCollection = $block->getLoadedProductCollection() ?>
<div class="block block-product-slider slider-list">
  <div class="block-title">
    <h2>List</h2>
  </div>
  <div class="block-content">
    <?php if (count($productCollection)): ?>
      <ul>
        <?php foreach ($productCollection as $product): ?>
          <li><?php echo $product->getName() ?></li>
        <?php endforeach; ?>
      </ul>
```

```
        <?php endif; ?>
    </div>
</div>
```

13. On the widget configuration, configure a valid category ID. When you save the configuration and open the homepage, you will see a list of product names of that category, as shown in the following screenshot:

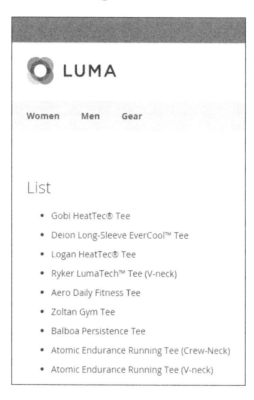

 You can find the category ID while navigating to a category in the backend. Navigate to **Products | Categories** and select the category that you want in the tree. When selecting a category, the ID appears near the name.

How it works...

The first thing that we did was to create a `Block` class that extends the product list class (`Magento\Catalog\Block\Product\ListProduct`) from the `Magento_Catalog` module.

When the class is created, we updated the configuration in the `widget.xml` file to use this class.

With only a `Block` class, we can't display the output to the frontend. So, we create the template files. We created two template files that we can use to generate a different output with the same data.

To configure the templates in the widget, we have to add an extra `<parameter>` configuration. Templates are always configured with a `<parameter name="template">` configuration. In the `<options>` child tag, the different templates are set as options from the dropdown.

The widget configuration is now finished, so by completing the form, the widget will be placed on the frontend.

To show a widget on the frontend, you have to create a **layout update** in the widget configuration page. In a layout update, you can configure the page type, container, and template where the widget needs to be displayed. In this example, the displayed is shown in the content area of the homepage.

The last thing we did was displaying the product names of the configured category. We created a loop that shows the product names for a category. Using the `getLoadedProductCollection()` method, all the products that are in a configured category are returned. The category ID needs to be configured in the `category_id` field of that block (this is something that is done using the `category_id` widget parameter).

Creating a custom configuration parameter

At this point, we have a working widget. It shows up in the frontend and the right products are displayed for the given category ID.

To configure the category ID, we have to know the ID of the category. We have to copy it from the category page and paste it in the textbox.

For better usability, we will create a custom configuration field to select a category. We will create a button that opens an overlay where we can choose the right category ID.

Getting ready

We will create a similar configuration field that is used for the **Catalog Category Link** widget type in the backend. You can look at this configuration widget's configuration to see how it works.

Also, ensure that you have the right start files installed because we will build further on the module that we created in the previous recipes.

How to do it...

Using the following steps, we will create a category chooser that will be used on the widget configuration page.

1. When we look at the **Catalog Category Link** widget, we see that they use a custom widget to select the category ID. We will use this widget in our module.

2. Open the `widget.xml` file that is placed in the `/etc` folder of the `Packt_ProductSlider` module. Replace the parameter of the `category_id` parameter with the following highlighted code:

```
. . .
  <label translate="true">Title (frontend)</label>
</parameter>
<parameter name="category_id" xsi:type="block" visible="true"
required="true">
  <label translate="true">Category</label>
  <block class="Magento\Catalog\Block\Adminhtml\Category\
  Widget\Chooser">
    <data>
      <item name="button" xsi:type="array">
        <item name="open" xsi:type="string">Select
        Category.</item>
      </item>
    </data>
  </block>
</parameter>
<parameter name="template" xsi:type="select"
required="true" visible="true">
  <label translate="true">Template</label>
. . .
```

3. Clean the cache and open the widget configuration page for the product slider widget type. When you click on the **Select Category** button, a popup opens with the category tree, as shown in the following screenshot:

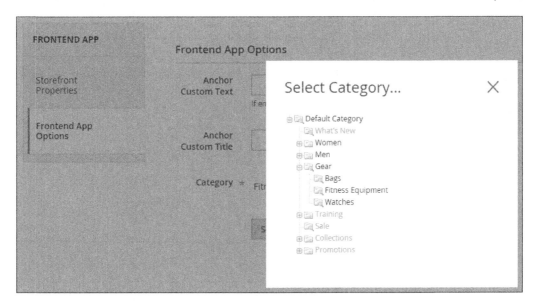

4. When you inspect the **Select Category** button and navigate to the hidden form field in the HTML code, you see that the value is similar to the following pattern:

   `category/<category_id>`

5. This widget requires a category ID that is the number after the slash. Now, we have the category path that is used to generate URLs. To fix this problem, we have the choice to implement one of the following things:

   ❑ Extract the ID from the path with string functions

   ❑ Ensure that a proper ID is set in the widget configuration page

   ❑ The most stable option is the second one, so we will implement it

6. We will create a new `Block` class that extends the standard one so that we can inherit a lot of functionality. Create the `app/code/Packt/ProductSlider/Block/Adminhtml/Catalog/Category/Widget/Chooser.php` file with the following content:

```php
<?php

namespace Packt\ProductSlider\Block\Adminhtml\Catalog\
Category\Widget;

class Chooser extends \Magento\Catalog\Block\Adminhtml\
Category\Widget\Chooser {

}
```

7. To use the previously created block in the configuration field, we have to update the `widget.xml` file. The `widget.xml` file will look as shown in the following code. The highlighted code is the line that you have to change:

```xml
<?xml version="1.0" encoding="UTF-8"?>
<widgets xmlns:xsi="http://www.w3.org/2001/XMLSchema-
instance"
  xsi:noNamespaceSchemaLocation=
  "urn:magento:module:Magento_Widget:etc/widget.xsd">
  <widget
    id="category_product_slider"
    class="Packt\ProductSlider\Block\Catalog\Product\
    ProductSlider"
    is_email_compatible="false"
    placeholder_image="Magento_Widget::placeholder.gif">
    <label translate="true">Category product slider</label>
    <description translate="true">List of Products for a
    given category in a slider widget</description>
    <parameters>
      <parameter name="title" xsi:type="text" required=
      "true" visible="true">
        <label translate="true">Title (frontend)</label>
      </parameter>
      <parameter name="category_id" xsi:type="block"
      visible="true" required="true">
        <label translate="true">Category ID</label>
        <block class="Packt\ProductSlider\Block\Adminhtml\
        Catalog\Category\Widget\Chooser">
          <data>
            <item name="button" xsi:type="array">
            <item name="open" xsi:type="string">Select
            Category...</item>
            </item>
          </data>
        </block>
      </parameter>
      <parameter name="template" xsi:type="select"
      required="true" visible="true">
        <label translate="true">Template</label>
        <options>
          <option name="default" value=
          "product/slider/list.phtml" selected="true">
            <label translate="true">Product list
            slider</label>
          </option>
```

```
           <option name="teaser"
           value="product/slider/teaser.phtml">
             <label translate="true">Product teaser slider
             </label>
           </option>
         </options>
       </parameter>
     </parameters>
   </widget>
</widgets>
```

8. When you clean the cache and reload the configuration page of the widget, you will see that nothing has changed because the class that we created contains no functionality. To change the behavior that we want, we will add three methods to the `app/code/Packt/ProductSlider/Block/Adminhtml/Catalog/Category/Widget/Chooser.php` file. The highlighted code shows the differences between the methods from the extended class:

```php
<?php

namespace Packt\ProductSlider\Block\Adminhtml\Catalog\
Category\Widget;

class Chooser extends \Magento\Catalog\Block\Adminhtml\
Category\Widget\Chooser {
  protected function _construct() {
    $this->setModuleName('Magento_Catalog');

    parent::_construct();
  }

  public function prepareElementHtml
  (\Magento\Framework\Data\Form\Element\AbstractElement
  $element) {
    $uniqId = $this->mathRandom->getUniqueHash($element-
    >getId());
    $sourceUrl = $this->getUrl(
      'productslider/catalog_category_widget/chooser',
      ['uniq_id' => $uniqId, 'use_massaction' => false]
    );

    $chooser = $this->getLayout()->createBlock(
      'Magento\Widget\Block\Adminhtml\Widget\Chooser'
    )->setElement(
      $element
```

```
    )->setConfig(
      $this->getConfig()
    )->setFieldsetId(
      $this->getFieldsetId()
    )->setSourceUrl(
      $sourceUrl
    )->setUniqId(
      $uniqId
    );

    if ($element->getValue()) {
      $categoryId = $element->getValue();

      $label = $this->_categoryFactory->create()-
      >load($categoryId)->getName();
      $chooser->setLabel($label);
    }

    $element->setData('after_element_html', $chooser-
    >toHtml());
    return $element;
}

public function getNodeClickListener() {
  if ($this->getData('node_click_listener')) {
    return $this->getData('node_click_listener');
  }
  if ($this->getUseMassaction()) {
    $js = '
      function (node, e) {
        if (node.ui.toggleCheck) {
          node.ui.toggleCheck(true);
        }
      }
    ';
  } else {
    $chooserJsObject = $this->getId();
    $js = '
      function (node, e) {
        ' .
      $chooserJsObject .
      '.setElementValue(node.attributes.id);
        ' .
      $chooserJsObject .
```

```
            '.setElementLabel(node.text);
            '  .
          $chooserJsObject .
          '.close();
          }
        ';
      }
      return $js;
    }
}
```

9. The code that we added in the previous step contains a call to an AJAX controller that we will create. To register the admin router for this module, we will create the app/code/Packt/ProductSlider/etc/adminhtml/routes.xml file with the following content:

```xml
<?xml version="1.0"?>
<config xmlns:xsi="http://www.w3.org/2001/XMLSchema-
instance" xsi:noNamespaceSchemaLocation="
urn:magento:framework:App/etc/routes.xsd">
  <router id="admin">
    <route id="productslider" frontName="productslider">
      <module name="Packt_ProductSlider"
      before="Magento_Backend" />
    </route>
  </router>
</config>
```

10. The next step is to create the controller action that matches the URL that we call in the prepareElementHtml() method. Create the app/code/Packt/ProductSlider/Controller/Adminhtml/Catalog/Category/Widget/Chooser.php file with the following content:

```php
<?php

namespace Packt\ProductSlider\Controller\Adminhtml\Catalog\
Category\Widget;

class Chooser extends \Magento\Catalog\Controller\
Adminhtml\Category\Widget\Chooser {
  protected function _getCategoryTreeBlock() {
    return $this->layoutFactory->create()->createBlock(
      'Packt\ProductSlider\Block\Adminhtml\Catalog\Category\
      Widget\Chooser',
      '',
      [
        'data' => [
```

```
                    'id' => $this->getRequest()->getParam('uniq_id'),
                    'use_massaction' => $this->getRequest()-
                    >getParam('use_massaction', false),
                ]
            ]
        );
    }
}
```

The highlighted code shows the differences between what is changed in the code.

11. Clean the cache and reload the configuration page of the widget. When you click on the **Select Category** button, a popup opens with the category tree. When you select a category and you inspect hidden input field, you will see that a number (the category ID) is set instead of the path.

12. Save the widget and reload the home page. You will see that the right products are shown for the chosen category.

How it works...

In this recipe, we created a custom configuration parameter to develop a better user experience for the admin users.

We based this configuration field on the existing category tree pop-up window that is used in other widget types, such as the **Catalog Category Link** type. To use an existing field, we just have to modify some configurations in the widget.xml file and the field is ready to use.

However, this type of configuration field is not exactly what we are looking for. The frontend representation was OK, but a wrongly formatted category ID was returned in the background.

To solve this, we created a custom configuration field that extends the behavior from the standard category chooser. We only had to change some things that are responsible for returning a correctly formatted category ID.

The first thing we did was creating a new Block class that extends from the standard class at the Magento\Catalog\Block\Adminhtml\Category\Widget\Chooser location. In this class, we override three methods. First, we added the setModuleName() method in the _construct() method. We called this method so that we can use the templates from the Magento_Catalog module in the Packt_ProductSlider module.

In the prepareElementHtml() method, we configured an AJAX URL to render the right block when the popup shows up. Later in this method, we stripped some logic to extract the category ID from the path.

In the last method, `getNodeClickListener()`, we did a change so that only the category ID is returned to the form instead of the category path.

When the **Select Category** button is clicked, an AJAX call is done and a block will be rendered to show the category tree. We also needed to change the block that is rendered in that AJAX call, so we had to overwrite this call.

We did this by creating a new controller action in our module that extends from the standard controller action, `Magento\Catalog\Controller\Adminhtml\Category\Widget\ Chooser`. In this action, we changed the `Block` class to our custom class using the _ `getCategoryTreeBlock()` method.

There's more...

Like we did in this recipe, it is possible to create configuration fields that use a custom HTML output.

A lot is possible to show a configuration parameter, but you have to return a value that will be saved in the widget configuration. This is always done with a input form element, which has the naming convention `<input name="parameters[<parameter_name>]">`.

Replace the `<parameter_name>` tag with the name of your custom configuration parameter and the values of this element will be handled like all the other configuration parameters of that widget.

Finalizing the theming

The frontend representation of the widget that we just created is not something that invites people to buy some products. It is just a list of the product names for a given category.

The last step of this chapter is to finalize the theming of the widget. We will create an HTML output that shows an image, name, and price of the given products.

With a jQuery plugin, we will convert the HTML output to a slider, so we can scroll through the products.

Getting ready

On the Internet, there are a lot of good JavaScript carousel plugins. In this recipe, we will use the following:

`http://kenwheeler.github.io/slick/`

For the code, we will build further on the things that are created in the previous recipes of this chapter. Ensure that you have the right files installed.

How to do it...

In the following steps, the last actions are described to complete the widget with a good-looking carousel:

1. The first thing is to generate a good HTML output that is usable for the jQuery plugin. Add the following code to the `list.phtml` file of the `Packt_ProductSlider` module:

```php
<?php
$productCollection = $block->getLoadedProductCollection();
$_helper = $this->helper('Magento\Catalog\Helper\Output');
?>
<div class="block block-product-slider slider-list">
  <div class="block-title">
    <h2>><?php echo $block->getTitle() ?></h2>
  </div>
  <div class="block-content">
    <?php if (count($productCollection)): ?>
      <div class="product-slider">
        <?php foreach ($productCollection as $product): ?>
          <div class="product">
            <div class="product-image">
              <a href="<?php echo $product->getProductUrl()
              ?>">
                <?php echo $block->getImage($product,
                'category_page_grid')->toHtml() ?>
              </a>
            </div>
            <strong class="product-name">
              <a
                href="<?php echo $product->getProductUrl()
                ?>">
                <?php echo $_helper->productAttribute
                ($product, $product->getName(), 'name'); ?>
              </a>
            </strong>
            <?php echo $block->getProductPrice($product) ?>
          </div>
        <?php endforeach; ?>
      </div>
    <?php endif; ?>
  </div>
</div>
```

2. When we reload the frontend, we see a simple list of products with their name, price, and image.

3. The next step is to initialize the carousel script. Go to the following URL and download the latest version of the plugin:

   `http://kenwheeler.github.io/slick/`

4. Unzip the archive on your local PC. For this recipe, we need the following two files of the archive:

   ❑ `slick/slick.js`

   ❑ `slick/slick.css`

5. When you want to add the CSS file to the module, create the `app/code/Packt/ProductSlider/view/frontend/web/css/source/module/_slick.less` file and copy the content of the `slick/slick.css` file to that file.

6. To load the LESS file, link it in the `_module.less` file. Create the `app/code/Packt/ProductSlider/view/frontend/web/css/source/_module.less` file with the following content:

   `@import 'module/_slick.less';`

7. The next step is to add the JavaScript file. In Magento 2, we use the **RequireJS** library to include the file. First, we copy the `slick/slick.js` file to the following location: `app/code/Packt/ProductSlider/view/frontend/web/js/slick.js`.

8. To register the JavaScript file, we have to create a RequireJS configuration file. Create the file at `app/code/Packt/ProductSlider/view/frontend/requirejs-config.js` with the following content:

```
var config = {
  map: {
    '*': {
      slick: 'Packt_ProductSlider/js/slick'
    }
  }
};
```

9. We added JavaScript and LESS files, so this means that we have to clear the previously generated static content. We can do this by removing the following folders:

   ❑ `pub/static/frontend/`

   ❑ `pub/static/_requirejs/`

   ❑ `var/view_preprocessed/`

10. Clean the cache and reload the frontend. Because the static content needs to be generated, it can take some time to load the frontend.

11. The last thing that we have to do is to initialize the slick carousel. Add the following code at the end of the `app/code/Packt/ProductSlider/view/frontend/templates/product/slider/list.phtml` file:

```javascript
<script type="text/javascript">
require(['jquery', 'slick'], function($){
  $(function(){
    $('.product-slider').slick({
      dots: false,
      infinite: false,
      speed: 300,
      slidesToShow: 5,
      slidesToScroll: 5,
      responsive: [
        {
          breakpoint: 1024,
          settings: {
            slidesToShow: 4,
            slidesToScroll: 4,
            infinite: true
          }
        },
        {
          breakpoint: 770,
          settings: {
            slidesToShow: 3,
            slidesToScroll: 2
          }
        },
        {
          breakpoint: 600,
          settings: {
            slidesToShow: 2,
            slidesToScroll: 2
          }
        },
        {
          breakpoint: 400,
          settings: {
            slidesToShow: 1,
            slidesToScroll: 1
          }
        }
      ]
    });
  });
});
</script>
```

12. Reload the home page and you will see that the carousel is initialized, as shown in the following screenshot:

13. The JavaScript configuration contains some breakpoints for responsive devices. When you have a smaller screen, you will see something as shown in the following screenshot:

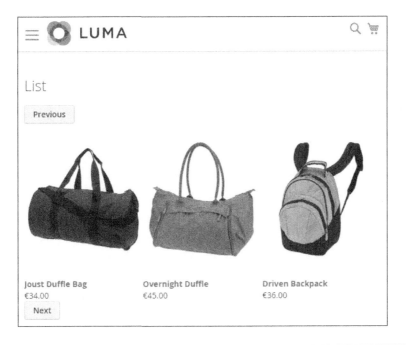

14. To finish this chapter, we can make the title of this widget configurable. In the widget configuration, there is a title field that we can use for this. When we change the following highlighted code of the `list.phtml` file to the following, the title of that field is used in the frontend.

```
. . .
<div class="block-title">
  <h2><?php echo $block->getTitle() ?></h2>
</div>
. . .
```

How it works...

In the first step, we created a good HTML output that is compatible with the slick JavaScript plugin. For every product, we show an image, name, and price. Behind every image and name is a link that redirects to the respective product detail page.

The product slider script contains a JavaScript and CSS file that we have to include in the shop. For the CSS file, we converted the content to a LESS file so that it is rendered with the CSS of the whole shop.

For every module, Magento looks for a `_module.less` file in the `view/frontend/web/css/source/` directory. In that file, we included a `_slick.less` file that contains the CSS code of the plugin.

For the JavaScript file, we used the RequireJS system of Magento to include the file. We placed the `slick.js` file in the `view/frontend/web/js/` folder.

The script is initialized in the `view/frontend/requirejs-config.js` file. With the code in that file, the `slick.js` file is initialized but not loaded. To load the file, we had to use the `require` function as shown in the following code:

```
require(['jquery', 'slick'], function($) {

});
```

With the previous code, the `jQuery` library and the `Slick` library are loaded before the code between the brackets is executed.

To initialize the product slider, we used the JavaScript code that is used in the documentation of the slick plugin. With that configuration, we created some breakpoints to make the plugin responsive.

10
Performance Optimization

In this chapter, we will cover the following recipes:

- ▶ Benchmarking a website
- ▶ Optimizing the frontend of the website
- ▶ Optimizing the database and MySQL configurations
- ▶ Optimizing the Apache web server
- ▶ Finding performance leaks in Magento
- ▶ Configuring OPcache, Redis, and Memcached
- ▶ Optimizing the PHP configurations

Introduction

In a sport competition, every second, millisecond, decide whether a player wins a competition or not. Every small aspect that improves the performance is a step in the right direction to win a competition. For websites, this is the same. The faster a website is, the better it is. A fast website gives a better user experience and it is better for SEO. So, the faster, the better.

Magento is a framework that calls a lot of operations when loading a page. All these operations take some time. This means that Magento is not one of the best performing systems in the world, especially when you are working with a lot of products, attributes, multiple store views, and more.

However, with a good setup and the right tools, you can improve the performance of your shop so that it will perform very fast.

The performance of a website has a lot of impact on your visitors. Here are some facts about the performance of a website:

- ▸ When your site is 100 milliseconds slower, you lose 1% of the total sales.
- ▸ When a site is slower than 2-3 seconds, users will leave because your site is slow. A quickly loading page has a positive influence on your SEO results.
- ▸ More and more people have mobile devices without the fastest Internet connection.

As you can see, the performance is an important thing when you want to improve the conversion of your website. Customers will leave your site when it is slow, and search engines will give you a lower rank when your site is slow.

The improvement of the performance is mostly one of the last steps in the development workflow of a site. People build something and when it is ready, they begin to look at how that they can optimize some parts to make it faster.

In this chapter, we will explore, detect, and fix performance leaks in a Magento webshop using some performance tools.

Magento delivers some tools by default, but we have to look at the whole picture. Two identical Magento installations can have a different performance that can be caused by the following reasons:

- ▸ Hardware
- ▸ Network
- ▸ Load
- ▸ Device of the client

Benchmarking a website

When you have a high-traffic site, you would probably want to know the limits of the website. What will be the capacity of my website when I launch a marketing campaign? What is slowing down my site? Which optimizations have the most effect?

To know the limits of a website, we have to use benchmarking tools. With a benchmarking tool, we will create a load on the website and log the response time to a file. By increasing or decreasing some values, we can determine the load that is the limit of a website.

In this recipe, we will benchmark the Magento site by doing some tests with **ApacheBench** and **Siege**. With these tools, we can measure the performance of different pages.

Getting ready

For this recipe, we need some tools that need to be installed on the webserver. Ensure that you have the following tools installed:

- **ApacheBench** (ab): This tool can be installed using the `sudo apt-get install apache2-utils` command. When this is installed on the server, you can use the `ab -h` command to display the usage information.

- **Siege**: We will do some benchmarking tests with Siege that is installed on the same server as the Magento instance. To see if it is installed, you can run the following command:

  ```
  siege -V
  ```

  - Ensure that the `-V` option is in uppercase. When Siege is installed, you will see its version number, as shown in the following screenshot:

    ```
    SIEGE 3.0.5

    Copyright (C) 2013 by Jeffrey Fulmer, et al.
    This is free software; see the source for copying conditions.
    There is NO warranty; not even for MERCHANTABILITY or FITNESS
    FOR A PARTICULAR PURPOSE.
    ```

  - If it is not installed, you can run the following command when you are using a Debian-based Linux distribution:

    ```
    sudo apt-get install siege
    ```

  - Another option is to download the installation file and install it using the following steps:

    1. Download the archive using the following `wget` command:

       ```
       wget http://download.joedog.org/siege/siege-3.1.0.tar.gz
       ```

    2. Extract the file by running the following command:

       ```
       tar xfz siege-3.1.0.tar.gz
       ```

3. Move the folder to the preferred location and go to that directory using the `cd` command.

4. When you are in that folder, you can install Siege using the following command:

```
sudo ./configure
```

How to do it...

1. To get an idea of the response time with a load of a number of concurrent users, we can use ApacheBench to perform some simple tests. With the following command, we will run a test that writes the result to a CSV file:

```
ab -c 10 -n 50 -e apachebench.csv http://magento2.local
```

2. In the previous command, we did a load test with the following parameters:

   - `-c`: This parameter represents the number of concurrent users. In this test, we ran 10 requests at the same time throughout.

   - `-n`: This parameter represents the number of requests, which is 50 in this case. So, we will have 50 results in the file.

   - `-e`: This parameter represents the output file. The output is written to the given CSV file.

> The `-g` option means the same as the `-e` option, but a `-g` option will generate a **TSV (Tab Separated Value)** file, also known as a `gnuplot` file.

3. When you run the preceding command, it will return an output as shown in the following screenshot:

```
This is ApacheBench, Version 2.3 <$Revision: 1528965 $>
Copyright 1996 Adam Twiss, Zeus Technology Ltd, http://www.zeustech.net/
Licensed to The Apache Software Foundation, http://www.apache.org/

Benchmarking magento2.local (be patient).....done


Server Software:        Apache/2.4.7
Server Hostname:        magento2.local
Server Port:            80

Document Path:          /
Document Length:        35192 bytes

Concurrency Level:      10
Time taken for tests:   40.735 seconds
Complete requests:      50
Failed requests:        0
Total transferred:      1788500 bytes
HTML transferred:       1759600 bytes
Requests per second:    1.23 [#/sec] (mean)
Time per request:       8146.937 [ms] (mean)
Time per request:       814.694 [ms] (mean, across all concurrent requests)
Transfer rate:          42.88 [Kbytes/sec] received

Connection Times (ms)
              min  mean[+/-sd] median    max
Connect:        0    1   1.5      0       4
Processing:  5508 8130 4178.0   6265   16409
Waiting:     5119 7696 4099.0   5871   15777
Total:       5508 8131 4179.5   6266   16413

Percentage of the requests served within a certain time (ms)
  50%    6266
  66%    6869
  75%    6988
  80%   16261
  90%   16376
  95%   16385
  98%   16413
  99%   16413
 100%   16413 (longest request)
```

4. This report shows the general statistics of the test. The specific results of each request are saved in the CSV file (apachebench.csv).

5. Load testing with Siege.

   Siege is another load testing tool like ApacheBench. The difference between Siege and ApacheBench is that Siege has more functions than ApacheBench. It is designed to perform a stress test with a number of concurrent users. Siege also provides the ability to work with HTTP authentication, cookies, sessions, and more. When you write a good script, you can simulate a real stress situation.

6. For a load test with Siege, we will use a text file where we will configure some URLs that will be used during the Siege load test. When we do a test with different URLs, we will test more pages, and we can find more pitfalls on the website. Create a file called `siege_url.txt` with the following content:

- ❏ `http://magento2.local/`
- ❏ `http://magento2.local/pub/static/frontend/Magento/luma/en_US/mage/calendar.css`
- ❏ `http://magento2.local/pub/static/frontend/Magento/luma/en_US/css/styles-m.css`
- ❏ `http://magento2.local/pub/static/frontend/Magento/luma/en_US/images/logo.svg`
- ❏ `http://magento2.local/pub/static/frontend/Magento/luma/en_US/requirejs/require.js`
- ❏ `http://magento2.local/women/tops-women.html`
- ❏ `http://magento2.local/women/tops-women.html?cat=28`
- ❏ `http://magento2.local/checkout/cart/add/?product=1`
- ❏ `http://magento2.local/checkout/`
- ❏ `http://magento2.local/pub/static/frontend/Magento/luma/en_US/js-translation.json`
- ❏ `http://magento2.local/pub/static/frontend/Magento/luma/en_US/Magento_Ui/templates/block-loader.html`
- ❏ `http://magento2.local/pub/static/frontend/Magento/luma/en_US/Magento_Ui/templates/modal/modal-popup.html`
- ❏ `http://magento2.local/pub/static/frontend/Magento/luma/en_US/Magento_Checkout/template/onepage.html`
- ❏ `http://magento2.local/pub/static/frontend/Magento/luma/en_US/Magento_Checkout/template/progress-bar.html`
- ❏ `http://magento2.local/pub/static/frontend/Magento/luma/en_US/images/loader-1.gif`
- ❏ `http://magento2.local/pub/static/frontend/Magento/luma/en_US/images/select-bg.svg`
- ❏ `http://magento2.local/customer/account/login/`
- ❏ `http://magento2.local/contact/`
- ❏ `http://magento2.local/catalog/product_compare/add/?product=1`
- ❏ `http://magento2.local/pub/static/frontend/Magento/luma/en_US/js/theme.js`

- ❑ http://magento2.local/catalog/product_compare/index/
- ❑ http://magento2.local/catalogsearch/result/?q=watch
- ❑ http://magento2.local/catalogsearch/advanced/result/?nam
  e=Watch&sku=&description=analog&short_description=&price
  %5Bfrom%5D=50&price%5Bto%5D=100&tax_class_id=
- ❑ http://magento2.local/pub/media/catalog/product/cache/1/
  small_image/240x300/e9c3970ab036de70892d86c6d221abfe/
  sample_data/m/g/mg05-br-0.jpg
- ❑ http://magento2.local/customer/account/forgotpassword/
- ❑ http://magento2.local/search/term/popular/

7. Change the URLs so that they match your Magento configurations. Ensure that you are testing your development environment with valid URLs.

8. With the following command, we can start a load test with 50 concurrent users based on the URLs that we entered in the `siege_url.txt` file:

```
siege -c50 -i -t 1M -d 3 -f siege_url.txt
```

9. The time taken by this command to complete, depends on the webshop's performance. The output of the command will be similar to the following:

```
$ siege -c50 -i -t 1M -d 3 -f siege_url.txt

** SIEGE 3.0.5

** Preparing 50 concurrent users for battle.

The server is now under siege...[alert] socket: 1772328704 select
timed out: Connection timed out

[alert] socket: 1998931712 select timed out: Connection timed out

[alert] socket: 1671616256 select timed out: Connection timed out

socket: 2024109824 select timed out: Connection timed out

[alert] socket: 1713579776 select timed out: Connection timed out


Lifting the server siege...       done.


Transactions:                 171 hits

Availability:                 86.80 %

Elapsed time:                 59.44 secs

Data transferred:             1.02 MB

Response time:                6.08 secs

Transaction rate:             2.88 trans/sec

Throughput:                   0.02 MB/sec
```

Concurrency:	17.49
Successful transactions:	190
Failed transactions:	26
Longest transaction:	27.51
Shortest transaction:	0.00

 In the preceding output, we can see some timeouts. This means that there are requests that are not successful.

10. With the `siege -h` command, you can see all the available options of that command.

How it works...

We started this recipe with a load test using ApacheBench. This is a tool that was previously a part of the Apache Web Server. Currently, it is packaged in the `apache2-utils` bundle. This package also contains tools such as log rotation, generation of `htpasswd` files, and more.

With ApacheBench, we performed a load test with a number of concurrent users. A concurrent user is a user that is generating load on the website. When we test with 10 concurrent users, we will simulate a continuous load of 10 processes during the time of the test. When one of the requests is finished, a new one is fired, so there are always 10 requests running.

When we you a limit of 30 seconds, we can see how many requests are successfully finished during that time. This can give you a good idea of the capacity of your website.

With Siege, we can do the same as with ApacheBench. The main difference between ApacheBench and Siege is that Siege has more features when you compare it with ApacheBench.

In this recipe, we performed a load test with a list of generic Magento URLs such as some pages, static content, product images, and more. We also added some products to the cart with the query string URL so that we can simulate a human workflow on the website.

A lot of pages are cached in Magento, but we also have to test the session-specific pages, such as the cart, checkout, search, and more.

 With ApacheBench and Siege, you can create load on a website. When you do this on a remote site, it is possible that you will be blocked by a firewall because a lot of requests from the same IP will give the impression of an attack.

Optimizing the frontend of the website

When you look at the performance of a website, there are many points that you can optimize. Between the start of a request and the rendered page in the browser, a lot of operations are carried out.

In this recipe, you will learn how to spot bottlenecks and optimize some things that increase the performance.

Getting ready

For this recipe, we will use two browser plugins where we can measure some metrics:

> **app.telemetry**: With this simple browser plugin, we can monitor the load time of each page. We can download the plugin from the following website:
>
> http://www.apptelemetry.com/en/page-speed-monitor.html
>
> This will add an icon in the browser bar where we can read the response time.

> **YSlow**: With this browser plugin, can we generate a report of things that we can optimize in the website. You can install the YSlow plugin to Chrome or Firefox from the following URL:
>
> http://yslow.org/

How it works...

The following steps describe how we can find pitfalls in the frontend of Magento to decrease the page load time:

1. When you have the app.telemetry plugin installed, you will see an icon on the browser bar, as shown in the following screenshot:

2. To analyze a page load, you have to reload a page, and when the page is loaded, you will see the time taken for loading in the browser bar icon. When you click on the icon, you can see more details, as shown in the following screenshot:

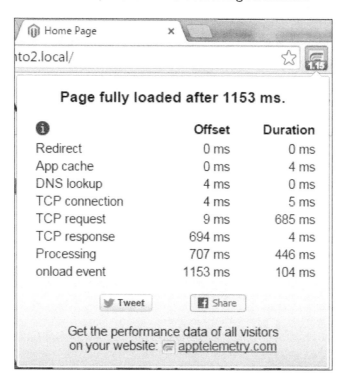

3. When we do the same on a remote website, we will see different results. The time taken by the TCP and DNS steps will be longer.

4. We will continue by generating a performance analysis with YSlow. YSlow is a browser plugin that needs to be installed in your browser. When you have installed the browser plugin, you can click on the icon in the browser bar.

5. A window will show up and when you click on the **Run Test** button, the report will be generated.

6. When the report is ready and you click on the **Grade** tab, you will see the report, as shown in the following screenshot:

7. With a default Magento instance, you will have a good score. But we can increase this with some simple optimizations.

8. The first thing that we can optimize is to add `Expires` headers. With the following code, we can add `Expires` headers to some static files. Add this code in the `.htaccess` file by replacing the `<IfModule mod_expires.c>` section with the following code:

```
<IfModule mod_expires.c>

#############################################
## Add default Expires header
## http://developer.yahoo.com/performance/rules.html
#expires

    ExpiresDefault "access plus 1 year"

    ExpiresActive On
    ExpiresByType image/gif "access 1 year"
    ExpiresByType image/jpg "access 1 year"
    ExpiresByType image/jpeg "access 1 year"
    ExpiresByType image/png "access 1 year"
    ExpiresByType image/x-icon "access 1 year"
    ExpiresByType text/css "access 1 month"
    ExpiresByType application/x-javascript "access 1 month"

</IfModule>
```

9. When we add this code, we will have to reload the website in order to check that the site is not broken after the change in the `.htaccess` file. When this is done, we can run the test again. We will see that the **Add Expires Headers** is now changed to an **A**.

10. Another improvement is to minify JavaScript and CSS. There are a lot of tools to minify JavaScript and CSS files but this also a setting in the configuration of Magento. In the backend, navigate to **Stores** | **Configuration** | **Advanced** | **Developer** and change the following settings to **Yes**:

   ❑ **Merge JavaScript files: Yes**

   ❑ **Minify JavaScript files: Yes**

   ❑ **Merge CSS files: Yes**

   ❑ **Minify CSS files: Yes**

11. After saving these settings, the configuration will look as shown in the following screenshot:

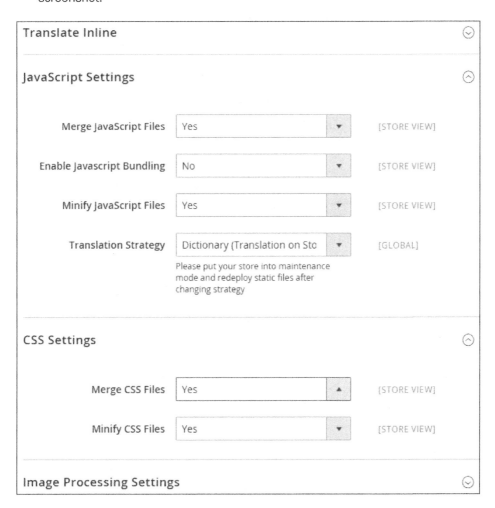

12. When you run the test again, you will see that the overall score is raised again. There are two points that need more attention: **Use a Content Delivery Network** and **Use cookie-free domains**. You can use an existing CDN provider to host your static files, but you can also create another domain such as `static.magento2.local` that also points to the Magento root. In the backend, you can configure Magento to use this domain for static content. You can configure this by navigating to **Stores | Configuration | General | Web**. In the base URLs section, you can configure the values as shown in the following screenshot:

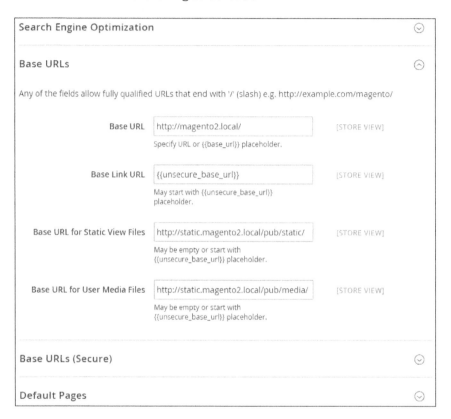

How it works...

We started this recipe using the `app.telemetry` plugin to show the different parts of a page load. When we click on the icon of that plugin, we see the following parameters:

► `Redirect`: This is the time that is taken to redirect this page (if there is a redirect).

► `App Cache`: This is the time of your local cache.

► `DNS Lookup`: This is the time taken to resolve the IP address for the given domain name.

- ▸ `TCP Connection`: This is the time taken to send a request to the server. This is mostly longer when sending a large POST request.

- ▸ `TCP Request`: This is the time that the server needs to process your response. In this timeframe, the server will build the HTML file of the page.

- ▸ `TCP Response`: This is the time taken to download the response to your local device. With slow networks, this time will be more.

- ▸ `Processing`: This is the time it takes to render your HTML, CSS, JavaScript, and other stuff.

- ▸ `Onload event`: This is the time that the onload event takes. After this, the page is fully loaded.

In the first column, **Offset**, you see the time from the start of the request. In the second column, **Duration**, you can see how much time is taken for each step.

In the next step, we did an analysis of the page with YSlow. YSlow will test a website on different topics. All these topics are based on a ruleset. With the Chrome plugin, the YSlow(v2) ruleset is automatically selected. You can also choose the Classic(v1) ruleset.

The YSlow(v2) ruleset will test on the following topics:

- ▸ Minimizing HTTP requests
- ▸ Using a Contend Delivery Network
- ▸ Avoiding empty `src` or `href` instances
- ▸ Adding `Expires Headers` or a `cache-control` header
- ▸ Using compression for static files
- ▸ Placing stylesheets at the top
- ▸ Placing JavaScript at the bottom
- ▸ Avoiding CSS expression
- ▸ Making JavaSript and CSS external
- ▸ Reducing DNS lookups
- ▸ Minifying JavaSript and CSS
- ▸ Avoiding redirects
- ▸ Removing duplicate JavaScript and CSS
- ▸ Configuring ETags
- ▸ Making AJAX cacheable
- ▸ Using GET fo AJAX requests
- ▸ Reducing the Number of DOM elements
- ▸ Reducing the number of 404 errors

- ▸ Reducing the cookie size
- ▸ Using cookie-free domains for static files
- ▸ Avoiding filters
- ▸ No scaling of images in HTML
- ▸ Making `favicon.ico` small and cacheable

When we did the test on a standard Magento 2 shop, the overall score was quite good. When you develop your own stuff, you will have to keep the previous rulesets in mind because these points reduce the load of the page.

The YSlow ruleset mostly increases the performance of the frontend (the loading of JavaScript, CSS, images, and so on). It doesn't give advice on how to optimize your PHP processes.

First, we added some `Expires headers` instance to the static files. With these headers, we configured how long static files will be cached in the browsers of the visitors. For every MIME type, we can specify a different time.

The second point to optimize is to merge the JavaScript and CSS files. Loading one big file is faster than loading 100 small files. This can be declared by the following reasons:

- ▸ For every file, an HTTP request will be created. Also, headers and cookies are sent for every request.
- ▸ Some webservers can only handle a limited number of HTTP requests at a time. So, if there are a lot of requests, they will be queued.
- ▸ Sometimes, it may happens that one of the requests hangs, so your page keeps loading. With fewer requests, you have lesser chances that this happens.

Finally, we configured a different domain to the static content. When you have a different domain (or a cookie-free domain), the cookies are not sent to the server for every request, so this reduces the bandwidth.

There's more...

If you go to the site `gtmetrix.com`, you can enter a URL that you want to analyze. This tool will do a **PageSpeed** and **YSlow** test on the given URL.

Because this is an online tool, you have to ensure that your site is accessible by the **GTmetrix** server.

Optimizing the database and MySQL configurations

The Magento applications use a database to store all the data, including products, customers, orders, and more. The database is the central storage of all the data that is available in the Magento instance. Scaling Magento to multiple frontend servers is not that hard but scaling the database is much harder because the data is something that needs to be in sync.

In this recipe, we will see how we can optimize the database and the MySQL server.

Getting ready

Ensure that you have access to a database client where you can do some queries to your database. In this recipe, we will use **phpMyAdmin**.

How to do it...

In the first part of this recipe, we will optimize the table structures of the Magento database. Take a look at the following steps:

1. Open **phpMyAdmin** and click on the Magento database. You will see an overview of all the tables.

2. At the bottom of this page, click on the **Check All** button.

3. When you click on the dropdown list, you can repair the table and optimize it, as shown in the following screenshot:

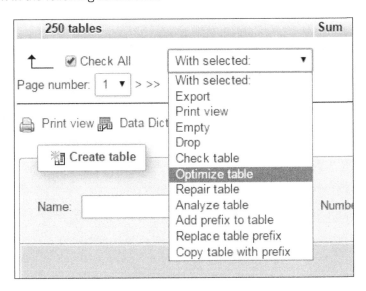

Ensure that you run this action for all the tables in the Magento database. It can happen that the list is divided in multiple pages. A Magento 2 shop has over 300 tables. The phpMyAdmin installation shows by default 250 tables per page.

4. We have now optimized the tables of Magento. The other thing that you can do is run the database repair tool to check whether some relations are missing.

We are now at the second part of this recipe. In this part, we will see some optimizations that we can do on the MySQL server:

1. A good MySQL server starts with good hardware and the right operating system. To run Magento, it is recommended that you use a dedicated server or a VPS. You can also use a shared hosting environment, but this is not the best option because the RAM and CPU load is shared between other users on that server. With a VPS or dedicated server, you have a fixed number of CPUs and RAM available.

2. When your server has enough RAM available, you can turn off the swapped devices. Sometimes, the swap option will be automatically used even when there is enough memory available.

3. On your server, open the /etc/mysql/my.cnf file. Look for the skip-external-locking setting under the [mysqld] section. If the setting isn't there, you can add this on a new line.

4. To show the size of the key buffer for **MyISAM** tables, we can run the following query on the MySQL prompt:

```
mysql> SHOW VARIABLES LIKE '%key_buffer%';
```

5. For Magento, the recommended value is 512 MB. To set this value, we can run the following command on the MySQL prompt:

```
mysql> SET GLOBAL key_buffer_size = 536870912;
```

6. Next, we will change some default configuration parameters. We can set these in the main configuration file of the MySQL server that is located at /etc/mysql/my.cnf.

7. Open that file and paste the following configuration under the [mysqld] section:

```
key_buffer = 512M
max_allowed_packet = 64M
thread_stack = 192K
thread_cache_size = 32
table_cache = 512
query_cache_type = 1
query_cache_size = 52428800
tmp_table_size = 128M
expire_logs_days = 10
```

```
max_binlog_size = 100M
sort_buffer_size = 4M
read_buffer_size = 4M
read_rnd_buffer_size = 2M
myisam_sort_buffer_size = 64M
wait_timeout = 300
max_connections = 400
```

8. Save the file and restart your MySQL server. You can do this by running the following command:

```
sudo service mysql restart
```

How it works...

When optimizing a MySQL server, you have to know the capabilities of your server and the traffic that you except. With these parameters, you can calculate a good value for the `key_buffer`, `query_cache` and `table_cache`.

With the following commands, you can view the MySQL server status:

Command	Description
`mysql> SHOW STATUS;`	This command shows the current status of the MySQL server. It is available in MySQL 5.0 and later, and is the standard query to show all the global variables.
`mysql> SHOW VARIABLES;`	This command shows all the MySQL variables.
`mysql> SHOW ENGINE INNODB STATUS;`	This command shows the current status of the **INNODB** engine.
`mysql> SHOW GLOBAL STATUS;`	This query shows values of the current load on the database server for all connections.
`mysql> SHOW LOCAL STATUS;`	This command shows the same as the last one but now only for the current connection.
`$ mysqladmin extended -i100 -r`	You need to run this command in a Linux prompt. This command shows what is happening with the MySQL server.

Database optimization is one of the key aspects to tune your Magento webshop. Database processes are responsible for a big part of the page load, so a good performing database is very important.

Optimizing the Apache web server

Magento can be run on **Apache** or **Nginx**. Configuration files for both systems are available in the code base (`.htaccess` and `nginx.conf.sample` in the root folder).

The performance of the web server depends on what hardware the server is running. Network card, RAM, disk, OS, and CPU are the most important hardware components that you have to think about when choosing a server.

How to do it...

1. The first thing to think about is a good operating system to run your web server. It is highly recommended that you use a Linux distribution because it is the standard for PHP applications.

   In the recipes of this book, we used an Ubuntu server (a Debian-based Linux distribution).

    Don't use a Windows server to run Magento. It will work, but it is less efficient and you can have issues with file permissions, code, and more.

2. Update the operating system to the latest stable version. An updated software is safer and faster. Use at least the Apache 2.4. At the time of writing, this is the latest stable release and has some improvements for performance.

3. Install only the required software on your webserver. Less is more! When a lot of software is installed that you don't use, you will have background tasks that are running for nothing.

4. Use a fast filesystem. Use an SSD in your server because this is much faster than a disk. Never use a file system that is shared over a network because this is very slow.

5. You have to configure your web server so that it doesn't swap. When your web server begins to swap, all requests will be served slower. The first thing to do is to compare the volume of RAM on the server with the average memory load of a request and a number of requests. The second thing that you can do is configure the `MaxClients` setting. This setting controls the number of child processes when the server is swapping.

6. Look at the `HostnameLookups` setting and check whether this is configured with the `Off` value.

7. Enable the Apache modules `mod_deflate` and `mod_headers`. We can do this with the following commands:

   - ❏ `sudo a2enmod deflate`
   - ❏ `sudo a2enmod headers`

8. Open the `.htaccess` file in the Magento root and go to the `mod_deflate` configuration tag. Uncomment some lines so that the block looks like the following code:

```
<IfModule mod_deflate.c>

############################################
## enable apache served files compression
## http://developer.yahoo.com/performance/rules.html#gzip

    # Insert filter on all content
    SetOutputFilter DEFLATE
    # Insert filter on selected content types only
    AddOutputFilterByType DEFLATE text/html text/plain
    text/xml text/css text/javascript

    # Netscape 4.x has some problems...
    BrowserMatch ^Mozilla/4 gzip-only-text/html

    # Netscape 4.06-4.08 have some more problems
    BrowserMatch ^Mozilla/4\.0[678] no-gzip

    # MSIE masquerades as Netscape, but it is fine
    BrowserMatch \bMSIE !no-gzip !gzip-only-text/html

    # Don't compress images
    SetEnvIfNoCase Request_URI \.(?:gif|jpe?g|png)$ no-gzip
    dont-vary

    # Make sure proxies don't deliver the wrong content
    Header append Vary User-Agent env=!dont-vary

</IfModule>
```

When you get an internal server error after the change, it is possible that the headers module is nog enabled. Run the `sudo a2enmod headers` command and restart the server to fix this.

9. Take a look at the `KeepAlive` setting of your Apache server. When this setting is active, the Apache server can handle multiple requests trough the same TCP connection.

10. Configure the **Multi-Processing Modules** (**MPM**) for your case. The values of these configurations depend on the resources and load that you expect on your server:

```
StartServers 50
MinSpareServers 15
MaxSpareServers 30
MaxClients 225
MaxRequestsPerChild 4000
```

11. When you run some load tests again, you can compare the current result with the results before the optimization. Usually, you will see some differences.

How it works...

The performance of a web server depends on many factors. The key parts are the application, hardware, operating system, and the network.

- ▶ **Application**: Ensure that the application that you are running is working efficiently with the resources on your server. If your application expects a lot of resources for a simple task, maybe you can optimize this.

- ▶ **Hardware**: Ensure that the hardware resources are high enough to serve the expected load and peaks.

- ▶ **Operating system**: The operating system and the web server version are among the important factors. Use a Linux server to run Magento with an Apache or Nginx web server on it. Always use the latest stable versions of the software because they are faster and more secure.

- ▶ **Network**: The web server sends the response trough the network to the client. When that network is slow, the download time of a request will be long. Host your web server with a good network connection and host it geographically in the region of your target audience. For example, host your website in Italy for an Italian website.

As you can see, you can optimize a lot of things on your web server. But every case is different. Normally, people have a standard server setup. They deploy the application on it and then they start optimizing. Every application is different (in terms of code, load, and so on).

Finding performance leaks in Magento

When optimizing a website, we can do lots of things to the server environment but the application that runs on it can always be faster.

When you have a Magento store and one kind of page is significantly slower than other pages, it could possible be that there is a performance issue on that page.

To find performance issues, we can use the Magento Profiler. With the Magento Profiler, we can see how much time every process takes to render a page.

Getting ready

To enable the profiler, we have to modify the apache environment variables. We can do this in the `VirtualHost` configuration or in the `.htaccess` file. Ensure that you have access to one of these files.

How to do it...

In the following steps, we will specify how we can use the Magento profiler:

1. To enable the profiler, add the following code in the `VirtualHost` or the `.htaccess` file:

   ```
   SetEnv MAGE_PROFILER html
   ```

2. If you changed this setting in the `VirtualHost` file, reload the Apache server.

3. Reload a page in the frontend and you will see that the profiler output is shown at the end of the page, as shown in the following screenshot:

Timer Id	Time	Avg	Cnt	Emalloc	RealMem
cache_frontend_create	0.008444	0.004222	2	919,496	786,432
cache_load	0.004327	0.001442	3	428,176	524,288
magento	1.742083	1.742083	1	28,880,032	28,049,408
· cache_load	0.003832	0.000547	7	406,032	262,144
· init_stores	0.017420	0.017420	1	1,733,504	1,835,008
· · EVENT:core_collection_abstract_load_before	0.001165	0.000388	3	230,800	262,144
· · · cache_load	0.000559	0.000280	2	40,648	262,144
· routers_match	0.186264	0.186264	1	13,476,696	13,631,488
· · cache_load	0.001788	0.000358	5	170,040	262,144
· · session_start	0.000379	0.000379	1	22,880	0
· · EAV: Magento\Eav\Model\Config::_initEntityTypes	0.000776	0.000776	1	46,168	0
· · EAV: Magento\Eav\Model\Config::getEntityType	0.000482	0.000482	1	66,168	262,144
· · load_area:frontend.design	0.001269	0.001269	1	16,808	0
· · load_area:frontend.translate	0.001508	0.001508	1	91,464	262,144
· · EVENT:controller_action_predispatch	0.006372	0.006372	1	615,248	524,288
· · · OBSERVER:register_form_key	0.000344	0.000344	1	16,304	0

4. It is possible that the profiler output will break some functionality when you have JSON responses with AJAX. For this reason, it is also possible to write the profiler output to a `.csv` file. To enable this, we have to change the `SetEnv` rule in `.htaccess` or `VirtualHost` to the following:

```
SetEnv MAGE_PROFILER csvfile
```

5. The profiler output will be written to the `var/log/profiler.csv` file.

6. When we switch the profiler back to the HTML output, we can analyze the page.

7. Open a product detail page and take a look at the **Time** and **Count** column. We see the steps of a page load in a tree. When we look for the most time consuming parts, we see that the **LAYOUT** part is the slowest of the whole page.

How it works...

When you enable the Magento profiler, the profiling results will be showed in the HTML file, CSV file, or Firebug.

In the profiling results, you have the following columns:

- **Timer Id**: This is the code of a profiled statement. In the code, you can profile a block of code by surrounding it with the following code:

```
\Magento\Framework\Profiler::start('profiler_name');

//Your code to profile

\Magento\Framework\Profiler::stop('profiler_name');
```

- **Time**: This is the time taken to complete the code between a profiler start and stop.

- **Avg**: When a profiler statement is executed more than one time, this will show the average time to complete one statement.

- **Cnt**: This shows the number of times a profiler statement is called.

 The **Avg** column multiplied by the **Cnt** column gives the same value as the **Time** column.

- **Emalloc**: This is the amount of memory that is allocated for the profiler statement.

- **RealMem**: This is the same as the Emalloc option but this is the amount of memory that is allocated to the system.

It is possible to run profiler statements in each other. When this is done, the HTML output will show dots for the items that are executed in a parent statement. This will give you a tree overview so you can see how a page is executed.

Configuring OPcache, Redis, and Memcached

The default caching mechanism of Magento is based on file caching. All the cache files are written to the `var/cache` folder. For a simple webshop, this is enough, but if you are scaling your shop with many products and high traffic, you will need to use some extra caching systems.

Redis is a replacement of the standard file caching of Magento. This system works faster when you have a lot of cache files.

Memcached is similar to Redis. It is a system in which you can cache objects.

Zend OPcache is an opcode caching system. When these caching techniques are enabled, the PHP code will be cached to these systems.

Getting ready

When we want to configure the caching tools Zend OPcache, Memcached, and Redis, we have to install them on our server. To install these, run the commands explained in the following topics:

Zend OPcache

This package is normally standard installed with PHP 5.5. When you execute a `phpinfo()` method or run the `php -i | grep opcache` command, you can search for the `opcache` settings.

Memcached

Install Memcached with the `sudo apt-get install php5-memcached`. command.

Redis

Install Redis with the `sudo apt-get install redis-server` command.

How to do it...

In the following steps, we will use Zend OPcache and Memcached for Magento:

1. When you run a `phpinfo()` method in the browser or execute the `php -i | grep opcache` command, you will see the OPcache settings. The following settings must be set to On to ensure that OPcache is enabled:

    ❏ `opcache.enable`
    ❏ `opcache.enable_cli`

2. When these settings are not set to *On*, we have to set it in the `php.ini` file. Normally, this is located in the `/etc/php5/apache2` and `/etc/php5/cli` folders. This configuration is for a Ubuntu server.

3. To enable Redis, we have to modify the `app/etc/env.php` file. In this file, we have to add the cache configuration so that Magento knows which cache type it has to use. Add the following code to this file. You have to paste this code in the existing array:

```
'cache' => array (
  'frontend' => array (
    'default' => array (
      'backend' => 'Cm_Cache_Backend_Redis',
      'backend_options' => array (
        'server' => '127.0.0.1',
        'port' => '6379',
        'persistent' => '',
        'database' => '0',
        'force_standalone' => '0',
        'connect_retries' => '1',
        'read_timeout' => '10',
        'automatic_cleaning_factor' => '0',
        'compress_data' => '1',
        'compress_tags' => '1',
        'compress_threshold' => '20480',
        'compression_lib' => 'gzip',
      ),
    ),
    'page_cache' => array (
      'backend' => 'Cm_Cache_Backend_Redis',
      'backend_options' => array (
        'server' => '127.0.0.1',
        'port' => '6379',
        'persistent' => '',
        'database' => '1',
        'force_standalone' => '0',
        'connect_retries' => '1',
        'read_timeout' => '10',
        'automatic_cleaning_factor' => '0',
        'compress_data' => '0',
        'compress_tags' => '1',
        'compress_threshold' => '20480',
        'compression_lib' => 'gzip',
      ),
    ),
  ),
),
```

4. Clean all the Magento caches and restart your Apache server. When you do a load test with ApacheBench, you will see that there is an improvement with the performance.

 Magento uses **Full Page Caching** to cache every content page. If you want to test the performance of uncached pages, you can disable it.

5. To end this recipe, we will configure Memcached to store the Magento sessions. In your `phpinfo()` method, ensure that Memcached is enabled.

6. Open the `app/etc/env.php` file and add the following code in that file. You have to paste it in the existing array:

```
'session' => array(
  'save' => 'memcached',
  'save_path' => '127.0.0.1:11211?persistent=1&weight=
  2&timeout=10&retry_interval=10',
),
```

7. The last thing that we can do is store the `var/cache` folder in memory. We can do this by mounting the folder using TMPFS:

```
mount tmpfs /var/www/magento2/var/cache -t tmpfs -o size-
64m
```

How it works...

Zend OPcache is an opcode caching mechanism. This will cache PHP files so that they don't have to load from the disk every time they are called. Zend OPcache is the replacement of **APC**, which is available in older versions of PHP.

APC is deprecated in PHP 5.4 and is not available from PHP 5.5. To replace this, Zend OPcache is the tool that we have to use. That's also the reason why it is standard enabled when you install PHP 5.5 or higher.

The second thing that we configured is Redis. Redis is a caching tool in which we can cache objects. It is a replacement of the default file caching of Magento. The advantage of Redis is that it uses cache tags. When you have a lot of cache files, a file caching mechanism will open every file to see that it is relevant. With Redis, every cache object is tagged, so it can be opened quickly when there is a lot of cache.

This is also the reason that a file caching system becomes slow when there is a lot of cache. The caching mechanism will become slow because it has to open lots of files.

At last, we used Memcached to store the sessions in. Memcached is a system similar to Redis. Memcached doesn't use cache tags, so in theory, it is slower than Redis, but practically, you have to see which of these two systems is the best for you.

Optimizing the PHP configurations

In the previous recipe, we explained how some caching systems of PHP work. Since PHP 5.5, we have Zend OPcache that is used as the opcode cache.

In this recipe, we will tune some PHP settings to optimize this for Magento.

Getting ready

We will make some changes in the `php.ini` file, so ensure that you have access to it.

How to do it...

In the following steps, we give some tips to optimize PHP:

1. At this moment, PHP 7 is in Beta version. But when it is stable, it is recommended that you use this version because this is much faster than PHP 5.x.

2. Always use the latest stable PHP version because this is more secure and fast.

3. Try running PHP with an efficient process manager such as `php-fpm` that runs on an impressive speed with `FastCGI`.

4. Use the `realpath_cache_size` configuration setting to configure the size of the real path cache in PHP. On systems where PHP opens and closes a lot of files, this value needs to be increased. You can use the following setting for Magento:

   ```
   realpath_cache_size=1M
   realpath_cache_ttl=86400
   ```

5. The following settings can improve the performance of PHP:

Setting	Description	Recommended value
max_execution_time	This setting sets the maximum time (in seconds) that a process can execute.	120
max_input_time	With this property, we set the time (in seconds). A script will wait for input data.	240

Setting	Description	Recommended value
`memory_limit`	This setting sets the amount of memory that a process can use.	For Magento, it is recommended to use 768 MB
`output_buffering`	With this setting, you can set the amount of bytes to buffer before sending the response to the client.	4096

6. Ensure that Xdebug is not enabled on a production environment.

7. Finally, we can disable some error reporting levels when your site is live. This can be configured with the following setting:

```
error_reporting = E_COMPILE_ERROR|E_ERROR|E_CORE_ERROR
```

How it works...

The values in the `php.ini` configuration depend mostly on the application that you are running and the load that you expect on your system. If your application has some processes that will run for a long time (this is possible with some re-indexing processes with large amounts of products), it is required to increase the values of `max_execution_time` and `max_input_time`. The same goes for the `memory_limit` parameter where the recommended value is 768 MB.

Disabling **Xdebug** will give a better performance because no debug data will be processed.

Disabling the error reporting on a production system is recommended for warnings and notices but critical errors needs to be reported because you need this information when you want to solve a possible bug.

11
Debugging and Unit Testing

In this chapter, we will cover the following recipes:

- ▶ Logging into Magento 2
- ▶ Getting started with Xdebug
- ▶ Running automated tests from Magento
- ▶ Creating a Magento test case

Introduction

Debugging a website in an efficient way is one of the most important jobs of PHP developers. These days, a website is a lot more than a few simple HTML pages. In a Magento store, you have a lot of complex business logic that is used in the flow of an e-commerce transaction.

Debugging in PHP is not out of the box like in other programming languages, such as .NET and Java. There are many ways to configure a PHP debugger (such as Xdebug). With a good code editor and debugger, debugging in Magento is much easier.

Another part of debugging and code testing are automated tests. Automated tests, or Unit tests, are developed to test the output of functions for a given input. When some code is changed, you can run the tests and a report will be generated about the failed and passed tests.

Logging into Magento 2

The standard debugging techniques in PHP are `echo $variable`, `die($variable)` and `var_dump($variable)`. These simple debugging tricks don't always work (when you are working with AJAX and JSON) when it is printed in a hidden HTML section.

If you want to do a simple debugging trick without changing the HTML output of a page, you can use the Magento logging. This will write the debugged results to a log file.

Getting ready

We will print some data to the Magento log files. To easily view the content of these files, we need command line access. Also, open your IDE because we will add some logging statements in the Magento code.

How to do it...

Perform the following steps to describe how we can use logging in Magento 2:

1. If we want to debug some data on a category page, we can use the logger interface to write something to a file. Open the category page controller, which is in the following file: `app/code/Magento/Catalog/Controller/Category/View.php`.

    If you installed Magento with the composer, you will have to edit the `vendor/magento/module-catalog/Controller/Category/View.php` file.

2. In that file, we have to add the following highlighted code to the `_initCategory()` function:

```
try {
  $this->_eventManager->dispatch(
    'catalog_controller_category_init_after',
    ['category' => $category, 'controller_action' => $this]
  );
}
catch (\Magento\Framework\Exception\LocalizedException $e)
{
  $this->_objectManager->get('Psr\Log\LoggerInterface')-
  >critical($e);
  return false;
}
```

```
$this->_objectManager->get('Psr\Log\LoggerInterface')->debug(
  print_r($category->debug(), true)
);
return $category;
```

3. We need to add the highlighted code before the return statement of that code.

4. Open a category page and the data of the category page will be written to the `var/log/debug.log` log file.

 Make sure that the full page caching is not enabled. If it is enabled, the cache will skip the execution of the logging statement.

With the following command, we can follow the new lines that are added to the log file:

```
tail -f var/log/debug.log
```

5. To exit this mode, we can use the shortcut *Crtl* + *C* in the terminal.

How it works...

In Magento 1, we could use the `Mage::log()` function that wrote messages to the log files. In Magento 2, the `Mage` class is gone and a logging interface is created to do the Magento logging.

The logger interface is the `Psr\Log\LoggerInterface` instance. With this interface, we can call the following functions to write data to log files:

*   `alert()`
*   `critical()`
*   `debug()`
*   `emergency()`
*   `error()`
*   `info()`
*   `log()`
*   `notice()`
*   `warning()`

When you log data to files, you can use the function that fits to your log message. In this recipe, we used the `debug()` function to log some debug data. If you want to log the message of an error, you can use the `error()` function.

The logging method only accepts string variables, so it is not possible to pass arrays or objects to this method. To fix this issue, we used the `print_r()` function to convert the content of the array to a string.

We logged the data of a category, but the category is an object. If you apply a `print_r()` method to an object, you will get a huge output, which is not easy to read. To solve this, we can use the `debug()` method on Magento entities. This method will convert the data of the object to a readable array.

Getting started with Xdebug

With a real debugger, you can pause the execution of the script. It allows you to have a look at the variables and values that they have at that point. In a debugger, you can also change values, skip statements, and a do much more.

In PHP, there is the Xdebug extension that enables you to use a debugger in combination with an IDE. In this recipe, we will see how to install Xdebug and integrate it with the IDE **NetBeans**.

Getting ready

In this recipe, we will start an Xdebug session with the NetBeans IDE. Open NetBeans and set the **Magento Project** as **Main Project**. Ensure that all the URLs are configured correctly in the **Property** settings of the project.

To install Xdebug, you have to ensure that the `php5-dev` and `php-pear` packages are installed on your server. If not, you can install them using the following commands:

```
sudo apt-get install php5-dev
sudo apt-get install php-pear
```

How to do it...

The following steps describe how you can install Xdebug on your development server:

1. First, we will install the `xdebug` library. You can do this using the following command:

   ```
   sudo pecl install xdebug
   ```

   This command will give the following output:

   ```
   Build process completed successfully
   Installing '/usr/lib/php5/20121212/xdebug.so'
   install ok: channel://pecl.php.net/xdebug-2.3.2
   configuration option "php_ini" is not set to php.ini location
   You should add "zend_extension=xdebug.so" to php.ini
   ```

2. As you can read in the screenshot, we have to locate the `xdebug.so` file in the `php.ini` file. To find the path of the `xdebug.so` file, we can use the following command:

   `find / -name "xdebug.so"`

3. When we know the path, we have to add the following line in the `php.ini` files. On an Ubuntu server, we have to add the same configuration to the following files:

   ❏ `/etc/php5/apache2/php.ini`

   ❏ `/etc/php5/cli/php.ini`

4. In these files, add the following line at the end of the file. Ensure that the path to the `xdebug.so` file matches the one on your server:

   `zend_extension="/usr/lib/php5/20121212/xdebug.so"`

5. Restart the apache server using the following command:

   `sudo service apache2 restart`

6. When we want to test that Xdebug is correctly installed, we can check this in two ways:

   ❏ The first method is to create a PHP script and call the `phpinfo()` function. When you open this script in the browser, you will see all the PHP settings that are active in that session.

   ❏ The second method is to use the command `php -i`. This gives the same information as `phpinfo()` but now for `php` over `cli`.

7. When we run the `php -i | grep xdebug` command, we will see the following output. These are the Xdebug settings:

```
xdebug
xdebug support => enabled
xdebug.auto_trace => Off => Off
xdebug.cli_color => 0 => 0
xdebug.collect_assignments => Off => Off
xdebug.collect_includes => On => On
xdebug.collect_params => 0 => 0
xdebug.collect_return => Off => Off
xdebug.collect_vars => Off => Off
xdebug.coverage_enable => On => On
xdebug.default_enable => On => On
xdebug.dump.COOKIE => no value => no value
xdebug.dump.ENV => no value => no value
xdebug.dump.FILES => no value => no value
xdebug.dump.GET => no value => no value
xdebug.dump.POST => no value => no value
xdebug.dump.REQUEST => no value => no value
```

```
xdebug.dump.SERVER => no value => no value
xdebug.dump.SESSION => no value => no value
xdebug.dump_globals => On => On
xdebug.dump_once => On => On
xdebug.dump_undefined => Off => Off
xdebug.extended_info => On => On
xdebug.file_link_format => no value => no value
xdebug.force_display_errors => Off => Off
xdebug.force_error_reporting => 0 => 0
xdebug.halt_level => 0 => 0
xdebug.idekey => no value => no value
xdebug.max_nesting_level => 256 => 256
xdebug.max_stack_frames => -1 => -1
xdebug.overload_var_dump => On => On
xdebug.profiler_aggregate => Off => Off
xdebug.profiler_append => Off => Off
xdebug.profiler_enable => Off => Off
xdebug.profiler_enable_trigger => Off => Off
xdebug.profiler_enable_trigger_value => no value => no
value
xdebug.profiler_output_dir => /tmp => /tmp
xdebug.profiler_output_name => cachegrind.out.%p =>
cachegrind.out.%p
xdebug.remote_autostart => Off => Off
xdebug.remote_connect_back => Off => Off
xdebug.remote_cookie_expire_time => 3600 => 3600
xdebug.remote_enable => Off => Off
xdebug.remote_handler => dbgp => dbgp
xdebug.remote_host => localhost => localhost
xdebug.remote_log => no value => no value
xdebug.remote_mode => req => req
xdebug.remote_port => 9000 => 9000
xdebug.scream => Off => Off
xdebug.show_exception_trace => Off => Off
xdebug.show_local_vars => Off => Off
xdebug.show_mem_delta => Off => Off
xdebug.trace_enable_trigger => Off => Off
xdebug.trace_enable_trigger_value => no value => no value
xdebug.trace_format => 0 => 0
xdebug.trace_options => 0 => 0
xdebug.trace_output_dir => /tmp => /tmp
xdebug.trace_output_name => trace.%c => trace.%c
xdebug.var_display_max_children => 128 => 128
xdebug.var_display_max_data => 512 => 512
xdebug.var_display_max_depth => 3 => 3
```

8. The next step is to configure the integration between NetBeans and Xdebug. To configure the integration, we have to add the following configuration at the end of the `php.ini` files:

```
xdebug.remote_enable=1
xdebug.remote_handler=dbgp
xdebug.remote_mode=req
xdebug.remote_host=localhost
xdebug.remote_port=9000
xdebug.idekey="netbeans-xdebug"
```

9. Restart your Apache server and look at the `phpinfo()` page to check whether the Xdebug settings have been applied.

10. Next, we have to configure NetBeans for Xdebug. In NetBeans, navigate to **Tools | Options** and configure it as shown in the following screenshot:

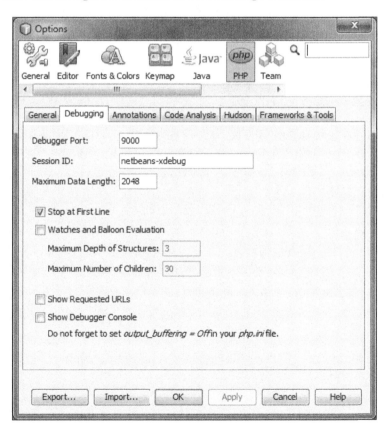

11. In the previous step, we configured the global NetBeans settings for Xdebug. In the next step, we will configure the project-specific settings. Open the **Project Properties** option (by right-clicking on project) and open the **Run Configuration** tab. Ensure that the **Project URL** field has the correct value, as shown in the following screenshot:

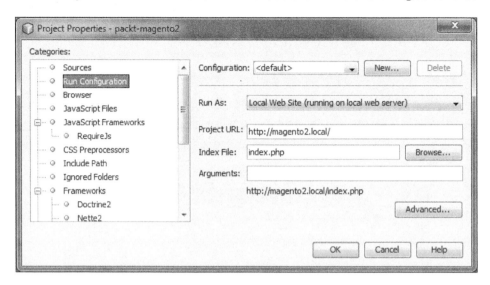

12. We are now ready to start the first debug session. To start it, we have to click on the debug button, which is near the **Run** button. We can also use the shortcut *Crtl + F5*.

13. When starting the debug session, your browser will be opened with a page that has the following URL:

    ```
    http://magento2.local/index.php?XDEBUG_SESSION_START=netbeans-
    xdebug.
    ```

14. The web page doesn't load because the debugger is interrupting the process. To continue, we have to use the debugger controls in NetBeans.

15. Add a breakpoint in the `index.php` file on the following line:

    ```
    $bootstrap = \Magento\Framework\App\Bootstrap::create(BP,
    $_SERVER);
    ```

16. On continuing with the debugger, you will see the actual values of the variables as shown in the following screenshot:

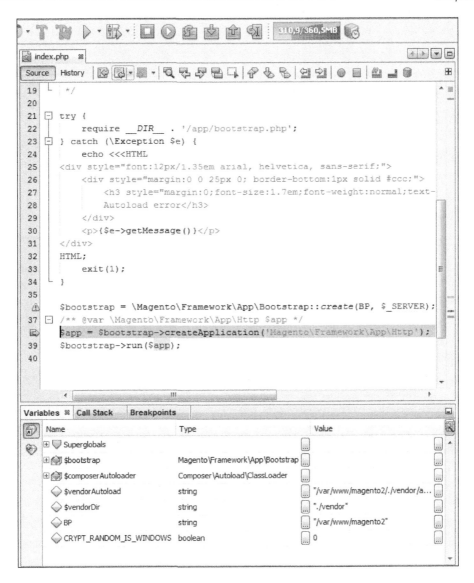

17. When you continue the debugger at the breakpoint, you will see that the page will be loaded.

18. The debug sessions stays alive until you hit the stop button in NetBeans. When you browse to other pages on your website, the debugger will continue as long as the session is alive.

19. To stop the debug session, click on the **Stop** button in NetBeans.

How it works...

We need to install Xdebug on the server where we want to debug a site on. In this recipe, it will be the server on which our Magento instance will run.

The installation of the Xdebug extension is done by PEAR. PEAR is an application repository for the PHP plugins. With PEAR, we downloaded and installed the `xdebug` library.

When Xdebug was installed on the server, we configured the `php.ini` file to use the `xdebug` library. We added some settings to make the Xdebug configuration compatible with NetBeans.

When using Xdebug on a remote server, ensure that you can connect to the server trough port `9000`. This is mostly disabled on the firewall of the server and your local PC.

When the server was correctly configured, we checked the configurations in NetBeans and we started the debug session. When this session was started, we were able to debug the Magento application like a debugger does it.

The debugger enables us to use the following advanced debugger features, among others:

- Setting breakpoints
- Executing the code statement by statement
- Browsing and changing values of variables

Running automated tests from Magento

When you build some functionality, you have to test that the functionality works like you would expect it. Testing is usually done at the end of your project and this can be automated.

With a unit test, we can specify what a specific part of code needs to do. What will be the input, how will it be processed, what is the output—these are all the things that you can specify in a unit test.

A new addition to Magento 2 is that unit tests are automatically included in the core. When you want to contribute to the Magento core with **GitHub**, it is required that your changes pass through the unit and integration tests.

Getting ready

For running the unit tests, we need the command-line tool of Magento. Ensure that you have access to it.

How to do it...

In the following steps, we describe how we can run automated tests from Magento:

1. First, we ensure that the `Magento_Developer` module is enabled. We can check this with the `php bin/magento module:status` command. This will output a list, and the `Magento_Developer` module needs to be in this list of enabled modules.

2. When the module is disabled, we can enable it using the following command:

   php bin/magento module:enable Magento_Developer

3. With the Magento command-line tool, we can start the execution of all tests in the installation. With the following command, we can see the available options:

   php bin/magento dev:tests:run --help

4. If we look at the output of that command, we know that the command will execute all tests without a parameter. If we want to run only the unit tests, we can use the following command:

   php bin/magento dev:tests:run unit

   This command will give the following output when it is running:

```
---- /var/www/magento2/dev/tests/unit> php /var/www/magento2/./vendor/phpunit/phpunit/phpunit

PHPUnit 4.1.0 by Sebastian Bergmann.

Configuration read from /var/www/magento2/dev/tests/unit/phpunit.xml.dist

...........................................................    59 / 15777 (  0%)
...........................................................   118 / 15777 (  0%)
...........................................................   177 / 15777 (  1%)
...........................................................   236 / 15777 (  1%)
...........................................................   295 / 15777 (  1%)
...........................................................   354 / 15777 (  2%)
...........................................................   413 / 15777 (  2%)
...........................................................   472 / 15777 (  2%)
...........................................................   531 / 15777 (  3%)
...........................................................   590 / 15777 (  3%)
...........................................................   649 / 15777 (  4%)
...........................................................   708 / 15777 (  4%)
...........................................................   767 / 15777 (  4%)
...........................................................   826 / 15777 (  5%)
...........................................................   885 / 15777 (  5%)
...........................................................   944 / 15777 (  5%)
...........................................................  1003 / 15777 (  6%)
...........................................................  1062 / 15777 (  6%)
...........................................................  1121 / 15777 (  7%)
.................SSSS.......................................  1180 / 15777 (  7%)
...........................................................  1239 / 15777 (  7%)
...........................................................  1298 / 15777 (  8%)
...........................................................  1357 / 15777 (  8%)
...........................................................  1416 / 15777 (  8%)
...........................................................  1475 / 15777 (  9%)
.....I.I...................................................  1534 / 15777 (  9%)
...........................................................  1593 / 15777 ( 10%)
...........................................................  1652 / 15777 ( 10%)
...........................................................  1711 / 15777 ( 10%)
...........................................................  1770 / 15777 ( 11%)
...........................................................  1829 / 15777 ( 11%)
...........................................................  1888 / 15777 ( 11%)
```

This is the result of the execution of all the unit tests that are available in Magento and this takes quite a lot of time. When we're developing a function, we only want to run one particular test. For this, we need some extra configuration.

5. To run specific tests, we have to create the following file: `dev/tests/unit/phpunit.xml`.

6. In that file, add the following content:

```xml
<?xml version="1.0" encoding="UTF-8"?>
<phpunit xmlns:xsi="http://www.w3.org/2001/XMLSchema-instance"
  xsi:noNamespaceSchemaLocation=
  "http://schema.phpunit.de/4.1/phpunit.xsd"
  colors="true"
  bootstrap="./framework/bootstrap.php"
  >
  <testsuite name="Specific Magento 2 unit tests">
    <directory suffix="Test.php">
    ../../../app/code/Magento/Catalog/Test/Unit</directory>
    <directory suffix="Test.php">
    ../../../app/code/Magento/Cms/Test/Unit</directory>
  </testsuite>
  <php>
    <ini name="date.timezone" value="America/Los_Angeles"/>
    <ini name="xdebug.max_nesting_level" value="200"/>
  </php>
  <logging>
    <log type="testdox-html" target="./test-reports/testdox.html" />
    <log type="testdox-text" target="./test-reports/testdox.txt" />
  </logging>
</phpunit>
```

 If you installed Magento with the composer, you have to ensure that the paths in the directory are going to the right path. With composer, you have to look for the Magento modules in the `vendor/magento/` folder.

7. With the previous configuration, we will run the tests that are available in these folders:

- ❑ `app/code/Magento/Catalog/Test/Unit`
- ❑ `app/code/Magento/Cms/Test/Unit`

8. To run the tests, we have to change the command-line prompt to the `dev/tests/unit` folder. We can do this by running the following command in our Magento root:

   `cd dev/tests/unit/`

9. When we are in that folder, we can run the following command to start the unit tests:

   `../../../vendor/bin/phpunit`

10. When this command has finished executing, we see that some tests are skipped but the full names of those tests are not displayed. To get some more information about unsuccessful tests, we can use the following command, which shows us more output:

    `../../../vendor/bin/phpunit --verbose`

11. When running this command, we get the following output:

```
Time: 14.47 seconds, Memory: 191.00Mb

There were 2 incomplete tests:

1) Magento\Catalog\Test\Unit\Model\CategoryTest::testMoveWhenCannotFindParentCategory
MAGETWO-31165

/var/www/magento2/app/code/Magento/Catalog/Test/Unit/Model/CategoryTest.php:188

2) Magento\Catalog\Test\Unit\Model\CategoryTest::testMoveWhenParentCategoryIsSameAsChildCategory
MAGETWO-31165

/var/www/magento2/app/code/Magento/Catalog/Test/Unit/Model/CategoryTest.php:240

OK, but incomplete, skipped, or risky tests!
Tests: 1213, Assertions: 3796, Incomplete: 2.
```

12. When we look in the test-reports folder, we see that the following log files are generated:

    ❑ `testdox.html`

    ❑ `testdox.txt`

How it works...

In Magento 2, we can find the unit tests in the code files of Magento. When we look in the `Test` directory of each module, we will find the files that will be used when running automated tests.

The `dev:tests:run` command in the Magento console is used to run all the tests in the Magento application. Normally, if you have changed something, you have to test the whole application because a small change can break tests in places that you do not expect.

The console tool uses **PHPUnit** to run the unit tests. This tool is a PHP executable and is delivered with Magento. The `phpunit` executable is available in the `vendor/bin` folder.

When running the `phpunit` executable, this will run unit tests that are configured in a `phpunit.xml` file. We created this file in the `dev/tests/unit` folder. A `phpunit.xml.dist` file is available in this folder, which contains an example configuration.

In this configuration file, we specified the following things:

- ▸ The path of the bootstrap parameter
- ▸ The folders of the tests that needs to be executed
- ▸ Some `php.ini` settings
- ▸ The path of log files

The bootstrap parameter refers to the `framework/bootstrap.php` file. This file initializes the Magento application by calling the necessary files and functions.

When running the `phpunit` tests, we get an output with dots. A dot means that the test result is OK. Sometimes, a dot is replaced with an `S` or `I`. An `S` means that a test is skipped and an `I` means that a test is invalid. With the `--verbose` option, we can get more information on why it is invalid or skipped.

Creating a Magento test case

As this is the last chapter of this book, we will write a test that we can execute with the Magento Testing Framework. This framework uses PHPUnit to execute the tests.

By following the pattern of the Magento tests (Unit tests, Integration tests, and more), the tests will automatically execute when the `dev:tests:run` console command will be executed.

Getting ready

In this recipe, we will create a unit test for the `Packt_HelloWorld` module that we created in *Chapters 4, Creating a Module, Chapter 5, Databases and Modules, Chapter 6, Magento Backend*, and *Chapter 7, Event Handlers and Cronjobs*.

If you don't have the complete code, you can install the starter files for this recipe.

How to do it...

Using the following steps, we will create a simple unit test for Magento:

1. For a unit test, we have to create the following folders:

   - ❑ `app/code/Packt/HelloWorld/Test/`
   - ❑ `app/code/Packt/HelloWorld/Test/Unit/`
   - ❑ `app/code/Packt/HelloWorld/Test/Unit/Block/`
   - ❑ `app/code/Packt/HelloWorld/Test/Unit/Block/Adminhtml/`
   - ❑ `app/code/Packt/HelloWorld/Test/Unit/Block/Adminhtml/Subscription/`

2. In the last folder, create a file called `GridTest.php`.

3. In this file, add the following content:

```php
<?php

namespace Packt\HelloWorld\Test\Unit\Block\Adminhtml\
Subscription;

class GridTest extends \PHPUnit_Framework_TestCase {
  /**
  * @var \Packt\HelloWorld\Block\Adminhtml\Subscription\Grid
  */
  protected $block;

  protected function setUp() {

  }

  protected function tearDown() {

  }

  public function testDecorateStatus() {

  }
}
```

4. We have now created a `test` class that is responsible to test the `Packt\HelloWorld\Block\Adminhtml\Subscription\Grid` class. To run this tests, we have to create a `phpunit.xml` file in the `dev/tests/unit` folder with the following content:

```xml
<?xml version="1.0" encoding="UTF-8"?>
<phpunit xmlns:xsi="http://www.w3.org/2001/XMLSchema-
instance"
  xsi:noNamespaceSchemaLocation="http://schema.phpunit.de/
  4.1/phpunit.xsd"
    colors="true"
    bootstrap="./framework/bootstrap.php"
  >
  <testsuite name="Packt HelloWorld module test">
    <directory suffix="Test.php">../../../app/code/Packt/
    HelloWorld/Test/Unit</directory>
  </testsuite>
  <php>
    <ini name="date.timezone" value="America/Los_Angeles"/>
    <ini name="xdebug.max_nesting_level" value="200"/>
  </php>
  <logging>
    <log type="testdox-html" target="./test-
    reports/testdox.html" />
    <log type="testdox-text" target="./test-
    reports/testdox.txt" />
  </logging>
</phpunit>
```

5. To run the tests, we have to open the terminal and open the `dev/tests/unit` folder. When you are in the Magento root, you can do this by running the following command:

`cd dev/tests/unit`

6. In this folder, run the following command to run the tests:

`../../../vendor/bin/phpunit --verbose`

The tests will pass as you can see in the following screenshot:

```
$ ../../../vendor/bin/phpunit --verbose
PHPUnit 4.1.0 by Sebastian Bergmann.

Configuration read from /var/www/magento2/dev/tests/unit/phpunit.xml

.

Time: 118 ms, Memory: 7.75Mb

OK (1 test, 1 assertion)
$
```

7. The tests will pass because the `test` class is empty. If we want to test the `decorateStatus()` method, we have to initialize the block in the `setUp()` method of the `GridTest` class. Add the highlighted code to the `setUp()` method:

```
protected function setUp() {
    $objectManager = new \Magento\Framework\TestFramework\Unit\
    Helper\ObjectManager($this);

    $this->block = $objectManager->getObject(
        'Packt\HelloWorld\Block\Adminhtml\Subscription\Grid'
    );
}
```

8. We also have to destruct the block when the tests are finished. We can do this by adding the highlighted code to the `tearDown()` method:

```
protected function tearDown() {
    $this->block = null;
}
```

9. We can now start writing our test. For this, we have to know what to test. If we look at the `decorateStatus()` method of the `Packt\HelloWorld\Block\Adminhtml\Subscription\Grid` class, we see that a specific HTML output is returned based on the input variable. To test the output of the input values, we have to add the highlighted code in the `testDecorateStatus()` method:

```
public function testDecorateStatus() {
    $this->assertContains('grid-severity-minor', $this->block->
    decorateStatus('pending'));
    $this->assertContains('grid-severity-notice', $this->block->
    decorateStatus('approved'));
    $this->assertContains('grid-severity-critical', $this->block-
    >decorateStatus('declined'));
```

```
    $this->assertContains('grid-severity-critical', $this->block-
    >decorateStatus(6));
    $this->assertContains('grid-severity-critical', $this->block-
    >decorateStatus(null));
}
```

10. Run the tests again using the `phpunit --verbose` command. You will see that the tests will pass (**1 test, 5 assertions**).

11. When you add the following asserts in the `testDecorateStatus()` method and run the test again, you will see that it fails:

```
$this->assertContains('grid-severity-minor', $this->block-
>decorateStatus('approved'));
$this->assertNull($this->block->decorateStatus(null));
```

How it works...

To create unit tests, we have to use PHPUnit. We created a `phpunit.xml` file where we configured that the `app/code/Packt/HelloWorld/Test/Unit` folder is the folder that contains the unit tests.

In Magento 2, every class has its own test class. We created a test class for the `Packt\HelloWorld\Block\Adminhtml\Subscription\Grid` class. In this class, there is a `decorateStatus()` method that we will test.

We created a `GridTest` class in the same folder structure as it is in the original module. The folder structure will come back in the `Tests/Unit` folder. Every class is suffixed with the word `Test`.

Every test method in a class starts with test followed by the name of the method that will be tested. For the `decorateStatus()` function, this will be `testDecorateStatus()`.

A `test` class extends from the `PHPUnit_Framework_TestCase` class. This class contains the framework that will execute the tests using PHPUnit.

The `setUp()` method is called before the tests are executed. It is like a constructor in a normal class. In this class, we initialize the original `Block` class that we will use in the test method.

The `tearDown()` method is called after the execution of the tests. It works like a destructor, and normally, we set all the class variables to `null` in this method.

A unit test will always pass when the code in a `test` function is empty. We created the `testDecorateStatus()` method where we added some assertion methods. In this recipe, we used the `assertContains()` method. When this method is used, the test will pass if the value of the second parameter will contain the variable of the first parameter.

We used this method to test different input variables of the `decorateStatus()` method. In the last step, we used a `assertNull()` method. The tests failed because the output of the `decorateStatus()` method was not `null` for the given input.

In large projects where unit tests are used, mostly the tests are written in the architectural phase of a project. A unit test can be used as a specification of what a method need to do when it is called. How we have to handle invalid input variables and other such things are specified in a unit test.

There's more...

In this recipe, we used the `assertContains()` and `assertNull()` methods to test the output of the `decorateStatus()` method. However, there are many more assertion methods that you can use with PHPUnit. For example, a method that compares a number, a method that compares the type of object, and many more.

A full list of assertion methods can be found at the following URL, which refers to the original documentation of PHPUnit:

`https://phpunit.de/manual/current/en/appendixes.assertions.html`

Index

database table
  creating, with models 104-111
  grid, creating 142-150
dependency injection
  about 92
  URL 94
downloadable product 42

E

email templates
  customizing 74, 75
empty module
  creating 204, 205
Entity Attribute Value (EAV) system 92
event observer
  adding 172-175
event types
  about 166-169
  URL 169

F

Facebook
  URL 42
fallback mechanism 65
file permissions
  URL 4
Full Page Caching 255

G

GitHub 268
Google Plus
  URL 42
grid
  creating, of database table 142-150
grouped product 41
Grunt
  configuring 66
  URL 66
GTmetrix server 244

H

HTML object
  embedding 44-46

HTML output
  customizing 55-59

I

IDE NetBeans 262
install script
  creating 100-104
Integrated Development Environment (IDE)
  about 20
  using 20-23
interceptor
  adding 92-94

J

jQuery slider script 203

L

layout updates
  adding 83-87
LESS
  working with 62-67
Luma theme 49

M

Magento
  about 1
  automated tests, running 268-272
  performance leaks, discovering 250-252
  URL 2
Magento 1
  upgrade, preparing 14-16
  website, creating with sample data 2-7
Magento 2
  about 2
  default themes, exploring 49-52
  logging in 260-262
  theme, creating 52-55
  website, creating 8-14
Magento Migration Whitepaper
  URL 20
Memcached
  about 253
  configuring 253-256

menu
extending 129-131
migration tool
URL 14
models
database table, creating with 104-111
module
adding, in frontend 199-202
configurations, initializing 186-193
files, creating 78, 79
Multi-Processing Modules (MPM) 250
MyISAM tables 246
MySQL
configurations, optimizing 245-247

N

NetBeans
about 20
URL 20
Nginx 248

O

OPcache
configuring 253-256

P

PageSpeed 244
page title
modifying 67, 68
PHP_CodeSniffer (PHP CS)
code, writing with 24-28
URL 24
PHP configurations
optimizing 256, 257
phpcsmd plugin
about 27
URL 27
PHP Mess Detector (PHPMD)
code, writing with 24-28
phpMyAdmin 245
PHP, settings
max_execution_time 256
max_input_time 256

memory_limit 257
output_buffering 257
PHPStorm
about 28
URL 28
PHPUnit
about 271
assertion methods, URL 277
product attributes
about 37
adding, programmatically 119-122
product page
URL, modifying 46-48
products
adding 89-92
product templates 33
product types
bundle product 41
configurable product 41
downloadable product 42
grouped product 41
simple product 41
virtual product 41
working with 37-40

R

Redis
about 253
configuring 253-256
RequireJS library 225
routing 47

S

shipping method
additional features, adding 197-199
Siege 231
simple product 41
slick
URL 223
social media buttons
adding 42-44
source models
working with 160-164

Thank you for buying
Magento 2 Development Cookbook

About Packt Publishing

Packt, pronounced 'packed', published its first book, *Mastering phpMyAdmin for Effective MySQL Management*, in April 2004, and subsequently continued to specialize in publishing highly focused books on specific technologies and solutions.

Our books and publications share the experiences of your fellow IT professionals in adapting and customizing today's systems, applications, and frameworks. Our solution-based books give you the knowledge and power to customize the software and technologies you're using to get the job done. Packt books are more specific and less general than the IT books you have seen in the past. Our unique business model allows us to bring you more focused information, giving you more of what you need to know, and less of what you don't.

Packt is a modern yet unique publishing company that focuses on producing quality, cutting-edge books for communities of developers, administrators, and newbies alike. For more information, please visit our website at www.packtpub.com.

Writing for Packt

We welcome all inquiries from people who are interested in authoring. Book proposals should be sent to author@packtpub.com. If your book idea is still at an early stage and you would like to discuss it first before writing a formal book proposal, then please contact us; one of our commissioning editors will get in touch with you.

We're not just looking for published authors; if you have strong technical skills but no writing experience, our experienced editors can help you develop a writing career, or simply get some additional reward for your expertise.

PUBLISHING

Magento: Beginner's Guide

ISBN: 978-1-84719-594-4   Paperback: 300 pages

Create a dynamic, fully featured, online store with the most powerful open source e-commerce software

1. Step-by-step guide to building your own online store.

2. Focuses on the key features of Magento that you must know to get your store up and running.

3. Customize the store's appearance to make it uniquely yours.

4. Clearly illustrated with screenshots and a working example.

Magento : Beginner's Guide
Second Edition

ISBN: 978-1-78216-270-4   Paperback: 320 pages

Learn how to create a fully featured, attractive online store with the most powerful open source solution for e-commerc

1. Install, configure, and manage your own e-commerce store.

2. Extend and customize your store to reflect your brand and personality.

3. Handle tax, shipping, and custom orders.

Please check **www.PacktPub.com** for information on our titles

Magento 1.8 Development Cookbook

ISBN: 978-1-78216-332-9   Paperback: 274 pages

Over 70 recipes to learn Magento development from scratch

1. Customize the look and feel of your Magento shop.

2. Work on theming, catalog configuration, module, and database development.

3. Create modules to modify or extend Magento's standard behaviour.

Mastering Magento

ISBN: 978-1-84951-694-5   Paperback: 300 pages

Maximize the power of Magento: for developers, designers, and store owners

1. Learn how to customize your Magento store for maximum performance.

2. Exploit little known techniques for extending and tuning your Magento installation.

3. Step-by-step guides for making your store run faster, better and more productively.

Please check **www.PacktPub.com** for information on our titles